D1477821

SOCIAL POLICY REVIEW 30

Analysis and debate in social policy, 2018

Edited by Catherine Needham, Elke Heins
and James Rees

First published in Great Britain in 2018 by

Policy Press
University of Bristol
1-9 Old Park Hill
Bristol BS2 8BB
UK
t: +44 (0)117 954 5940
e: pp-info@bristol.ac.uk
www.policypress.co.uk

North American office:
Policy Press
c/o The University of Chicago Press
1427 East 60th Street
Chicago, IL 60637, USA
t: +1 773 702 7700
f: +1 773-702-9756
e:sales@press.uchicago.edu
www.press.uchicago.edu

British Library Cataloguing in Publication Data
A catalogue record for this book is available from the British Library.

Library of Congress Cataloging-in-Publication Data
A catalog record for this book has been requested.

ISBN 978-1-4473-4999-0 hardback
ISBN 978-1-4473-5000-2 paperback SPA members' edition (not on general release)
ISBN 978-1-4473-5001-9 ePdf

Cover design by Policy Press
Front cover: photograph kindly supplied by istock
Printed and bound in Great Britain by CPI Group (UK)
Ltd, Croydon, CR0 4YY
Policy Press uses environmentally responsible print partners

Contents

List of figures and tables

Figures

Tables

Notes on contributors

Derek Birrell is Professor of Social Policy at Ulster University, Northern Ireland. He has published widely on devolution and social policy including books on the impact of devolution on social policy, governance and welfare, multi-level governance in Northern Ireland and Brexit and devolution.

Gideon Calder is Senior Lecturer in Social Sciences and Social Policy at Swansea University, where he directs the Social Policy programme. His research interests lie in the relationship between theory, policy and practice. His current work focuses on equality of children's life chances, and on the co-production of services. He is co-editor of the journal *Ethics and Social Welfare*.

Eleanor Carter is a post-doctoral Research Fellow at the Blavatnik School of Government, University of Oxford. She works with the Government Outcomes Lab where the team research outcomes-based commissioning, including the use of Social Impact Bonds. Her most recent research investigates the application of payment-by-results in employment support services.

Gary Craig is Emeritus Professor of Social Justice at the Wilberforce Institute, University of Hull, and a long-standing researcher, activist and writer on issues of modern slavery. He is co-convenor of the Modern Slavery Research Consortium and co-editor of *The modern slavery agenda* (Policy Press, 2018: forthcoming). He is editor of *Social justice: A global handbook* (Edward Elgar, 2018: forthcoming).

Richard Crisp is a Reader in the Centre for Regional, Economic and Social Research (CRESR) at Sheffield Hallam University. He specialises in research on poverty, social and spatial inequality and inclusive growth.

Rikki Dean is Post-doctoral Research Fellow in Democratic Innovations at Goethe University, Frankfurt. His research focuses on democratic theory, procedural preferences for democratic governance, the theory and practice of citizen participation, particularly in social policy, and adolescent social exclusion. In 2017 he was awarded the London School of Economics and Political Science's Titmuss Prize for Outstanding Scholarship in Social Policy for his PhD thesis 'Democratising bureaucracy'.

Matthew Donoghue is a Departmental Lecturer in Comparative Social Policy in the Department of Social Policy and Intervention, University of Oxford. His research interests focus on social citizenship and social cohesion in times of uncertainty, resilience, poverty and inequality, the role of discourse and ideology in policy, and lived experience of policy and politics.

Ann Marie Gray is Professor of Social Policy at Ulster University, Northern Ireland, and co-director of ARK, a joint Ulster University/ Queen's University research project. She has published on devolution and social policy, adult social care policy, social security and devolution and abortion policy.

Ian Greener is Professor of Social Policy at the University of Strathclyde. Ian has written over 50 peer-reviewed articles on social policy and public management, as well as several books. He is especially interested in the role of ideas in policy-making, and in how policy-makers try and justify the changes they make to public services.

Tina Haux is a Lecturer in Quantitative Social Policy at the University of Kent. Her research spans two broad areas, namely, the practice and policies around post-separation parenthood as well as the role of evidence in policy-making. Her chapter in this book is part of a larger project that includes interviews with 15 Social Policy professors about their impact over their academic career.

Elke Heins is Lecturer in Social Policy at the School of Social and Political Science, University of Edinburgh. Her research interests mainly focus on comparative and European social policy as well as the politics of welfare in the UK. She has recently co-edited (with Caroline de la Porte) *The sovereign debt crisis, the EU and welfare state reform* (Palgrave Macmillan, 2016) and *Social Policy Review 29* (with John Hudson and Catherine Needham, Policy Press, 2017).

Stuart Hodkinson is Associate Professor of Critical Urban Geography at the University of Leeds. His research focuses on 'new urban enclosures' such as the privatisation of public housing, state-led gentrification, residential displacement, and welfare reform. He has a specific interest in the rise of public–private partnerships and outsourcing in housing, and conducted an ESRC-funded investigation into residents' experiences of public housing regeneration in England under the Private Finance Initiative (2011–14). He is a co-author of *Precarious lives: Forced labour, exploitation, and asylum* (Policy Press, 2015).

Markus Ketola joined Ulster University in 2013 as a Lecturer in Social Policy. He received his PhD from the London School of Economics and Political Science (LSE) in 2011, where he also taught Social Policy from 2011–13 with a focus on international social policy and the role of non-governmental organisations (NGOs) in social policy. Prior to this, Markus studied European Studies (BA) at Leeds University (2002) and NGO Management (MSc) at LSE (2004).

Ruth Lupton is Professor of Education at the University of Manchester where she heads the Inclusive Growth Analysis Unit. She researches spatial inequalities, neighbourhood dynamics and the effects of policy responses.

Catherine Needham is Professor of Public Policy and Public Management in the Health Services Management Centre, University of Birmingham. Her research focuses on new approaches to public service workforce development, as well as social care and policy innovation.

Johan Nordensvard joined University of Southampton in 2014. Johan studied Political Science at the University of Lund (MA), Sweden and the University of Oldenburg (PhD), Germany. His PhD thesis was about civic education. Prior to his employment at the University of Southampton, Johan was a Fellow and Researcher in Social Policy at the London School of Economics and Political Science (LSE) (2010–13) and a Lecturer in Social Policy at the University of Brighton (2008–09 and 2012–13).

Robert M. Page is Reader in Democratic Socialism and Social Policy at the University of Birmingham, UK. He has written extensively about the political history of the welfare state in Britain since the Second World War, including, most recently, *Clear blue water? The Conservative Party and the welfare state in Britain since 1940* (Policy Press, 2015). He is currently working on a companion volume entitled *Towards a red and pleasant land? Labour governments and the welfare state in Britain since 1945*.

James Rees is Senior Research Fellow at the Centre for Voluntary Sector Leadership in the Open University Business School. His research focuses on the third sector, public service delivery and reform, as well as leadership, governance and citizen involvement.

Adrian Sinfield is Professor Emeritus of Social Policy at the University of Edinburgh. He has worked on social security, unemployment, poverty, inequality and the social division of welfare. He has been chair and president of the Social Policy Association, and the recipient of its first lifetime achievement award, co-founder and chair of the Unemployment Unit and vice-chair of the Child Poverty Action Group.

Moira Wallace is a former senior civil servant who served in the Treasury, No 10 Downing Street, the Cabinet Office and Home Office before taking up the role of Permanent Secretary of the Department of Energy and Climate Change from 2008 to 2012. At No 10 she was Economic Affairs Private Secretary to Prime Ministers Major and Blair, and from 1997 to 2001 she was Director of the Government's Social Exclusion Unit. From 2000 to 2008 she was a Visiting Fellow at Nuffield College, Oxford, and is currently Provost of Oriel College Oxford. Her chapter in this volume draws on work she undertook as a Visiting Professor of Practice at the Centre for the Analysis of Social Exclusion at the London School of Economics and Political Science.

Part One
Developments in social policy

Catherine Needham

In the UK we have lived for over a decade with austerity-driven policies that shrink the welfare state, stigmatise people who receive state benefits and deepen child poverty. The private affluence/public squalor distinction made by J.K. Galbraith in the 1950s seems particularly apposite for our times. The fire that destroyed Grenfell Tower in West London, in which 71 people are confirmed to have died, was a horrifying visible display of the myriad failings of social housing policy. Critique of the modes of governance that contributed to the fire has been a key element of social policy scholarship, along with the articulation of modes of resistance. As the immediate horror of Grenfell fades in the public mind, those strategies of resistance – and the commitment to vigilance that go alongside – remain vital if anything is to change.

This 30th edition of *Social Policy Review* opens with Stuart Hodkinson's eviscerating account of the Grenfell fire, and the multiple threads that combined to produce the tragedy. Using the language of 'social murder', Hodkinson traces the roots of the fire to three interconnected policy drivers. The first is the planned destruction of the postwar public housing model under policies of privatisation, demunicipalisation and commercialisation. The second is the interaction between business deregulation and austerity. The third is the gentrification of urban neighbourhoods and the way that this has reshaped the housing market, particularly in London. He concludes that the structural drivers and policy failures behind the Grenfell Tower disaster were rooted in decades of neoliberal policy dominance in Britain. He frames it as a disaster 'foretold', not just by the Grenfell residents but also the long lineage of neoliberal critics, and hopes that it will represent 'the moment in history when policy changed course'. This requires overhauling building and fire safety regulations, regulating the construction industry and ensuring that standards are enforced for all existing and new homes of all tenures.

Gary Craig's chapter on modern slavery has a related focus on the people who are the casualties of hyper-charged capitalism and who continue to be let down by lack of regulation or enforcement. His focus is the Modern Slavery Act 2015, and the chapter outlines the developments leading to this legislation, summarises it and evaluates subsequent progress. In the chapter Craig points to a range of issues underlying the need for a major reform programme to ensure that the legislative and policy tools required effectively to combat modern slavery are in place, usable and used. The UK government claimed that the Act was 'world leading', and it clearly did constitute a great advance in raising the profile of the issue and the sanctions that could be applied. However, the chapter argues that the Act was a missed opportunity and that there are critical issues to be addressed such as training, victim support, increasing the effectiveness of the criminal justice system in responding to modern slavery, strengthening the supply chain legal framework and revising arrangements for domestic workers. Craig anticipates that the Act will soon be back in Parliament for significant revision.

Childcare is the focus of Gideon Calder's chapter, with a focus on the full range of ways in which children receive care, within and outside the family. The chapter considers the relationship between the 'life chances' agenda and persistent questions about the intersection of childcare and social justice. It focuses on childhoods themselves as the focal point when looking at inequality between children rather than focusing on the future destinations of children. Following a discussion of the existing life chances agenda and of why a child-focused analysis is needed, the chapter suggests that we address childcare as a 'relationship good' – a uniquely valuable form of relationship, the distribution of which should be treated as a basic matter of social justice, and of a viable approach to 'life chances' in policy terms. This enables a flourishing childhood to be established as a core parameter rather than as simply a pathway to future thriving.

Outcomes occupy a privileged position within social policy analysis. They offer a move away from a naive focus on outputs (number of care visits a day, number of operations performed), which can hide poor-quality service, into a more sophisticated account of wellbeing. Outcomes are, however, much more elusive than output or process measure: they are compromised by attribution problems and the absence of counter-factuals (Talbot, 2010). Public policy academics have used terms such as 'outcome theology' and 'fool's gold' to convey this sense that an outcome orientation in performance measurement relies on faith and wishful thinking as much as hard metrics (Bovaird, 2012; Tunstill and Blewett, 2013). In the final chapter of this section, Derek Birrell and Ann Marie Gray focus on the outcomes-based approaches taken in the three devolved administrations of the UK (Scotland, Wales and Northern Ireland). The chapter focuses on the outcomes-based accountability (OBA) model in particular, assessing the conceptual issues arising from the OBA methodology and its application. While there has been substantial buy-in to the principle of an outcomes-based approach in the three administrations, the chapter highlights ways in which long-standing issues relating to performance measurement have continued to dog attempts to take an outcome focus. They conclude that the OBA methodology has not produced any robust evidence regarding the impact on policy-making, and tells us little about how to do policy intervention better.

References

Bovaird, T. (2012) 'Attributing outcomes to social policy interventions – "gold standard" or "fool's gold" in public policy and management?', *Social Policy and Administration*, vol 48, no 1, pp 1-23.

Talbot, C. (2010) *Theories of performance: Organizational and service improvement in the public domain*, Oxford: Oxford University Press.

Tunstill, J. and Blewett, J. (2013) 'Mapping the journey: outcome-focused practice and the role of interim outcomes in family support services', *Child and Family Social Work*, vol 20, no 2, pp 234-43.

ONE

Grenfell foretold: a very neoliberal tragedy

Stuart Hodkinson

Introduction

At around 12.50am on 14 June 2017, a fire broke out on the fourth floor of Grenfell Tower, a 24-storey public housing tower block in North Kensington, London. Ten minutes later, firefighters were handling an apparently routine job − Grenfell had been designed to contain fires from spreading. However, within 15 minutes flames had reached the top floor, and shortly after the whole building was ablaze. It would take 250 firefighters, 70 fire engines and 60 hours to extinguish the fire that killed at least 72 people and made 208 households homeless. The fire's rapid spread was immediately linked to cladding fitted during a recent refurbishment scheme about which Grenfell Tower residents had made repeated fire safety warnings to various public agencies to no avail (ASH, 2017). Attention focused on the main contractor, Rydon, the chain of private companies that fitted the cladding, the Conservative-controlled local authority − the Royal Borough of Kensington and Chelsea (RBKC), which owned Grenfell Tower − and the arm's-length company, Kensington and Chelsea Tenant Management Organisation (KCTMO), that managed the homes. Nine days after Grenfell, 800 homes in five public housing tower blocks on the Chalcots Estate in Camden, London, also refurbished by Rydon between 2006 and 2011, were evacuated, and soon hundreds more tower blocks across England were deemed a fire risk as cladding samples failed government-ordered tests.

In the aftermath of Grenfell, a more fundamental political question was soon posed: how, less than a decade after the deadly Lakanal House fire in Southwark that had prompted calls by the investigating authorities for fundamental changes to building regulations, could this have been possible? With the Conservative government floundering after a disastrous snap general election, an emboldened Labour Party began shifting the focus onto the political and structural causes of the tragedy. Labour's Shadow Chancellor, John McDonnell, claimed the victims had been 'murdered by political decisions that were taken over recent decades' including housing privatisation, deregulation and recent cuts to local authority and fire service budgets under the Conservatives' austerity programme (quoted in BBC News, 2017a). McDonnell was evoking the concept of 'social murder' that Friedrich Engels had first articulated in *The condition of the working class in England* to capture the mass of premature yet preventable deaths among the industrial working class at the hands of unregulated capitalist exploitation and state indifference:

> ... when society places hundreds of proletarians in such a position that they inevitably meet a too early and an unnatural death ... [and] knows that these thousands of victims must perish, and yet permits these conditions to remain, its deed is murder just as surely as the deed of the single individual.... (Engels, 1845 [2008], p 95)

Although the Grenfell disaster raises the enduring issues of class and race inequalities in the UK with the vast majority of the dead of non-white ethnicity (Whitehead, 2017), this chapter focuses on the main 'political decisions' that have guided public policy over the past four decades that arguably contributed to the Grenfell disaster and the subsequent discovery of other 'Grenfells in waiting'. Three specific yet interconnected policy drivers are discussed in the following order:

- The planned destruction of the postwar public housing model under policies of privatisation, demunicipalisation and commercialisation, and more specifically, the creation of the unaccountable public–private partnership vehicle under which Grenfell Tower was renovated.
- The interaction between the long-term drive to deregulate business, particularly with respect to the building industry, and the more recent cuts to public expenditure that compromised fire safety and neutered residents' agency.
- The wider urban processes of gentrification-based housing market restructuring, most extreme in London, which arguably underpinned Grenfell's largely aesthetic renovation and fuelled the housing crisis that Grenfell's homeless survivors now find themselves in.

All of these political decisions and processes were either led or informed by the disastrous ideas of neoliberalism, namely, the 'market revolution' in public policy since the 1970s global economic crisis inspired by Hayek (1960) and Friedman's (1962) urges to liberate both capitalist enterprise and individuals from state intervention in favour of a social order driven by unrestrained economic competition between private firms for consumer markets and profit. This anti-collectivist philosophy has driven the continual rolling-back of postwar working-class gains once embedded in the Keynesian Welfare State era through policies aimed at the (re)commodification of all spheres of economic and social life with housing taking centre-stage (Marcuse and Madden, 2016). Given that warnings about the disastrous consequences of these policies have gone largely unheeded over many decades, I conclude that while the fire may have been *accidental*, the destruction of Grenfell and the lives of its residential community was very much a modern-day act of social murder, and must mark a radical turning point in policy-making towards restoring housing stability, security and safety for all in law.

The slow death of public housing

Public housing developed out of the long struggle for decent housing over the 19th and 20th centuries forged in the Victorian working-class slums of unregulated private landlordism and capitalism (Englander, 1983). From 1875 onwards, an emergent cross-party consensus on the need for state intervention, famously enshrined in the 1919 'Homes for Heroes' programme, saw local authorities gradually empowered and financed to demolish slums, borrow to purchase land, and build public housing for rent, as well as regulate new developments and plan for housing need (Cole and Furbey, 1994). A postwar housing 'arms race' between Conservative and Labour governments produced a massive state-financed public house-building programme. Although private home ownership became the dominant tenure over the course of the 20th century, by 1979, public housing had grown to 6.6 million homes, a third of the UK's total housing stock, making it a mainstream rental alternative to home ownership and private landlordism for 40 per cent of the population (Hills, 2007).

Grenfell Tower was completed in 1974 during the last major wave of slum clearance and improvement as part of the 1,000-home Lancaster West public housing estate in North Kensington. It represented a dramatic improvement for residents in an area of West London once home to the notorious private slum-lord of the 1950s and early

1960s, Peter Rachman, whose exploitation, harassment and unlawful eviction of tenants, especially West Indian immigrants, led to the term 'Rachmanism'. With its iconic 'brutalist' design, 67 metre height and solid concrete structure, Grenfell symbolised the high-rise phenomenon of postwar building that between 1955 and 1975 built nearly 440,000 tower blocks, the vast majority in inner urban areas (Dunleavy, 1981). The architectural and construction quality of high-rise towers has attracted long-standing critique. The 1968 Ronan Point disaster in East London, in which a new 21-storey tower block partially collapsed following a gas explosion, killing four people, highlighted inadequate building regulations, insufficient public funding and the corrupting influence of major building companies promoting profitable (that is, cheap) industrialised systems of prefabricated building. Paradoxically, the resulting policy changes meant Grenfell Tower was built to far higher design and construction standards.

Privatisation and permanent austerity

Despite its variable quality and valid critiques of municipal landlord–tenant relations, public housing like Grenfell Tower transformed housing conditions as part of a wider postwar housing–welfare consensus that the state should provide for the poor, meet housing need, regulate private sector tenancies and rents, provide secure and affordable tenancies and rehouse vulnerable homeless groups (Malpass, 2005). However, in the 40 years since Grenfell's construction, public housing in the UK – and England in particular since devolution after 1999 – has changed beyond recognition. Most striking is its decline to less than 8 per cent of the overall housing stock with a net loss of 4.5 million homes (DCLG, nd, a). This transformation stems from the 1979 electoral victory of Thatcherism that brought the proactive application of a neoliberal project to create a property-owning democracy in which public housing would be privatised and the state would guarantee an 'ambulance service' for the genuinely 'weak' (Harloe, 1978).

Privatisation was spearheaded by giving tenants a statutory Right to Buy (RTB) their council homes at large discounts in 1980, which laid the basis for the subsequent sale of 2.5 million homes (Murie, 2015).[1] While Grenfell Tower had arguably survived the privatisation assault – only a handful of flats were sold under the RTB – the disastrous chain of events leading up to the fire reflect the 'neoliberal straitjacket' (Hodkinson, 2011a) placed on public housing since 1979. One arm of this straitjacket has been *permanent austerity* (to varying degrees over time), with funding cuts, caps and conditions curtailing local authorities' ability to build new housing and adequately maintain, repair and modernise their existing housing stock (Davis, 2013). Consequently, more than 85 per cent of homes sold under RTB UK-wide have never been replaced. Although New Labour partially relaxed local borrowing controls after 2004 to enable local authorities to address the estimated £23 billion housing repair backlog, it blocked a return to public house building. These controls largely remain despite the introduction of 'self-financing' under the Localism Act 2011 that was originally sold to English local authorities as a vehicle for making long-term investments in their existing and new public housing stock. As a result, less than 9,000 new public housing units were started between 2012 and 2016 compared to over 100,000 started in 1974 when Grenfell Tower was opened (DCLG, nd, b).

Demunicipalisation and commercialisation

Another arm of the neoliberal straitjacket on public housing not privatised by the RTB has been *demunicipalisation*. Both Conservative and Labour governments set about breaking up what they saw as an undesirable 'municipal monopoly' model of local authorities acting as both developer and landlord, directly responsible for the design, construction, management and maintenance of the public housing stock, using in-house direct labour organisations (DLOs) or more typically tendering work to the private sector (Cole and Furbey, 1994). One route has been the diversion of government subsidy for new social house building from local authorities to charitable housing associations (Registered Social Landlords, RSLs), and, since 2008, for-profit providers (Davis, 2013). Around 750,000 social rented homes have been built UK-wide by housing associations on less secure tenancies and at higher rents than public housing on average. Various initiatives have also sought to transfer the management, repair and ownership of public housing to independent, charitable and for-profit private landlords and contractors.

For instance, as part of its 2000–10 Decent Homes programme in England to ensure minimum standards in the social housing sector, New Labour made desperately needed funding conditional on local authorities agreeing to one of three options: (i) selling off their housing to RSLs, subject to a successful statutory ballot of tenants who were told that voting 'no' would mean no investment in their homes; (ii) establishing an 'arm's-length management organisation' (ALMO) owned by the local authority but run as a separate company to manage its public housing stock; or (iii) contracting out a discrete regeneration scheme to a private sector consortium for up to 30 years under the Private Finance Initiative (PFI) (Hodkinson, 2011b). This context helps to explain why the management of Grenfell Tower was initially transferred in 1996 to a tenant management organisation – KCTMO – with tenants elected to the company board as a way of protecting residents from the planned privatisation of housing management under the Conservatives' compulsory competitive tendering (CCT) regime (Apps, 2017), and why, in 2002, KCTMO itself was transformed into an ALMO in order to access Decent Homes finance (Apps, 2017).

Over time, the ever-fragmented social housing sector in England has been increasingly commercialised, with both providers and tenants further exposed to market forces. Between 2002 and 2016, council and social housing rents were increased above inflation as part of a harmonisation policy aimed at convergence towards the local private market average. Under the Coalition government, capital funding for affordable housing was cut by 60 per cent between 2010 and 2015, and subsidies for new social rented housing diverted into a new 'affordable rent' tenure on fixed-term tenancies that can reach 80 per cent of local market rents. At the same time, there have been major cuts to welfare support for housing costs in both private and social rental sectors since 2010, discussed later in the chapter. Since 2015, social landlords have had the legal power to charge market rents to tenants with a household income of over £60,000. The Localism Act 2011 also abolished new council tenants' statutory right to a secure lifetime tenancy, leaving it to local discretion, and ended statutory homeless people's right to a lifetime social housing tenancy by allowing local authorities to discharge their duty by offering private sector accommodation for a fixed term of at least 12 months. The Housing and Planning Act 2016 went further, making it mandatory for local authorities to grant fixed-term tenancies of between 2 and 10 years (Davies and Compton, 2016).

Over the past four decades, neoliberalism's recommodification of 'home' has transformed the public housing model from an imperfect form of 'housing commons' into a highly financialised world of 'housing assets', owned, managed and periodically regenerated by commercial organisations where board members are legally obliged to act in the interests of the company, not the wider resident body (Goulding, 2018). The analysis now turns to ways in which the neoliberal policies of austerity, deregulation and outsourcing may have interacted with this privatisation context to produce the Grenfell disaster.

A deadly renovation

Although Grenfell Tower received some investment under Labour's Decent Homes programme, between June 2014 and July 2016 a major renovation project took place to fit new cladding, double-glazed windows, heat and hot water systems, to reconfigure the existing nursery and boxing club, create two additional floors of housing and improve the outdoor public realm. Four main companies were employed to partner with the local authority and KCTMO: French-owned Artelia UK managed the project; Studio E Architects designed the scheme; Max Fordham advised on the building's thermal insulation; and Rydon acted as the main refurbishment contractor. Significantly, Grenfell Tower residents repeatedly warned of fire safety fears before, during and after the refurbishment, and in November 2016 made this chilling prediction online about their future:

> It is a truly terrifying thought, but the Grenfell Action Group firmly believe that only a catastrophic event will expose the ineptitude and incompetence of our landlord, the KCTMO, and bring an end to the dangerous living conditions and neglect of health and safety legislation that they inflict upon their tenants and leaseholders.... It is our conviction that a serious fire ... is the most likely reason that those who wield power at the KCTMO will be found out and brought to justice! (Grenfell Action Group, 2016)

The devastating fire that residents foretold began from an exploding fridge-freezer that residents suspect was caused by the faulty electrical system first reported in 2013 (Hosken, 2017). Instead of being contained within the flat in line with Grenfell's original design, the fire managed to spread rapidly to the tower's new external cladding, trapping residents in the upper storeys. The cladding's combination of low fire resistant aluminium panels with a combustible polyethylene plastic core and long air cavities within the physical structure appears to have then fuelled the fire (ASH, 2017). Survivors report that two-thirds of the recently installed gas pipes were not covered in fire resistant material, and that both central fire alarm and emergency fire escape lights failed, causing residents to scramble and fall in the pitch-black stairwells (Doward, 2017).

Austerity and the race to the bottom

As the opposition Labour Party has suggested, the deficit reduction policies of austerity undoubtedly played some role in the tragedy. Local government has been most affected with grant cuts of nearly 40 per cent to councils in England, leading to an overall 26 per cent reduction in local budgets in real terms between 2009/10 and 2016/17, albeit with large variations by authority and region that have hit the poorest local authorities and places hardest (Amin-Smith et al, 2016; Beatty and Fothergill, 2016). Government spending cuts have particularly hurt non-ring-fenced regulatory services such as Building Control, Planning, and Environmental Health: between 2010 and 2015 funding for stand-alone fire and rescue authorities fell by an average of 28 per cent in real terms, savings predominantly coming from reduced staffing, audits, inspections and fire risk checks (NAO, 2015). Fire safety checks in tower blocks fell 25 per cent in the most recent five years (Tombs and Whyte, 2017). These cuts may well have undermined both local authority and fire service inspections at Grenfell Tower as, despite being one of the world's wealthiest and least deprived geographies, RBKC has experienced a 38 per cent cut in government funding over this period, and contains some of the 10 per cent most deprived areas in the country, including the Lancaster West Estate.

Austerity was also a factor in the Coalition and Conservative governments' refusal to lift borrowing caps on local Housing Revenue Accounts (HRAs). This apparently left a £46 million shortfall in Kensington and Chelsea's housing maintenance budget for 2015–20, reducing the Grenfell Tower renovation budget to £9.7 million that was funded mainly from the private market sale of 23 flats created from converting basements in existing council houses elsewhere in the borough (Apps, 2017). While this budget was deemed too low by two separate contractors, Rydon's bid of £8.7 million offered 'the most economically advantageous tender' (RBKC, 2014). Crucially, it has been reported that in June and July 2014, political pressure by RBKC on KCTMO to cut costs led to the replacement of non-combustible zinc panels with fire-retardant cores with cheaper, more combustible cladding, saving a further £293,000 (O'Neill and Karim, 2017). Austerity thus created the 'value engineering' race-to-the-bottom environment of doing 'more with less' seen across the public sector in which a cheaper, flammable cladding was chosen to meet spending targets.

Fire safety: a casualty of self-regulation?

If austerity influenced the decision to change the cladding, Grenfell has raised more fundamental questions about the fitness and enforcement of building and fire safety regulations. Grenfell's cladding failed government-ordered tests less than nine minutes into what should have a 40-minute resistance (Cook, 2017). The government has stated that the cladding did not comply with Approved Document B of the UK's Building Regulations 2010, which states that the 'external envelope of a building should not provide a medium for fire spread' in buildings over 18 metres high (Richards, 2017). Identical and similar forms of combustible cladding have since been removed from many tower blocks across England. However, alternative analyses of Approved Document B suggest that the cladding was lawful because of ambiguous wording in the regulations (Ledbetter, 2017). Moreover, while separate components may meet regulations, the testing regime and regulations have hitherto failed to assess the safety combinations of materials in relation to the building's original design (Webb, 2017). Crucially, the Grenfell refurbishment works passed all relevant local authority Building Control inspections (Booth, 2017).

In the 30 years prior to the disaster, these regulatory failures were foretold in at least seven major fires and 11 deaths in high-rise council tower blocks linked to flammable cladding across the UK, each time generating the same three demands: the fitting of sprinkler systems to all new and existing blocks; clear rules that require cladding to be non-combustible and actively resistant to the spread of fire; and consistent, appropriate and published guidance to residents over whether to 'stay put' or 'get out' in the event of fire (Webb, 2017). However, while governments in Scotland and Wales have taken steps to address some of these issues under their devolved powers (Huckle, 2017), England has taken a markedly different approach. For instance, sprinklers are still only required in new-build residential tower blocks higher than 30 metres with no requirement for retrospective action, compared to any new building above 18 metres in Scotland since 2005, and all new or refurbished residential buildings in Wales. A BBC Panorama investigation revealed that the All-Party Parliamentary Fire Safety and Rescue Group of MPs had privately warned four separate government ministers about the need for urgent action since 2013, each time being rebuffed (BBC News, 2017b). The government's opposition to new building regulations was illustrated in comments made by a government minister, Brandon Lewis MP, during a parliamentary debate in February 2014 on Fire Sprinklers Week:

> We should intervene only if it is entirely necessary, and only as a last resort.... We believe that it is the responsibility of the fire industry, rather than the Government ... to encourage their wider installation.... (Hansard, 6 February 2014, col 188)

In line with Wacquant's (2010) figure of the 'centaur state' that rewards those at the top while punishing the poor, this ideological refusal to re-regulate business reflects the neoliberal 'regulatory orthodoxy' championed by Thatcherism but systematically rolled out under New Labour's Better Regulation programme since 1997 aimed at 'removing the "burden" of inspection from most premises' (Tombs, 2016a, p 116). Following recommendations from the government-appointed 2004 Hampton Review of regulatory inspection and enforcement (chaired by a leading business figure, Philip Hampton), regulation was shifted to a default position of a risk-based model in which businesses would be made legally responsible for ensuring their own compliance with regulations, including fire safety, with the threat of detection and prosecution negligible. A key plank of self-regulation has been the roll-out of 'self-certification' for compliance with building regulations since 2002. An estimated 85 per cent of all building work that previously required either local authority or approved private sector inspectors to inspect and certify for a fee is now self-certified without charge under competent person schemes where contractors are registered and thus approved by a professional body (DCLG, nd, c). Similarly, since October 2006 the first line of responsibility for fire safety enforcement in England and Wales passed from the fire services authority to the responsible person for each building – the owner, landlord or managing agent (The Regulatory Reform [Fire Safety] Order 2005).

The Coalition and Conservative governments have continued to construct this self-regulatory regime under their Cutting Red Tape review programme, including the 'one-in, two-out' rule where for every £1 of additional net cost imposed on business by new regulations, other regulation must be cut by £2; the 2012 abolition of the Tenant Services Authority (TSA), which had regulated 'consumer' standards in social housing; the 2015 abolition of the Audit Commission, which has weakened auditing and enforcement against fraud and poor value for money in local government; and a 46 per cent cut in the Health and Safety Executive's budget between 2009/10 and 2019/20, reducing its capacity to investigate complaints about unsafe workplace practices by companies (Applebey, 2016). Overall, in the decade spanning these reforms and the onset of austerity (2004–13), research has found 'a long-term downwards trend in every form of enforcement activity' by statutory regulators (Tombs, 2016b, p 4).

The rise of self-regulation, long sub-contracting chains of private companies and austerity appear to have interacted in deadly fashion in the Grenfell Tower disaster. Self-certification has been linked to insufficient compliance with Building Regulations (DCLG, 2012, p 5) as well as major health and safety failures in public buildings constructed under largely self-monitored PFI contracts (Aitken, 2017). The ability of Building Control inspectors to check cladding systems and the standard of workmanship, or for landlords and contractors to identify who the designated fire risk assessor is in large renovation projects, has become increasingly difficult, with a complex chain of contractors self-certifying a large part of their own work and no single contractor or authority having oversight of all the works. This complexity is illustrated by reports that the London Metropolitan Police has identified no less than 383 companies involved in the construction or refurbishment of Grenfell Tower (Barratt, 2017). Government funding cuts are creating additional pressures on local authority building control teams to win contracts against private companies with speed of sign-off taking priority over rigorous inspection (London Fire and Emergency Planning Authority, 2014).

Grenfell residents repeatedly warned KCTMO, the local authority and the fire service of their safety fears, yet were largely ignored. Incredibly, several residents were threatened with legal action over making their claims public (Fifield, 2017). In reality, the residents of Grenfell Tower, like all council tenants, had very little legal power to pursue their concerns. Following the Housing Act 2004 and its risk assessment approach to housing safety – since April 2006 the Housing Health and Safety Rating System (HHSRS) – there has, in effect, been no minimum legal fitness standard for rented housing in England. Tenants can therefore only take legal action for any of 29 defined 'hazards' if they are caused by disrepair or relate to a relevant tenancy term (Huckle, 2017). Moreover, as singular legal entities, local housing authorities' environmental health officers, who have enforcement and prosecution powers to tackle unsafe rental housing, are unable to take action against themselves, only private landlords and RSLs (Peaker et al, 2017). Despite KCTMO being an independent company, Grenfell tenants thus had no protection against fire safety hazards from their local authority landlord:

The KCTMO manages the Council housing stock and as such the Council cannot take enforcement action against it. The Council's Environmental Health Team can however speak to the KCTMO on a tenant's behalf to try to address any problems informally. (RBKC, nd)

Labour MP Karen Buck's Private Member's Bill in 2015–16, and Labour amendments to the Housing and Planning Bill 2015–16, sought to reintroduce a 'fitness for human habitation' test to all rental accommodation in England. These initiatives were defeated by Conservative MPs with the official government line that they would 'result in unnecessary regulation and cost to landlords' (Jones, 2016).

Placing Grenfell: gentrification, social cleansing and the housing crisis

Grenfell has also drawn attention to the increasingly contested nature of urban regeneration and the wider housing crisis. Grenfell Action Group was, in fact, formed in 2010, long before the Tower refurbishment, by local residents opposed to plans for a new secondary school that would remove a large part of Lancaster West Estate's existing green space used by Grenfell Tower residents who lacked balconies or private amenity space (Grenfell Action Group, nd). The struggle soon widened to the local authority's proposed 15-year comprehensive redevelopment of the 1,800 homes on the Lancaster West and Silchester council estates in order to unlock land for 'high-end, high-value market housing' and 'maximise the overall value' of the wider area (Urban Initiatives, 2009, p 5). Grenfell Tower was originally earmarked for demolition because its mono-tenure population and architecture were held to 'blight' the local property market. RBKC eventually opted to retain and refurbish Grenfell Tower, arguably due to the development viability problems after the 2008 global financial crisis and housing market crash. However, for Grenfell Action Group, the masterplan was proof that RBKC and KCTMO wanted to 'socially cleanse' their working-class residents out of central London. In this context, the cladding of Grenfell Tower was perceived as less about thermal efficiency and more about aesthetic beautification to support the council's wider regeneration and housing market plans (ASH, 2017).

The displacement pressure felt by Grenfell and other local social housing residents speaks to a much wider spatial frame of speculative urban development and social cleansing in London under the logics of what the late Neil Smith (2002) called 'state-led gentrification'. This approach underpinned New Labour's urban regeneration policies after 2000 with their mantra of 'social mixing' and 'tenure diversification' aimed at bringing the middle classes back to the city. Urban regeneration schemes explicitly stigmatised the residents and architecture of public housing estates, most notably dozens of large postwar inner urban London estates characterised by brutalist design, before targeting them for wholesale demolition and regeneration as predominantly private housing (Lees, 2013; Watt, 2009). This agenda was continued under David Cameron's short-lived 'sink estates' policy announced in January 2016 to pump-prime the demolition and redevelopment of the UK's worst 100 estates, specifically targeting the 'brutal high-rise towers and dark alleyways that are a gift to criminals and drug dealers' and which he said were behind the 2011 riots in several UK cities (Cameron, 2016).

Housing and austerity policies since 2010 have accelerated this trend in London, in part due to extreme house price and land value increases that have made it the second most over-valued property market in the world and a target for increased demand from profit-seeking investors (Minton, 2017). With slashed council budgets meeting high real estate values, many London urban authorities, mostly Labour-run, are now seeking to expand the overall housing supply and raise finance for other services at the expense of affordable and secure housing through demolition and redevelopment of almost exclusively luxury private housing for sale or rent. A London Assembly Housing Committee (2015) report found that 50 estates subject to regeneration from 2004 to 2014 saw a *net loss* of around 8,300 social rental homes while the total number of homes almost doubled due to a massive increase in market provision. Some local authorities, such as Lambeth and Barnet, are even setting up their own for-profit Local Housing Companies outside of their housing revenue accounts to become speculative developers of private housing for sale and rent themselves (Beswick and Penny, forthcoming).

This gentrification-based regeneration and the speculative effects of foreign investment are part of a wider housing crisis affecting all tenures. Despite historically low mortgage interest rates, home ownership is currently at its lowest level in England since 1985, falling from its 2003 peak of 71 per cent to 63 per cent in 2015-16 (DCLG, 2017). Unaffordable home ownership and privatisation have driven the private rental sector, which was deregulated in 1988, to more than double in size over the past two decades, with around 36 per cent of former council homes sold under the RTB in London now owned by buy-to-let landlords (Copley, 2014). High demand has seen average private rents rise to 35 per cent of household income compared to 18 per cent for average mortgage costs: almost one in seven private renters spends over half their income on rent (LGA, 2017). This picture is set to deteriorate further as the RTB has been reinvigorated in England since 2012 with the Coalition and Conservative governments increasing maximum discounts from £38,000 to £104,900 in London and £78,600 elsewhere. The Housing and Planning Act 2016 introduced a new privatisation front in England – the sale of vacant higher-value local authority housing – which will force local authorities to sell on the open market all council houses located in an as yet undefined top price tier of the local housing market once they become empty (Davies and Compton, 2016).

The growing mismatch between housing costs and incomes is partly a function of the lowest peacetime building output at the hands of the 10 largest building companies that currently control around half of all housing production (compared to just 9 per cent in 1960), deliberately restricting supply so as to increase the price of new housing and make large profits (Archer and Cole, 2016). But it is also driven by the impact of austerity on the demand side, with falling average real wages since 2008 further undermined by huge welfare cuts since 2010 that will reach £27 billion a year by 2021 – equivalent to £690 a year for every working-age adult (Beatty and Fothergill, 2016). Nearly 90 per cent of council tenants on the Universal Credit system are in rent arrears (National Federation of ALMOs, 2017), and a record number of official evictions are taking place, up by a third between 2010 and 2016, to over 40,000 a year (Clarke et al, 2017). Homelessness has risen by nearly 60 per cent since 2009 (Shelter, 2017), pushing over 120,000 children into temporary accommodation (LGA, 2017). Shelter (2017) predicts that by 2020 over a million households in the UK could be put at risk of homelessness unless the current uprating freeze on Housing Benefit levels is lifted. This housing insecurity crisis is most acute in London where average house prices and rents are more than double the rest of England and almost 40 per cent of all evictions take place. When combined with welfare cuts and the growing shortage of social housing, an unprecedented social cleansing is in motion. Indeed, Housing Benefit cuts for private sector tenants have been explicitly linked by ministers and civil servants to forcing those dependent on welfare to lower-value areas (Powell, 2015). Tens of thousands of London households in temporary accommodation are being moved to other local authority areas each year, most within London, but a growing proportion to other cities and regions, including Newcastle upon Tyne (Greenwood, 2017).

But the London housing crisis that faced the 255 survivors of the fire, many bereaved and suffering from post-traumatic stress, was arguably the most extreme. Kensington and Chelsea is home to the highest average house prices in the UK, at £1.4 million (ONS, 2017), and the most expensive street in the UK with an average property price of £35.6 million (Odams, 2017). The borough's status as a destination for foreign property investment has led to 1,652 homes being left empty by distant owners treating them only as a pure financial asset (Batty et al, 2017). Since 1979, the Borough has lost around a quarter of its public housing stock to the RTB, and existing shortages mean that 72 per cent of homeless households placed in temporary accommodation by the council are housed outside of the borough (Trust for London, 2017). This is why, six months after the fire, only 42 out of the 208 households made homeless had been permanently rehoused, the rest remaining in temporary accommodation at the time of writing (Gentleman, 2017). In a final twist of cruelty, a small number of migrants resident in Grenfell Tower at the time of the fire have not made themselves known to the authorities because of their fear of being deported, and are reportedly sleeping rough.

Conclusion

In this chapter I have argued that the structural drivers and policy failures behind the Grenfell Tower disaster were rooted in neoliberalism's decades of policy dominance in the UK. It was neoliberalism that: produced the now ubiquitous privatised model of housing regeneration with for-profit companies empowered to operate long, badly monitored sub-contracting chains under a regime of self-certification and privatised governance; rolled back health and safety protections previously embedded in building regulations and planning controls; enabled the recommodification of housing under privatisation and the gentrification of urban policy that has created an acute shortage of affordable and secure housing for the Grenfell survivors; and created the corporatised structures of housing management that put money before the warnings of residents. If this was a disaster foretold, not just by the Grenfell residents but also by the long lineage of neoliberalism's discontents, then perhaps Grenfell will also represent the moment in history when policy changed course. Policy-makers must now ensure that all homes are both secure and safe to live in, and that residents' voices are democratically enshrined in housing governance. This means restoring the main features of the public housing model set out in this chapter, and regulating the private rental sector again. But post-Grenfell, better-quality housing requires that we overhaul all building and fire safety regulations, regulate the construction industry, and ensure that standards are enforced for all existing and new homes of all tenures. That means ending the neoliberal disaster before it kills again.

Note

[1] The Right to Buy was abolished in Scotland in 2016 and Wales in 2017.

References

Aitken, K. (2017) 'Scottish schools found with significant structural defects', *Public Finance*, 13 April (https://goo.gl/AOK0Ek).

Amin-Smith, N., Phillips, D. and Simpson, P. (2016) 'Council-level figures on spending cuts and business rates income', London: Institute for Fiscal Studies, 28 November (www.ifs.org.uk/publications/8780).

Applebey, L. (2016), 'HSE's funding will be cut £100m over ten years', *Safety and Health Practitioner*, 5 April (www.shponline.co.uk/hses-funding-will-be-cut-100m-over-ten-years/)

Apps, P. (2017) 'Grenfell: The paper trail', *Inside Housing* (www.insidehousing.co.uk/news/news/grenfell-the-paper-trail-51907)

Archer, T. and Cole, I. (2016) *Profits before volume? Major housebuilders and the crisis of housing supply*, Sheffield: Centre for Regional, Economic and Social Research, Sheffield Hallam University (www4.shu.ac.uk/research/cresr/sites/shu.ac.uk/files/profits-before-volume-housebuilders-crisis-housing-supply.pdf).

ASH (Architects for Social Housing) (2017) *The truth about Grenfell Tower: A report by Architects for Social Housing* (https://architectsforsocialhousing.wordpress.com/2017/07/21/the-truth-about-grenfell-tower-a-report-by-architects-for-social-housing/)

Barratt, L. (2017) 'Police investigation reveals 383 companies were involved in Grenfell refurbishment', 11 December, *Inside Housing*, 11 November (www.insidehousing.co.uk/news/news/police-investigation-reveals-383-companies-were-involved-in-grenfell-refurbishment-53557)

Batty, D., McIntyre, M., Pegg, D. and Asthana, A. (2017) 'Grenfell: Names of wealthy empty-home owners in borough revealed', *The Guardian*, 1 August (www.theguardian.com/society/2017/aug/01/names-of-wealthy-empty-home-owners-in-grenfell-borough-revealed).

BBC News (2017a) 'John McDonnell: Grenfell victims "murdered by political decisions"', 26 June (www.bbc.co.uk/news/uk-politics-40401314).

BBC News (2017b) 'Four ministers were warned about tower block fire risks', 21 June (www.bbc.co.uk/news/uk-40330789).

Beatty, C. and Fothergill, S. (2016) *The uneven impact of welfare reform: The financial losses to places and people*, Sheffield: Sheffield Hallam University (www4.shu.ac.uk/research/cresr/sites/shu.ac.uk/files/welfare-reform-2016_1.pdf).

Beswick, J. and Penny, J. (2018: forthcoming) 'Demolishing the present to sell off the future? The emergence of "financialized municipal entrepreneurialism" in London', *International Journal of Urban and Regional Research*.

Booth, R. (2017) 'Flammable Grenfell Tower cladding "passed" by council officer in 2015'*, 14 July, *The Guardian* (www.theguardian.com/uk-news/2017/jul/14/grenfell-tower-cladding-passed-by-council-officers-in-2015).

Cameron, D. (2016) 'Estate regeneration: Article by David Cameron', 10 January (www.gov.uk/government/speeches/estate-regeneration-article-by-david-cameron).

Clarke, A., Hamilton, C., Jones, M. and Muir, K. (2017) *Poverty, evictions and forced moves*, York: Joseph Rowntree Foundation (www.cchpr.landecon.cam.ac.uk/Projects/Start-Year/2016/Poverty-evictions-and-forced-moves/OutputTemplate/DownloadTemplate

Cole, I. and Furbey, R. (1994) *The eclipse of council housing*, London: Routledge.

Cook, C. (2017) 'Grenfell Tower: Government to review building regulations', BBC News Online, 14 July (www.bbc.co.uk/news/uk-40602991).

Copley, T. (2014) *From Right to Buy to Buy to Let*, London: Greater London Assembly (http://tomcopley.com/wp-content/uploads/2014/01/From-Right-to-Buy-to-Buy-to-Let-Jan-2014.pdf).

Davies, L. and Compton, J. (2016) 'A devastating blow to social housing in England', July, Legal Action Group (www.lag.org.uk/magazine/2016/07/a-devastating-blow-to-social-housing-in-england.aspx).

Davis, C. (2013) *Finance for housing: An Introduction*, Bristol: Policy Press.

DCLG (Department for Communities and Local Government) (no date, a) 'Live table 101: Dwelling stock by tenure, United Kingdom (Historical Series)' (www.gov.uk/government/uploads/system/uploads/attachment_data/file/609286/LT_101.xls).

DCLG (no date, b) 'Live table 208: Permanent dwellings started, by tenure and country' (www.gov.uk/government/uploads/system/uploads/attachment_data/file/639717/LiveTable208.xlsx).

DCLG (no date, c) 'Competent person scheme – Current schemes and how schemes are authorised' (www.gov.uk/guidance/competent-person-scheme-current-schemes-and-how-schemes-are-authorised#types-of-building-work).

DCLG (2012) *Changes to the conditions of authorisation for building regulations competent person self-certification schemes: Final impact assessment* (www.gov.uk/government/uploads/system/uploads/attachment_data/file/8405/2157372.pdf).

DCLG (2017) *English Housing Survey: Headline report, 2015-16* (www.gov.uk/government/uploads/system/uploads/attachment_data/file/658478/2015-16_EHS_Headline_Report.pdf).

Doward, J. (2017) 'The chronicle of a tragedy foretold: Grenfell Tower', 17 June, The *Guardian* (www.theguardian.com/uk-news/2017/jun/17/grenfell-tower-government-councils-fire-safety).

Dunleavy, P. (1981) *The politics of mass housing in Britain, 1945-1975: A study of corporate power and professional influence in the welfare state*, Oxford: Oxford University Press.

Engels, F. (1845 [2008]) *The condition of the working class in England*, New York: Cosimo Classics.

Englander, D. (1983) *Landlord and tenant in urban Britain, 1838-1918*, Oxford: Clarendon Press.

Fifield, N. (2017) 'Two women feared dead in Grenfell Tower tragedy were threatened with legal action – after raising alarm about fire safety', *The Mirror*, 17 June (www.mirror.co.uk/news/politics/two-women-feared-dead-grenfell-10640944).

Friedman, M. (1962) *Capitalism and freedom*, Chicago, IL: University of Chicago Press.

Gentleman, A. (2017) 'Four out of five Grenfell families still need homes, says support group', *The Guardian*, 7 December (www.theguardian.com/uk-news/2017/dec/07/grenfell-families-need-home-support-group).

Goulding, R. (2018) 'Governing risk and uncertainty: Financialisation and the regulatory framework of housing associations', in H. Carr, B. Edgeworth and C. Hunter (eds) *Law and the precarious home: Socio-legal perspectives on the home in insecure times*, Oxford: Hart Publishing, Chapter 8.

Greenwood, G. (2017) 'Homeless families rehoused out of London "up five-fold"', BBC News, 3 April (www.bbc.co.uk/news/uk-england-london-39386587).

Grenfell Action Group (no date) 'History – From Core Strategy to Kensington Academy' [Online] (https://grenfellactiongroup. wordpress.com/beginnings-3/).

Grenfell Action Group (2016) 'KCTMO – Playing with fire!', 20 November (https://grenfellactiongroup.wordpress.com/2016/11/20/ kctmo-playing-with-fire/).

Hansard HC Deb vol 575 col 188 (6 February 2014) [Electronic version].

Harloe, M. (1978) 'The Green Paper on housing policy', in M. Brown and S. Baldwin (eds) *The year book of social policy in Britain 1977*, London: Routledge and Kegan Paul, pp 3-21.

Hayek, F. (1960) *The constitution of liberty*, Chicago, IL: University of Chicago Press.

Hills, J. (2007) *Ends and means: The future roles of social housing in England*, CASEReport 34, London: London School of Economics and Political Science.

Hodkinson, S. (2011a) 'Housing regeneration and the private finance initiative in England: Unstitching the neoliberal urban straitjacket', *Antipode*, vol 43, pp 358-83. doi:10.1111/j.1467-8330.2010.00819.x

Hodkinson, S. (2011b) 'The private finance initiative in English council housing regeneration: A privatisation too far?', *Housing Studies*, vol 26, no 6, pp 911-32.

Hosken, A. (2017) 'Electricity problems at Grenfell Tower "never resolved"', 18 July, BBC News (www.bbc.co.uk/news/uk-40632705).

Huckle, T. (2017) 'Grenfell Tower – A different perspective', *New Law Journal*, issue 7753, pp 9-10 (www.newlawjournal.co.uk/content/ grenfell-tower-different-perspective).

Jones, M. (2016) House of Commons Debate on Housing and Planning Bill, 12 January (https://publications.parliament.uk/pa/cm201516/ cmhansrd/cm160112/debtext/160112-0003.htm).

Ledbetter, S. (2017) 'Fact Check: Is the type of cladding used on Grenfell Tower actually banned in Britain?', The Conversation, 26 June (https://theconversation.com/fact-check-is-the-type-of-cladding-used-on-grenfell-tower-actually-banned-in-britain-79803).

Lees, L. (2013) 'The urban injustices of New Labour's "new urban renewal": the case of the Aylesbury Estate in London', *Antipode*, vol 46, no 4, pp 921-47.

LGA (Local Government Association) (2017) *Housing our homeless households*, London: LGA (www.local.gov.uk/sites/default/files/documents/5.12%20HOUSING%20AND%20HOMELESSNESS_v08_4.pdf).

London Assembly Housing Committee (2015) *Knock it down or do it up? The challenge of estate regeneration*, London: Greater London Authority.

London Fire and Emergency Planning Authority (2014) *Structural fire safety in new and refurbished buildings*, Strategy Committee, 11 July, Report by Deputy Commissioner, FEP 2265 (http://moderngov.london-fire.gov.uk/mgconvert2pdf.aspx?id=3106).

Marcuse, P. and Madden, D. (2016) *In defense of housing*, London, New York: Verso.

Malpass, P. (2005) *Housing and the welfare state: The development of housing policy in Britain*, Basingstoke: Palgrave Macmillan.

Minton, A. (2017) *Big capital: Who is London for?*, London: Penguin.

Murie, A. (2015) 'The Right to Buy: history and prospect', *History & Policy*, 11 November (www.historyandpolicy.org/policy-papers/papers/the-right-to-buy-history-and-prospect).

NAO (National Audit Office) (2015) *Impact of funding reductions on fire and rescue services. Report by the Comptroller and Auditor General*, Local Government report, London: NAO (www.nao.org.uk/wp-content/uploads/2015/11/Impact-of-funding-reductions-on-fire-and-rescue-services-A.pdf).

National Federation of ALMOs (2017) *Pause for thought: Measuring the impact of welfare reform on tenants and landlords – 2017 survey results* (www.almos.org.uk/include/getDoc.php?did=7944&fid=9326).

Odams, K (2017) 'Most expensive streets across Britain', Zoopla, 2 October (www.zoopla.co.uk/discover/featured-homes/the-most-expensive-streets-in-britain-s-top-10-counties/#eIPHKvRkElyZlMAb.97).

O'Neill, S. and Karim, F. (2017) 'Keep costs of cladding down, Grenfell Tower experts told', *The Times*, 30 June (www.thetimes.co.uk/article/keep-costs-of-cladding-down-grenfell-tower-experts-told-6qrhmwzxv).

ONS (Office for National Statistics) (2017) 'House Price Index, UK: June 2017', Statistical Bulletin (www.ons.gov.uk/economy/inflationandpriceindices/bulletins/housepriceindex/june2017).

Peaker, G., Bates, J. and Buck, K. (2017) 'Improving fire safety under housing legislation', Legal Action Group, 17 July (www.lag.org.uk/magazine/2017/07/improving-fire-safety-under-housing-legislation.aspx).

Powell, R. (2015) 'Housing benefit reform and the private rented sector in the UK: On the deleterious effects of short-term, ideological "knowledge"', *Housing, Theory and Society*, vol 32, no 3, pp 320-45

RBKC (Royal Borough of Kensington and Chelsea) (2014) Report by the Director of Housing, Grenfell Tower Major Works and Hidden Homes Project, Cabinet Meeting, 19 June (https://goo.gl/CmRXnh).

RBKC (no date) 'How we work with KCTMO' (www.rbkc.gov.uk/housing/living-healthy-homes/d-repair/how-we-work-kctmo).

Richards, A. (2017) 'Grenfell Tower: was the cladding really banned material?', Al's Law, 24 June (https://alrich.wordpress.com/2017/06/24/grenfell-tower-was-the-cladding-really-banned-material/).

Shelter (2017) *Shut out: Households at put at risk of homelessness by the housing benefit freeze*, London: Shelter (https://england.shelter.org.uk/__data/assets/pdf_file/0005/1391675/LHA_analysis_note_FINAL.pdf).

Smith, N. (2002) 'New globalism, new urbanism: Gentrification as global urban strategy', *Antipode*, vol 34, no 3, pp 427-50.

Tombs, S. (2016a) '"Better regulation": better for whom?', Briefing 14, London: Centre for Crime and Justice Studies (www.crimeandjustice.org.uk/sites/crimeandjustice.org.uk/files/Better%20regulation%20briefing%2C%20April%202016_0.pdf).

Tombs, S. (2016b) 'Making better regulation, making regulation better?', *Policy Studies*, vol 37, no 4, pp 332-49.

Tombs, S. and Whyte, D. (2017) 'One law for the poor at Grenfell Tower', Open Democracy UK, 21 June (opendemocracy.net/uk/steve-tombs-and-david-whyte/on-grenfell-one-law-for-rich-one-poor).

Trust for London (2017) 'London's poverty profile 2017, K&C' (www.trustforlondon.org.uk/news/new-analysis-poverty-kensington-chelsea-shows-big-divides-between-rich-and-poor/)

Urban Initiatives (2009) *Notting Barns South draft final masterplan report*, London: Urban Initiatives.

Wacquant, L. (2010) 'Crafting the neoliberal state: workfare, prisonfare, and social insecurity', *Sociological Forum*, vol 25, no 2, pp 197-220.

Watt, P. (2009) 'Social housing and regeneration in London', in R. Imrie, L. Lees and M. Raco (eds) *Regenerating London*, London: Routledge, pp 173-91.

Webb, S. (2017) 'New government fire safety advice is sensible and proportionate', *Inside Housing*, 6 October (www.insidehousing.co.uk/comment/comment/new-government-fire-safety-advice-is-sensible-and-proportionate-52700).

Whitehead, J. (2017) 'Grenfell Tower is about race and class', The F-Word Blog, 22 June (www.thefword.org.uk/2017/06/grenfell_tower_race_and_class/).

TWO

Modern slavery in the United Kingdom: an incoherent response

Gary Craig

Introduction

Ten years after the publication by the Joseph Rowntree Foundation (JRF) of the first national scoping study of modern slavery in the UK (Craig et al, 2007), discussion about modern forms of slavery is achieving some political and policy prominence, focused largely on the passage of the Modern Slavery Act 2015 (MSA, covering England and Wales) and its Scottish and Northern Irish counterparts. This chapter outlines developments leading to this legislation, summarises it and evaluates subsequent progress. It points to a range of issues underlying the need for a major reform programme to ensure that the legislative and policy tools required effectively to combat modern slavery are in place, usable and used. I also hope to encourage social policy and related academics/ teachers to take the issue of modern slavery seriously when reviewing taught curricula, given that modern slavery intersects with a range of key social policy themes including poverty, inequality, labour relations, gender, migration, criminal justice, the third sector, housing, social assistance and social work.

An earlier analysis (Craig, 2010) placed developing understanding and awareness of modern slavery in the UK in a global and historical context. In the eight years since then, although public understanding has grown and action to combat modern slavery in the UK is developing, there remains a long way to go. In 2010, the nature/scope and extent of modern slavery in the UK was poorly understood, with estimates of its extent extremely vague and based on little firm evidence. It was estimated in the mid-2000s that there were at any one time about 5,000 sex workers in the UK, most of them having been trafficked into the UK, 75 per cent of them female and 30 per cent under the age of 16 (UNICEF, 2006b). Possibly 10,000 adults had been trafficked into the UK by about 2008. Even now, the numbers of those said to be in modern slavery in the UK is disputed among those working in this area. In 2015 the Home Office suggested that, analysing accessible data sources, there were likely to be between 10,000 and 13,000 people in forms of modern slavery at any one time within the UK (Bales et al, 2015). This figure was widely challenged, not least on the basis that the numbers of those being referred into the National Referral Mechanism (NRM, the formal means for being identified as a victim of modern slavery) was nearing 4,000 in 2016 (NCA, 2017), substantially more than double the corresponding figure for 2013. It was recognised that many more identified as potentially fitting the official definition of victim of slavery were rejecting entry into the NRM because of its association with immigration procedures, hostility towards authority in general or because of fears about traffickers identifying and taking punitive action against them or their families. Doubtless many more, but necessarily an unknown number were not known to agencies charged with seeking them out.

By 2017, the government's National Crime Agency (NCA, one of the two main government bodies charged with overseeing the identification of victims), on the basis of its own investigations, suggested that the numbers were in the 'tens of thousands' (Grierson, 2017), and much higher than had previously been thought. This is reflective of a wider dynamic: slavery has changed its forms to reflect an industrialised and increasingly globalised world where the migration of labour – almost half of it female (OECD, 2013) – to new, strange contexts makes it more vulnerable to enslavement. Ironically, comprehensive data – which during the period when slavery was legal was diligently recorded – is now, in a context of illegality, far less accessible. Estimates of numbers and types of slaves in any country thus bear a health warning regarding their understated nature. The International Labour Organization (ILO, nd) estimates that there may be 211 million children aged 5-14 engaged in economic activity, many of them trafficked, most of them working in hazardous situations, and at least 8.4 million subjected to the 'worst forms of child labour'.

While the scope of modern slavery has also been substantially enlarged in recent years, the core definition of slavery remains the same, characterised by three elements:

- severe economic exploitation
- the absence of a framework of human rights and

- control of one person by another by the threat or reality of coercion or violence.

However, the contexts in which modern slavery was appearing had widened substantially from a focus largely on trafficking of women and children for sexual purposes into and within the UK; other types of modern slavery now identified include trafficking of male children also for sexual purposes both into and within the UK; severe labour exploitation/forced labour; domestic servitude; forced begging, pickpocketing and shoplifting, generally by young children; debt bondage; cannabis farming; and organ sales. Modern slavery has been identified in virtually every industrial sector within the UK including agriculture and horticulture, food production, clothing, various forms of manufacture, the sale of sexual services, leisure and hospitality, social care, construction, forestry and fishing, and personal services such as nail bars and car washes. Victims of modern slavery in the UK are now seen, from the NCA's annual reports, to come from many countries, although some predominate in terms of particular types of modern slavery: most young men freed from coercion in cannabis farms come from Vietnam and China; the largest numbers of young women trafficked into the country for sexual exploitation come from Albania, Nigeria, Romania and China; and many of those in domestic servitude from Nigeria or the Philippines.

Pressure for legislation

Contrary to the beliefs of many since the passage of the two British anti-slavery Acts of 1807 and 1834, slavery thus had never really disappeared (Quirk, 2009). It remained a potentially significant policy and political issue both outside the UK and through its links to goods and services consumed within the UK. This aspect has increasingly become a serious political issue within the UK itself, being increasingly framed not simply as something that happened in poor countries with inadequate governance and legal structures, but also within other countries with trading and/or transport links with such countries (now made much easier by the availability of cheap transport, ranging from normal air travel to the backs of lorries). Modern-day slavery was thus now seen as involving the production of commodities in slavery conditions brought (alongside human beings) into the UK to be sold on the high streets of every town and city, by criminal individuals and organised gangs and purchased through ignorance of their provenance.

The conditions driving people to migrate and to be trafficked are described in a series of vignettes in Gupta (2007). The impact of globalisation of labour markets is highly significant; essentially, trafficking for sexual purposes reverses the dynamic where those owning capital (sex tourists) move to labour (those offering sexual services, for example, in South East Asia) to the converse. Labour now moves to meet the demands of capital on the latter's own territory. Moldova is a typical example – one-seventh of the population is estimated to have emigrated during a few years in the early 21st century. In three years, 1,131 Moldovan victims of child trafficking were identified.

Broadly from the publication of the JRF report onwards (see Craig et al, 2007), pressure for legislation grew steadily, reacting in part to the rather grudging way in which the UK government had signed up to various European and international conventions on aspects of modern slavery. Pressure came from this report, the subsequent well-funded JRF programme of research into forced labour, together with some highly effective and well-publicised work by prominent non-government organisations (NGOs) such as ECPAT (which worked on issues of the trafficking of children and young people), Kalayaan (which supported overseas domestic workers, publicising the restrictive way in which employment visas were controlled by their employers), and some of the major children's organisations (which were beginning to report incidences of trafficking among their clientele). Also highly significant in building pressure for the Act was the broader lobbying work of umbrella organisations such as Liberty and Anti-Slavery International (which together inserted a clause into the Coroners and Justice Act 2009 making forced labour a freestanding offence in the UK), and the work of the very few academics active in the area. This all combined to provide a better evidence base for the relatively few MPs interested in the subject in the early years of lobbying.

The JRF programme led to a substantial number of influential reports (see, for example, Geddes et al, 2014; Allain et al, 2015), also significant in widening debates about modern slavery away from their narrow focus on sex trafficking. This higher profile led one MP, Anthony Steen, to sponsor a Private Member's Bill committing the UK to an annual anti-slavery day (18 October) and to the creation and active work of an All-Party Parliamentary Group, initially called the APPG on Human Trafficking, later changing its name to the APPG on Modern Day Slavery. As noted, the developing pressure for legislation emerged most of all from the campaigning work of NGOs. A group of them, coordinated by Anti-Slavery International under the title of the Anti-Trafficking Monitoring Group (ATMG),[1] was later to publish critical commentaries on aspects of the Act in policy and practice.

Early data collected by the UK government's Human Trafficking Centre (later subsumed within the NCA) showed that the numbers of those referred for sexual and labour exploitation were roughly similar, together accounting for more than 80 per cent of the total cases, although, as in many European countries, the numbers of those recorded for labour exploitation grew much more rapidly (ECPAT, 2014) – reflecting the consequences of the steady deregulation of the UK labour market (Standing, 2011; Waite et al, 2015) Early parliamentary discussion of modern slavery within the UK (and elsewhere) continued to focus on the issue of human trafficking for sexual purposes, despite the interest in forced labour arising from the creation of the Gangmasters Licensing Authority (GLA) consequent on the death of the 23 Chinese cockle-pickers in Morecambe Bay in 2004. This was reflected in early legislation with all forms of trafficking made illegal through the 2004 Sexual Offences, and Immigration and Asylum Acts. The emphasis on sexual trafficking was reflected elsewhere in the world. The US Department of State estimated that at least 800,000 people were trafficked annually across borders worldwide, mostly women and children for sexual purposes, not including people trafficked *within* countries (UNICEF, 2005). This may have been a modest estimate as it was believed that more than 500,000 were being trafficked into Europe annually. The United Nations (UN) suggested that 1.2 million children might be trafficked annually, internally and externally (UNICEF, 2006a).

Pressure for legislation also grew from outside the UK. The European Convention for the Protection of Human Rights and Fundamental Freedoms is the overarching policy and political framework covering the treatment of refugees, the right to be free from torture, inhumane or degrading treatment and the prohibition of slavery and forced labour. Here, slavery was also interpreted largely to imply a ban on trafficking. The Council of Europe, requiring binding standards of human rights among member states, introduced a treaty and, in 2000, the Palermo Protocol[2] specifically addressing trafficking. This proposed measures to prevent and combat trafficking and for better victim protection, establishing a monitoring body to review progress in implementation. However, although most countries adopted laws to combat trafficking, and there has been international cooperation and movement as a result of GRETA's work, policy and practice responses still vary quite widely between countries.[3]

The Modern Slavery Act

Growing clamour around issues of modern slavery within Parliament, still prompted largely by NGO lobbying (Centre for Social Justice, 2013), research findings and increasing media coverage, finally led to the government publishing a draft Modern Slavery Bill in December 2013. Since its inception, the Bill, now Act, and subsequent parliamentary work, has become an important element of Theresa May's parliamentary portfolio, whose sponsorship, while contradictory in light of her other political positions, has helped to keep a high profile for the issue. On the other hand, her claim and that of her successor Home Secretary, Amber Rudd, that the Act was 'world-leading', bore little scrutiny both in light of subsequent criticism of its provisions and the fact that other European Union (EU) countries were some way ahead in introducing legislation and adhering firmly to the terms of the Palermo Protocol.

The Bill's first draft was very weak, leading to substantial criticism from every side. Consequently, it went through an unusually detailed and highly critical process of scrutiny, both inside and outside Parliament, before reappearing in final form in June 2014. Most significantly, a joint committee of the Houses of Commons and Lords engaged in pre-legislative scrutiny, again informed by lobbying and briefings from NGOs and academics. The government response to this scrutiny paper (UK Government, 2014) outlines ways in which they accepted much of the Committee's critique, including issues such as the statutory defence for victims (Clause 42), the scope of offences, the role of the Anti-Slavery Commissioner, and the nature of prevention mechanisms such as Trafficking Prevention Orders. However, despite growing awareness of the much wider scope of modern slavery, most of the Bill still remained focused on the issue of human trafficking. This limited time available to debate or legislate on other aspects of modern slavery. One key argument involved the form precise protection for children might take, with one suggested scheme, involving children being provided by the state with advocates, to defend their best interests, being piloted by an NGO, Barnardo's (for an evaluation, see Kohli et al, 2016).

This was one of several initiatives the government, unusually, took while the Bill was still being debated. A second was to create a Modern Slavery Unit within the Home Office; a third was to move departmental responsibility for the GLA, which scrutinised businesses for evidence of forced labour and issued licences to agencies supplying labour to companies, from the Department for Environment, Food and Rural Affairs (Defra) to the Home Office. A fourth reviewed the

NRM in light of the scathing critique developed by many organisations (see ATMG, 2014); and a fifth created the post of Independent Anti-Slavery Commissioner (IASC). This role, claimed to be equivalent to that of a National Rapporteur, was required by the Council of Europe to be an independent one. However, although the Act alluded to an independent commissioner, it remains unclear that the commissioner can work entirely free from government interference (see GRETA, 2016, p 11). The commissioner reports to the Home Secretary who can redact reports, rather than directly to Parliament. The post was advertised even *before* being debated in Parliament.

The issue of trafficking for labour exploitation and of forced labour (which can occur whether or not trafficking is involved) still received far less attention. The number of cases for forced labour brought before the courts remained very low, and well-prepared cases of forced labour were thrown out or given lenient sentences by the judiciary who seemed to have a very limited understanding of how forced labour worked (*The Spectator*, 2014). One important victory was won late on by lobbyists with the government agreeing to include a clause (54) requiring companies to take some responsibility for exploring whether slavery might be found in their supply chains (see Allain et al, 2013). However, the government rejected very strong demands from inside and outside Parliament to protect overseas domestic workers from abusive employers.

There was also substantial pressure to extend the remit of the GLA from its early narrow focus. Initially it was only able effectively to investigate a small fraction of possible forced labour cases (Wilkinson et al, 2009). The Act required the government to complete a thorough review of the scope of the GLA within a year of enactment. This review was eventually subsumed into a wider review of immigration and labour market policy, thus confirming a widespread perception that modern slavery was an immigration issue rather than one of exploitation, confirmed by the insertion of various clauses about slavery into the Immigration Act 2016. In October 2016 the GLA became the Gangmasters and Labour Abuse Authority (GLAA). Although the government conceded that it should have a remit covering the whole of the labour market including a number of industrial sectors that had begun to be of wider concern (such as leisure and hospitality, construction, social care), and some additional quasi-policing powers, the GLAA is significantly under-funded. In late 2017 it received funding to enlarge its workforce by 60 per cent, although this was to deal with a labour market remit increased by 6,000 per cent!

The final debates in the weeks before Parliament rose for the 2015 General Election enabled the government to drive through clauses to which opposition parties were hostile: given that the Bill had all-party support in general, no one was prepared to prevent it from being enacted. The Act's final form thus reflected a substantial amount of unfinished business, some of it explicit as noted above, some of it implicit or contested.

Clearly the fact that the Acts (including the two parallel Acts in Scotland and Northern Ireland) are now part of the legislative and policy landscape is a great advance: this has not only put the issue firmly on the public and policy agendas, but it has also given a substantial boost to those arguing the case for action for many years. It provides a range of potential tools for the differing organisations (whether concerned with criminal justice, victim support, social care, advocacy and advice or ethical trading) to up their game. As a result, the number of prosecutions has increased (289 prosecutions brought in 2015 and 113 convictions obtained) (Inter-Departmental Ministerial Group on Modern Slavery, 2016), although not as many as might have been hoped given the scale of the problem, with some sentences regarded as derisory given the seriousness of the offences and a very small proportion of investigations resulting in the sentencing of perpetrators. There have also been some prosecutions relating to the supply chains clause (54) (McKevitt, 2017).

However, there remains continuing confusion about the use of the statutory defence for victims of slavery given that many of those victims freed from cannabis farms were then sentenced to imprisonment (Burland, 2017). Many police forces have begun to create modern slavery units which, with improvements in some data collection, have helped them to focus more clearly on modern slavery as a defined criminal offence, and in some areas they have helped create multi-agency modern slavery partnerships to coordinate local work. Worryingly, a scathing critique by the Inspector of Constabulary (HMICFRS, 2017) suggested that most police forces remain ill equipped to address the problem of modern slavery.

Despite limited gains, many have argued that the Act's provisions represent a missed opportunity in many ways. Some are cross-cutting, a prominent one being the question of training (see, for example, IASC, 2015; The Passage, 2017). It is clear from wide-ranging evidence that there is no group of concerned professionals, whether the police, judiciary, medical practitioners, NGOs, care workers or social care providers, where the level and quality of training for identifying and supporting victims of modern slavery, and of knowing how to progress their cases, is adequate.

Thinking about possible changes to legislation over the next few years, it is important to acknowledge the current UK political and policy context. Many commentators have suggested that the significant spike in race hate crimes following the Brexit vote of June 2016 reflected the more general antipathy to immigration and specifically to migrant workers that has been growing for some time (Institute of Race Relations, 2016). It is hardly a coincidence, then, that recent changes in the form of the GLA that claimed to address the issue of severe labour exploitation (Weatherburn and Toft, 2016) were introduced in an Immigration Act in late 2016, which presented a very 'hostile' face to migrants. This may compromise attempts to rescue workers found to be in severe labour exploitation. Meanwhile, concern is also growing about the potentially disastrous impacts in terms of European police cooperation, legal provision and human rights protection that may result from the current government stance towards Brexit (ATMG, 2017).

An agenda for further reform

Three Acts or one?

Along with the Westminster legislation, separate legislation was introduced in to both Scotland and Northern Ireland. The Scottish legislation initially appeared weaker than that of Westminster, and that in Northern Ireland even more narrowly conceived. Criticisms focused mainly on the fact that inconsistencies between law, policy and practice might lead to some jurisdictions becoming more attractive to traffickers and gangmasters. The IASC has made attempts to bridge these gaps and has been given a UK-wide role in some provisions, but important difficulties remain, and an independent evaluation of the legal framework across the UK has pointed to very significant problems (ATMG, 2016). It appears, however, that the legislation in Scotland and Northern Ireland has turned out to be more comprehensive and/or effective in certain areas such as the protection of children (ATMG, 2016). The difficulties include the following:

- There are 'significant differences' in a number of key areas across the three jurisdictions, including around the criminalisation of victims and in statutory support for adult victims (see below).

- There is a lack of monitoring arrangements to ensure coordination and calibration of the Acts' progress, as well as to assess the effectiveness of specific provisions.
- The wording of certain clauses or words such as 'travel' and 'duty to notify' is ambiguous.
- There are differences in provision and timetables in areas such as child guardianship.

The ATMG report proposes that the IASC be given a central role in terms of collecting and analysing data in order to identify specific gaps. It is also worth noting that Wales is the only UK territory with anything like a comprehensive centrally coordinated anti-slavery strategy (see Welsh Government, nd). Core elements of this strategy have been evaluated, the evaluators reaching broadly positive conclusions about the effectiveness of the key elements of the scheme, particularly training provision and the support arrangements for identified trafficking victims. The Welsh strategy is also developing freestanding critiques of aspects of the Act and guidance related to it (see Welsh Government, 2017, in relation to ethical practice in supply chains).

Role of the GLAA

The formal shift from the GLA to the GLAA occurred late in 2017 and it is not yet possible to make an authoritative statement on the impact of this change, although there remains a clear need for the issue of resources to be addressed. The GLAA, like its predecessor, is intelligence-led. Whether it will have the capacity to respond to claims that a whole sector such as construction or social care is infected by trafficking or by forced labour remains a moot point, although the Chief Executive Officer has indicated that targets are frequently reviewed. Construction is a case in point where the frequency of so-called self-employment may mask an equally frequent occurrence of severe labour exploitation. Other sectors where far-reaching investigations may be needed include food production and retailing, shown by research to be one possible focus for forced labour (Geddes et al, 2014), social care (Craig and Clay, 2017) and fishing, where deep sea fishing may require extensive resources for investigation.

The other major change to the GLAA has been in terms of institutional structures: although the GLAA still has a (smaller) Board of Directors, it appears that it may be more closely accountable to government through the new Director of Labour Market Enforcement, thus less open to change driven by external critiques. Given the high regard in which the GLA's work has been held to date by those active in this area, it would be unfortunate if these changes undermined its effectiveness.

Supply chains

Clause 54 of the Modern Slavery Act, inserted late on in the parliamentary process, required companies (numbering around 12,000) with a turnover of more than £36 million to ensure that slavery practices were not present in their supply chains, and to publish annual modern slavery statements. The clause, although welcome in terms of raising the profile of 'hidden' slavery within the goods and services found within the British economy, is weak, with no formal legal sanctions other than civil proceedings involving injunctions in the High Court, unlikely to impact significantly on profitability. An early analysis of some statements suggested that the response from businesses was uneven and in general, disappointing, with many companies appearing to rely on aspirational statements rather than action plans (Ergon Associates, 2017).

The government's view remains that the impact of naming and shaming on companies' reputations might be adequate to persuade companies to take effective action, a view challenged by early experience: relatively few companies have complied to date, most providing statements have failed to meet the Acts' requirements; and many remain ignorant of its provisions (CIPS, 2016). Meanwhile, 71 per cent of companies believe there is slavery in their supply chains (Fifty Eight, 2016), all suggesting a strong case for toughening sanctions against companies in line with the UN *Guiding principles on business and human rights* (OHCHR, 2011). Additionally, the Act only applies at present to private companies. Baroness Lola Young introduced a Private Member's Bill to extend the Acts' requirements to the public sector, many parts of which, such as hospital trusts and large local authorities, have substantial procurement budgets.[4] The Bill fell because of the 2017 General Election. The government also declined to coordinate the monitoring of anti-slavery statements, a task now undertaken by a group of NGOs (The Freedom Fund, 2016). A small industry has grown up of organisations advising companies on how to comply with the terms of Clause 54 (for example, Walk Free Foundation, 2014), sometimes on a minimal basis.

The NRM

As the Modern Slavery Act became operational, the government committed to reviewing the NRM, the system by which the claims of those alleging to be victims of modern slavery were assessed (see NCA, nd). The NRM had been widely criticised, including by the ATMG (2014), which argued, inter alia, that the NRM was racist, with those from countries outside the European Economic Area (EEA) (most of whom were Black or from other minority ethnic groups) standing only one-quarter of the chance of having their claims accepted as those from within the EU, most of whom were white). The NRM internal review undertaken by the Home Office led to a proposed simplification of structure with 'modern slavery leads' replacing the 'first responders' whose job it was to refer identified possible victims of modern slavery into the NRM via the NCA or UK Visas and Immigration. Pilot projects for the new structure were established to test the new system – a full evaluation of their effectiveness is still awaited. However, although the government asserts that the new system makes it easier for non-first responder NGOs to make referrals, this is disputed, and there has been little evidence of a greater volume of cases being processed.

The separation of the asylum/immigration and modern slavery elements within the assessment process is needed to ensure that alleged victims are not discouraged from reporting their experience, as noted earlier. It remains unclear whether the pilot system will be rolled out across the country or amended again. The IASC (2016) has published a scathing criticism of the NRM, which he regards as not fit for purpose, cumbersome and requiring radical change (IASC, 2017). He particularly criticises the need for a two-stage process for validating claims made by victims, other difficulties of accessing the NRM and the failure to provide adequate victim support, the last emphasised in a report produced by a coalition of NGOs (HTF, 2017). Late in 2017 the government announced limited changes to the NRM that appear to have satisfied no one: the removal of adjudication for potential victims from immigration officials had simply, in one view, 'contradicted the findings of the Home Office's own 2014 review of the decision-making process'.[5]

Child advocates

As noted, the government committed to introducing a system of child advocates whereby each child alleged to be the victim of trafficking would have a unique independent child trafficking advocate responsible for protecting their interests. This scheme was piloted by Barnardo's in 23 local authority areas and the scheme independently evaluated. Although some successes were noted, the government remained unconvinced by the scheme's effectiveness, arguing that it had not made much difference in terms of identifying or retaining trafficked children. It accepted that much more needed to be done to ensure the scheme's robustness, but has also acknowledged that it should not wait for these to be developed as it would put a number of children now at risk in danger. It therefore invested in a modest child protection fund targeted at alleged victims of child trafficking, highlighting the reasons why they might go missing, and on children from high-risk countries. It might be two further years before a system involving an agreed form of advocate is established, and this may still have territorial inconsistencies.

Domestic workers

Prior to 2010, domestic workers, typically employed by wealthy businesspeople or diplomats, had a degree of protection in that, although their visas were tied to a specific employer, if evidence of abuse emerged the worker could change employer without endangering their immigration status. The 2010 government changed this arrangement, and workers became liable to deportation (and thus also loss of income) if they tried to change employers (Mantouvalou, 2015). The government conceded an independent review of the visa arrangement and committed itself to accepting the findings in full. In the event, the Ewins review (UK Government, 2015) concluded that the visa arrangement aggravated the prospects of exploitation. The government has since backtracked on its commitment. Although the IASC intervened with the government to allow domestic workers on these visas to change employers during a six-month initial stay and those identified through the NRM as victims of modern slavery to stay for two years (IASC, 2016, p 19), this did not satisfy the government's promise to full implementation of the Ewins review. GRETA's (2016) monitoring report also noted that the government had fallen short of its promise, arguing that there was a need for inspections of private households to be encouraged, and that changes in employers should be more clearly facilitated. Contracts with those working for diplomats should, they felt, be concluded with Embassy Missions rather than individual diplomats, to prevent the latter using diplomatic privilege to escape prosecution.

Labour exploitation

The issue of labour exploitation and trafficking and forced labour in particular remains fairly marginal in UK modern slavery debates, even after the passage of legislation. Although the new GLAA has a wide-ranging remit, its limited resources make it unlikely that it can have a very strong impact; the effectiveness of the new Directorate of Labour Market Enforcement, whose remit covers employment agencies, low wages and labour exploitation, remains to be assessed. The Director is responsible to two government departments, making reporting arrangements difficult to manage, and its gestation, as a creation of new immigration legislation, suggests that it will focus much more on questions of irregular employment than in pursuing the perpetrators of labour exploitation.

A wider criticism of the Act is that it is, at heart, a criminal justice instrument linked strongly to issues of migration status rather than one focused strongly on victim support. In GRETA's view, more needs to be done to strengthen the role of the GLAA and parallel inspectorates including in relation to resources, training and remit. Trying to stop labour exploitation while all remaining government policy effectively encourages it represents the major contradiction at the heart of the Act, a contradiction barely addressed in the Taylor Review (Taylor, 2017), commissioned by the government to explore the idea of 'good work'. It is hardly surprising then that the Salvation Army, which oversees victim support, reported a four-fold rise in labour exploitation cases over the four years 2013-16.

Data collection and analysis

Effective data collection and analysis is critical to the successful implementation of the Act, yet the contested question of the numbers of those in modern slavery highlights the fact that data collection, recording and analysis remains inadequate. It was only in April 2015 that a separate crime recording category of modern slavery was introduced into police data systems, and it is clear that many police forces are still not exploiting the significance of this change. Compared with the more than 3,000 cases known to the NRM in 2016, less than one-third of that total were logged in police records, and an enquiry conducted on behalf of the IASC discovered that some police forces had no record of NRM referrals at all. In Northern Ireland, however, which has one police force, all modern slavery crimes were recorded in the appropriate category. The police lead on modern slavery has made data recording a priority, but much remains to be done, linked to the question of training. GRETA has noted 'gaps in the collection of data on human trafficking, limiting the possibility of analysing trends and adjusting policies.' This includes poor recording in other parts of the criminal justice system and no systemic information on possible child victims of trafficking missing from local authority care.

Support for victims of modern slavery

Current revised arrangements provide for a period of 45 days 'reflection' by alleged victims of modern slavery while their cases move from provisional acceptance of their claim to a final endorsement. Once formal acceptance of a claim has been confirmed, modern slavery victims have a very short period (typically two weeks) to make arrangements for establishing themselves in the community. With little knowledge of rights such as for housing and benefits and little formal support available (although NGOs and churches have stepped in to fill the gaps), victims may be vulnerable to poverty and isolation and possibly to re-trafficking if their traffickers have not been apprehended. The issue of support services for victims has thus become critical. The HTF has made this a strong focus for their work, publishing several reports arguing for improved care and support (HTF, 2016). There has yet to be a coordinated, strategic response to this issue, and much funding for this work has come from charities, leading to something of a postcode lottery for accessing effective support. Lord McColl has introduced a Private Member's Bill, pressing the government to provide better support. The government has also been required to ensure that victims can be treated with a great deal more sensitivity by benefits offices, the subject of a 2017 critical House of Commons enquiry.

Conclusion

These, and other issues not discussed here, represent a huge agenda of necessary political, structural and organisational change. Critical issues to be addressed immediately include training, victim support, increasing the effectiveness of the criminal justice system in responding to modern slavery, strengthening the supply chain legal framework (CLT Envirolaw, 2017), enlarging the GLAA's resources and revising arrangements for domestic workers. In terms of practice, evidence of the lack of effective training suggests that many organisations have yet to fully understand or implement the provisions of the Act; for example, a response to a parliamentary question in February 2017 indicated that six police forces in England and Wales had yet to identify a single victim of modern slavery within their areas.[6]

It was more than 200 years from the passage of Wilberforce's First Act to the passage of the MSA; based on this assessment it seems likely that it will be little more than two to three years before this Act returns to the statute book for significant revision. Having an Act, however incoherent its use, at least offers the possibility of future political leverage for change: wide-ranging campaigning will doubtless continue.

Notes
[1] See www.antislavery.org/what-we-do/where-we-work/uk/anti-trafficking-monitoring-group
[2] See www.ohchr.org/EN/ProfessionalInterest/Pages/ProtocolTraffickingInPersons.aspx
[3] GRETA is the Council of Europe's Group of Experts on Action against Trafficking.
[4] HL Bill 6, 56/2; see also House of Lords, In Focus LIF 2016/0035 Briefing Note.
[5] See www.labourexploitation.org/news/press-release-flex-condemns-ongoing-Home-Office-control-of-modern-slavery-victim-identification
[6] Personal communication from Diana Johnson MP to author, 2 March 2017.

References

Allain, J., Crane, A., LeBaron, G. and Behbahani, L. (2013) *Forced labour's business models and supply chains*, York: Joseph Rowntree Foundation.

ATMG (Anti-Trafficking Monitoring Group) (2014) *Proposals for a revised National Referral Mechanism*, London: ATMG.

ATMG (2016) *Class acts?*, London: ATMG.

ATMG (2017) *Brexit and the UK's fight against modern slavery* (www.antislavery.org/brexit-modern-slavery/).

Bales, K., Hesketh, O. and Silverman, B. (2015) 'Modern slavery in the UK: How many victims?', *Significance*, vol 12, no 3, pp 16-21.

Burland, P. (2017) *Guilty of being a victim? The continuing punishment of people trafficked for cannabis cultivation since the 2015 Modern Slavery Act*, York: Modern Slavery Research Consortium [copy available from the present author].

Centre for Social Justice (2013) *It happens here*, London: Centre for Social Justice.

CIPS (Chartered Institute of Procurement & Supply) (2016) *Procurement professionals unprepared for Modern Slavery Act* (www.cips.org/supply-management/news/2016/february/procurement-professionals-unprepared-for-modern-slavery-act).

CLT Envirolaw (2017) *The Modern Slavery Act: Act into action* (http://www.ardeainternational.com/?guide=modern-slavery-act-act-action).

Craig, G. (2010) '"Flexibility", xenophobia and exploitation: modern slavery in the UK', in I. Greener, C. Holden and M. Kilkey (eds) *Social Policy Review 22: Analysis and debate in social policy 2010*, Bristol: Policy Press, in conjunction with the Social Policy Association.

Craig, G. and Clay, S. (2017) 'Who is vulnerable? Social care and the Modern Slavery Act', *Journal of Adult Protection*, vol 19, no 1, pp 21-32.

Craig, G., Wilkinson, M., Gaus, A., McQuade, A. and Skrivankova, K. (2007) *Contemporary slavery in the United Kingdom*, York: Joseph Rowntree Foundation.

ECPAT (2014) *Parliamentarians against human trafficking, Final report to the European Union*, London: ECPAT UK.

Ergon Associates (2017) *Modern slavery statements: One year on*, London: Ergon Associates.

Fifty Eight (2016) 'How the Modern Slavery Act impacts companies and public procurement in the North West', Blog, 10 February (www.50eight.com/blog/how-the-modern-slavery-act-impacts-companies-and-public-procurement-in-the-north-west).

Freedom Fund, The (2016) 'Modern Slavery Act – First free and open registry makes 540 company statements available', Press release, 31 August (http://freedomfund.org/press-release/modern-slavery-act-first-free-open-registry/).

Geddes, A., Craig, G. and Scott, S. (2014) *Forced labour in the UK*, York: Joseph Rowntree Foundation.

GRETA (Group of Experts on Action Against Trafficking in Human Beings) (2016) *Report concerning the implementation of the Council of Europe Convention on Action against Trafficking in Human Beings by the United Kingdom* (https://rm.coe.int/CoERMPublicCommonSearchServices/DisplayDCTMContent?documentId=09000016806abcdc).

Grierson, J. (2017) 'Tens of thousands of modern slavery victims in UK, NCA says', *The Guardian*, 10 August (www.theguardian.com/world/2017/aug/10/modern-slavery-uk-nca-human-trafficking-prostitution).

Gupta, R. (2007) *Enslaved*, London: Portobello.

HMICFRS (Her Majesty's Inspectorate of Constabulary and Fire & Rescue Services) (2017) *Stolen freedom*, London: HMICFRS.

HTF (Human Trafficking Foundation) (2016) *Day 46*, London: HTF.

HTF (2017) *Supporting adult survivors of slavery to facilitate recovery and reintegration and prevent re-exploitation* (www.humantraffickingfoundation. org/sites/default/files/Long%20term%20survivor%20support%20 needs%20March%2017%202.pdf).

IASC (Independent Anti-Slavery Commissioner) (2015) *Independent Anti-Slavery Commissioner strategic plan 2015-17* (www.gov.uk/ government/uploads/system/uploads/attachment_data/file/468729/ IASC_StrategicPlan_2015.pdf).

IASC (2016) *Annual report*, London: IASC.

IASC (2017) Letter to Sarah Newton MP on improved National Referral Mechanism (www.antislaverycommissioner.co.uk/news-insights/letter-to-sarah-newton-mp-on-improved-national-referral-mechanism).

ILO (International Labour Organization) (no date) *Forced labour, modern slavery and human* trafficking, Geneva: ILO (www.ilo.org/global/ topics/forced-labour/lang--en/index.htm).

Institute of Race Relations (2016) *Racial violence and the Brexit state* (www.irr.org.uk/news/racial-violence-and-the-brexit-state).

Inter-Departmental Ministerial Group on Modern Slavery (2016) *Report of the inter-departmental ministerial group on modern slavery 2016* (www. gov.uk/government/uploads/system/uploads/attachment_data/ file/559690/Modern_Slavery_IDMG_Report_2016.pdf)

Kohli, R., Hynes, P., Connolly, H., Thurnham, A., Westlake, D. and D'Arcy, K. (2016) *Evaluation of independent child trafficking advocates trial: Final report*, London: Home Office.

Mantouvalou, V. (2015) 'Am I free now?', *Journal of Law and Society*, vol 42, pp 329-57.

McKevitt, J. (2017) 'Modern slavery prosecutions multiply in the UK', 6 June (www.supplychaindive.com/news/UK-modern-slavery-act-results-2016/444258/).

NCA (National Crime Agency) (2017) *National Referral Mechanism statistics – End of year summary 2016* (www.nationalcrimeagency.gov. uk/publications/788-national-referral-mechanism-statistics-end-of-year-summary-2016/file).

National Crime Agency (no date) *National Referral Mechanism* (www. nationalcrimeagency.gov.uk/about-us/what-we-do/specialist-capabilities/uk-human-trafficking-centre/national-referral-mechanism).

OECD (Organisation for Economic Co-operation and Development) (2013) *World migration in figures* (www.oecd.org/els/mig/World-Migration-in-Figures.pdf).

OHCHR (United Nations Human Rights Office of the High Commissioner) (2011) *Guiding principles on business and human rights* (www.ohchr.org/Documents/Publications/GuidingPrinciplesBusinessHR_EN.pdf).

Passage, The (2017) *Modern slavery in the homelessness sector*, London: The Passage.

Quirk, J. (2009) *Unfinished business*, Paris: UNESCO.

Spectator, The (2014) 'It's time for Britain to abolish slavery – Again', 5 July (www.spectator.co.uk/2014/07/lets-stop-slavery-again).

Standing, G. (2011) *The precariat*, London: Bloomsbury Books.

Taylor, M. (2017) *Good work: The Taylor review of modern working practices*, London: Department for Business, Energy & Industrial Strategy (www.gov.uk/government/publications/good-work-the-taylor-review-of-modern-working-practices).

UK Government (2014) *Draft Modern Slavery Bill* (www.gov.uk/government/uploads/system/uploads/attachment_data/file/318771/CM8889DraftModernSlaveryBill.pdf).

UK Government (2015) *Independent Review of the Overseas Domestic Workers Visa* (www.gov.uk/government/uploads/system/uploads/attachment_data/file/486532/ODWV_Review_-_Final_Report_6_11_15_.pdf]

UNICEF (2005) *The true extent of child trafficking*, London: UNICEF.

UNICEF (2006a) *Child trafficking*, London: UNICEF UK.

UNICEF (2006b) *Commercial sexual exploitation*, London: UNICEF UK.

Waite, L., Craig, G., Lewis, H. and Skrivankova, K. (eds) (2015) *Vulnerability, exploitation and migration*, Basingstoke: Palgrave.

Walk Free Foundation (2014) *Tackling modern slavery in supply chains. A guide 1.0* (http://business.walkfreefoundation.org).

Welsh Government (2017) *Code of practice: Ethical employment in supply chains* (www.gov.wales/code-of-practice).

Welsh Government (no date) *Research into the effectiveness of the anti slavery approach in Wales* (http://gov.wales/statistics-and-research/research-effectiveness-anti-slavery-approach/?lang=en).

Weatherburn, A. and Toft, A. (2016) 'Managing the risks of being a victim of severe labour exploitation', *Industrial Law Journal*, vol 45, no 2, pp 257-62.

Wilkinson, M., Craig, G. and Gaus, A. (2009) *Turning the tide*, Oxford: Oxfam.

THREE

Childcare, life chances and social justice

Gideon Calder

Introduction

In recent years the notion of 'life chances' has been moving ever closer to the centre of UK talk about social mobility and equality of opportunity. With the Welfare and Reform Act 2016, its official status was confirmed by the retrospective renaming of the Child Poverty Act 2010 as the Life Chances Act 2010. As a term it has been high on political resonance but low on definition. This chapter considers the relationship between the 'life chances' agenda – such as it is – and persistent questions about the relationship between childcare and social justice. 'Childcare' here refers to how children receive care in a general sense: not just to professional arrangements made by working parents, for example, but to the full range of ways in which children receive care, within and outside the family (Harding, 1996, pp 162-71). While 'life chances' (however conceived) reflect an array of factors ranging well beyond how a society arranges for the care of children, there is a strong case in favour of putting questions of childcare at the very centre of any strategy for fairer life chances.

Seen as a social justice issue, childcare can be approached from various angles – for example, in terms of gender, family autonomy and class inequalities. Each of these is vitally important to a critical understanding of how it features in social policy, and how the issues it raises might be addressed. But the chief focus here is on fairness among children themselves. There is a long-standing habit in policy circles – typified in 'life chances' talk – to take the future destinations of children as the yardstick for how fair their start in life has been. This chapter considers what happens when, instead, we take their childhoods themselves as the focal point, when gauging inequality between children. Looked at this way, the maldistribution of childcare in society is about the lives of children *now* just as much as it is about future life prospects: about childhood as 'a stage of life, with its own value' (CPAG, 2016, p 1).

This chapter looks first at the typical ways in which a 'life chances' agenda has been invoked in government strategies and ministerial speeches, and its role – as Ruth Lister has put it – as 'something of an empty vessel' (Lister, 2016, p 1). In the next section, seeking a firmer footing, it sets out a basic elaboration of how 'fair life chances' might be understood. It then turns to what might be called the 'yardstick problem': the difficulties encountered in finding a limited range of measures of how life chances pan out that capture the full significance of the concept. It then considers the pivotal place of childcare in any coherent 'life chances' agenda, and the value of a child-focused analysis as part of its wider articulation. The chapter concludes with a proposal that we address childcare as a 'relationship good' – a uniquely valuable form of relationship, the distribution of which should be treated as a basic matter of social justice and of a viable approach to 'life chances' in policy terms. This is not to distract from or downplay other senses in which childcare is a matter of social justice – with regard to gender, the family or class. Rather, it provides a way of establishing a flourishing childhood as a core parameter, alongside those others.

'Life chances' rhetoric

Politically, 2016 quickly came to be defined in terms of two world-changing and odds-defying votes: for Brexit, and for Trump. Both demand an explanation with reference to the divided, unequal and uneasy societies that the UK and the US have increasingly become (Ellison, 2017; Holden, 2017). Yet there was another, quieter casualty of that period, equally tied up with those same background trends. It was David Cameron's 'life chances' agenda. This was to be a defining project of Cameron's second and final term as Prime Minister. Its aim was to 'transform the life chances of the poorest in our country and offer every child who has had a difficult start the promise of a brighter future' (Cameron, 2016). Children who 'start behind', he pointed out, still get 'left behind'. Counteracting this would be a government priority. There would be a 'Life Chances Strategy', seeking to move beyond the 'old thinking' on child poverty characterised by 'statist' and 'free market' approaches. Instead, we would be offered a 'social' alternative, based less on economics and more on relationships. It would be based on a rich picture of 'how social problems combine, of how they reinforce each other, how they can manifest themselves throughout someone's life and how the opportunity gap [between poorer and richer children] gets generated as a result' (Cameron, 2016). In response, it would combine attention to families and the early years, education, widening opportunities, and the support and treatment of those in crisis.

This seemed a portentous moment. The agenda was grand and ambitious, whatever its arguable flaws. It promised an attempt at precisely the kinds of joined-up social policy that an effective approach to intergenerational inequality seemed to need. Whatever exactly the Life Chances Strategy would amount to, it seemed Cameron meant business and wanted to be judged by its success. The Strategy was due to be announced on 24 June 2016, the day after the Brexit referendum (Puffet, 2016a). Then came the result. The big moment was missed. Cameron stood down as Prime Minister. Attention turned to different things. In December 2016, a response to a question in the House of Commons confirmed that the Strategy would not now be published. An alternative 'Social Justice Green Paper' was promised for 2017 (Puffet, 2016b), but it has yet to be scheduled. Amid the immense political labour of Brexit, and the abrupt end of Cameron's own premiership, his Life Chances Strategy has been a kind of collateral damage.

Yet while that particular moment was short-lived in itself, it is part of a longer policy story that can be traced back to New Labour – most prominently, to its ambition to eliminate child poverty by 2020, and to the introduction of Sure Start in England. The key motivation for the latter was 'the wealth of evidence that what happens to students in their earliest years has a huge impact, for good or ill, on their life chances' (Eisenstadt, 2011, p 139). This case was reinforced by various initiatives introduced by the 2010–15 Coalition government with the aim of improving social mobility. The introduction of free school meals for all children in their first three years of primary school had the aim, said the then Deputy Prime Minister Nick Clegg, of ensuring that 'every child gets the chance they deserve' (Robinson, 2013).

The use of the term 'chance' is significant because of its versatility and apparent neutrality. Like 'social mobility' talk in general, the term 'fairer life chances' has taken on a non-ideological feel: it is a policy goal that politicians from across the political spectrum have felt equally comfortable with endorsing (Calder, 2016b). This mirrors the extent to which 'equality of opportunity' – giving everyone a 'fair go', regardless of background – has been treated as a non-controversial alternative to 'equality of outcome', or a more even distribution of income and wealth (Calder, 2016a, Chapter 4). As then-chancellor George Osborne once put it, 'you can't achieve equality of outcome, but ...

you should be able to achieve equality of opportunity. You should give everyone the best chance' (Osborne, 2013). This point was echoed in the education reforms of Michael Gove as Education Secretary from 2010–14, which were based on the idea that schools that 'were free to support and challenge all pupils' would themselves provide a kind of royal road to equality of opportunity, and level the playing field – notwithstanding the range of ways in which structural inequality and domestic factors might affect educational attainment (Gove, 2013). The theme reverberated. And it was reaffirmed on the grandest scale in Theresa May's famous declaration, on becoming Prime Minister, of her aim to fight against the 'burning injustices' persisting in a UK where the poor die younger, white working-class boys are the least likely to go to university, and state-educated children are less likely to enter the top professions. Her government would 'do everything we can to help anybody, whatever your background, to go as far as your talents will take you' (May, 2016). This, too, has yet to materialise in the form of a joined-up strategy – although there may be grounds to think that May's particular stress on meritocracy, and her affirmative views on the scope for state intervention in the service of the public good, give her particular motivations to make something more concrete of this agenda (Shipman, 2017, pp xxiii-xxvi; cf Guy, 2017).

While Brexit machinations have meant a pause in the life chances rhetoric, there is no reason to conclude that the general theme of fairer chances has been replaced by an alternative take on inequality. This does not, however, mean that the 'life chances' agenda has been clearly defined.

Unpacking 'fair life chances'

The term 'life chances' stands in need of definition. Cameron himself did not do this, beyond stating the aim 'to give every child the chance to dream big dreams, and the tools – the character, the knowledge and the confidence, that will let their potential shine brightly' (Cameron, 2016). The renamed Life Chances Act 2010 provides no elaboration of the term 'life chances' at all. The same goes for the key 2011 Coalition strategy document on social mobility. There is a tendency in such policy to proceed by referring to factors that *thwart* life chances without spelling out more affirmatively what exactly life chances *are*, beyond (at most) a general appeal to notions of opportunity. So Nick Clegg writes, in his Foreword to that document:

In Britain today, life chances are narrowed for too many by the circumstances of their birth: the home they're born into, the neighbourhood they grow up in or the jobs their parents do. Patterns of inequality are imprinted from one generation to the next. The true test of fairness is the distribution of opportunities. That is why improving social mobility is the principal goal of the Coalition Government's social policy. (Clegg, 2011, p 3)

Here we have the claim that having one's opportunities defined by one's background or geographical location is unfair, with the term 'life chances' being used as if synonymous with opportunities.

For more substance we need to look elsewhere. This account is given in the Fabian Commission on Life Chances and Child Poverty, in 2007, as part of a far fuller and more nuanced treatment of those questions:

As we define it, the concept of "life chances" refers to the likelihood of a child achieving a range of important outcomes, which occur at successive stages of the life course, from birth to early childhood, to late childhood and adolescence, and into adulthood. The life chances framework is premised on the idea that some kinds of experience and opportunity are fundamental to a person's future prospects. For this reason, we identify a number of dimensions as being particularly important: health and well-being, education, income, occupation, environmental quality, safety and security, social networks, and personal autonomy, all of which, we contend, are essential components of a flourishing life. (Fabian Society, 2006, p 21)

This definition makes it explicit that 'life chances' is an umbrella term, covering a range of dimensions. And it characterises the ultimate point of life chances in terms of the achievement of flourishing. Life chances are a means to that end.

What would a fair distribution of such chances look like? In his major recent work on equality of opportunity, Joseph Fishkin notes that while there are various versions of the principle of fair life chances, 'almost all would, at a minimum, endorse the idea that one's chances in life should not depend on the circumstances of one's birth' (p 26). A similar note is consistently struck in the rhetoric of Cameron, Clegg and May. Fishkin gives us this depiction:

Suppose we see some newborn babies in a hospital ward, and all we know about them is their races, their genders, their parents' income, the neighbourhoods where they will grow up, and other factors of a similar kind. We know nothing, for example, about their present or future individual traits or talents – just these demographic and geographic characteristics that we can view as circumstances of birth. If life chances are fair, we should not be able to predict to any degree of accuracy which of them will succeed in life and which will fail. (Fishkin, 2016, p 27)

Much here hangs on what we count as 'succeeding' – a point we return to later. But if we put together the Fabian Commission's definition of life chances and Fishkin's visualisation of what their fair distribution looks like, we have fleshed out the conceptual basis of a life chances agenda like this:

- *Life chances* are a means to human flourishing, understood in terms of outcomes across a range of dimensions, including health and wellbeing, education, income, occupation, environmental quality, safety and security, social networks, and personal autonomy.
- Life chances will be *fairly distributed* when we cannot, at birth, make predictions about the destinations of a cohort of human lives based on race, gender, parental income or neighbourhood of upbringing.

Beginning with birth highlights the connection between the circumstances of children's upbringing and their life chances. We can see a whole raft of policies associated with the Labour administration between 1997 and 2010 as geared towards greater fairness in the distribution of life chances, with shifts in policy focus not just to the eradication of child poverty, but also to the importance of early childhood experiences in forming prospects for later life. Policies from the baby tax credit to the extension of maternity leave, and from the expansion of nursery places to Sure Start, were indicative of a wider project to raise the threshold of the circumstances of children's upbringing and to even things up for the worse-off. And they represented a very deliberate zooming in on the early years as the period when life chances might be confirmed or adjusted. In the 10 years from 1997, spending on early years services in England increased by a factor of 3.5 (Stewart and Obolenskaya, 2016, p 36).

If this can be presented as a strategy to begin with early years in tackling inequalities in life chances, we can see equally how policy changes since the 2008 economic crisis have tended to undermine that ambition – precisely because austerity measures have tended to fall especially heavily on families with young children. If Cameron and May remain able to speak with such urgency of breaking the perniciously strong link between background and life chances, the urgency is, to an important degree, of recent government policy's own making. As Stewart and Obolenskaya conclude (2016, p 56), 'the rolling back of benefits and services for young children comes just at the point that policies appeared to be beginning to deliver convergence in outcomes between disadvantaged children and their peers'.

So the portents here are not good. But how we see their implications for life chances depends importantly on how such chances are tracked and compared. The indicators most commonly reached for may themselves be problematically one-dimensional. One of the central flaws of the 'life chances' agenda has been the tendency to presume that the value of interventions is measurable via indicators that offer only a patchy, incomplete picture of the processes at stake.

The yardstick problem

Any such 'yardstick' for measuring life chances outcomes will be limited for two salient reasons. One is that any available measure of 'success' will be partial, and often challengeable in itself. Thus educational attainment, income, status, wellbeing, longevity or any other indicator of what makes for a 'successful' life offers only one parameter – and will be contestable, in the sense that (say) educational qualifications, however much they may be an asset in general, are neither sufficient nor necessary for the achievement of a flourishing life. And there is no self-evident algorithm to trade these off against each other. For example, there is a perfectly reasonable debate to be had as to whether a shorter, flourishing life is preferable to a longer, unhappy one. There is no simple way of weighing the relative value of, say, status versus income, or of social versus cultural capital.

The other reason is that such yardsticks risk instrumentalising 'life chances' policy, or viewing the improvement of life chances primarily in terms of the needs of the economy rather than the wellbeing of those concerned. This concern arises wherever the mission of such interventions is cashed out in terms of (for example) 'ensuring people have the skills and qualities for future jobs, lives and citizenship' (Strategy Unit, 2005), in ways that betray a sense in which raising the bar for disadvantaged children may have its ultimate motivation not so much in the importance of fairness, but in the strategic requirements of a changing economy (Lister, 2006). On this model, investment in children is couched in terms of later destinations and levels of attainment – often *decades* further along the life course – rather than on the experience of childhood itself, or the wellbeing of children as children. It values them as future 'becomings' rather than as current 'beings', and tends towards narrowly utilitarian and monetised conceptions of what counts as a good destination in the first place (Fawcett et al, 2004; Gillies et al, 2017, Chapter 8). It risks reducing 'fulfilment' and 'success' down to GCSE results or earnings at age 37, as if the broader fabric of a life – relationships, contributions and achievements not measurable as grades or in monetised terms – were incidental to flourishing.

Still, it is destination-based yardsticks that have framed 'life chances' talk. They provide an unreassuring picture. We find a stalling or reversing of the redistribution of life chances in destination terms. So elite and professional occupations remain dominated by those who have attended independent schools, amid a general narrowing of access to higher-paid and higher-status work (Social Mobility and Child Poverty Commission, 2015). The publication of the Social Mobility Commission's annual *State of the nation* report in December 2017 confirmed – in line with each previous one since 2013 – that 'Britain's deep social mobility problem, for this generation of young people in particular, is getting worse not better' (Social Mobility Commission, 2017, p iii). Shortly afterwards, its chair Alan Milburn resigned along with his fellow commissioners, citing as a reason a lack of back-up of government rhetoric on social mobility with any clear commitment to give due priority to the reality of the challenges involved (Savage, 2017).

So whatever its shortcomings, we can safely say that a destination-based focus on fair life chances is not favoured for reasons of political convenience. There is little reassuring reading on current trends. On the one hand, recent articulations of the 'life chances' agenda – with Theresa May's talk of 'terrible injustices' included under this heading – have raised the stakes in terms of tackling the unfair distribution of opportunities. Yet while the Social Mobility Commission (at least, until those recent resignations) has continued to offer fresh analysis of those injustices, government has yet to follow that up with the kind of ambitious programme for tackling them that such analysis – along with the rhetoric of Cameron and May – seems to demand.

Childcare as a social justice issue: key dimensions

While childcare will only be one aspect of a rounded-out 'life chances' agenda, it is a core component. On the one hand, childcare relationships form a crucial part of early years experiences and development. Meanwhile, access to childcare, and its quality, are connected to the wider architecture of social life, across various realms of policy. Childcare provision plays a crucial role both in children's being children, and in their becoming the adults they become. And its provision is clearly a social justice issue – for the children concerned, for their carers, for those paying for that care, and for society at large (Calder, 2018). Both the costs of good childcare and the benefits that it provides have ripple effects. Those effects can partly be gauged in material terms. A 2014 survey of childcare costs by the Family and Childcare Trust found that they had risen by 27 per cent over the previous five years as wages remained the same – and that average childcare costs for a family with two children were 62 per cent higher than the cost of the average mortgage for a family home (Rutter and Stocker, 2014, p 3). The 2017 survey found that families working full time paying average childcare costs can spend up to 45 per cent of their disposable income on childcare – and that the scale of childcare costs often mean that for low- and middle-income parents of pre-school children there is little or no financial gain in moving from Universal Credit into work at the minimum wage (Harding et al, 2017, p 4). Thus childcare sits stubbornly at the intersection between aspects of policy affecting the livelihoods of families, and the prospects of their members.

As mentioned earlier, we tend to find childcare addressed as a social justice issue from four main angles: in terms of gender, family autonomy, class and the interests of children themselves. Clearly these areas intersect. Separating them out for analytical purposes may risk simply overlooking the ways in which, both at the structural level and in everyday lived experience, their implications are mutually entangled. Policy impinging on childcare tends to combine them, especially when aiming at a self-professedly holistic approach – as, for example, with New Labour's early years policy, with its identification of improving educational outcomes for disadvantaged children, removing barriers impeding women from entering work, and reducing child poverty (DSS, 1999; Flint, 2017). Even so, for the sake of weighing the social justice issues at stake, it is vital to address each on its own terms.

A focus on *gender* will address women as parents, and the relation between domestic dynamics and the world beyond – particularly in terms of work and social security. Prominent here are the ways in which the childcare burden has tended to fall disproportionately on women, work–life balance and the working of a 'double shift' (Hochschild, 2012 [1989]), the undervaluing of care work as a presumptively 'feminine' role, and on the restrictions such factors place on women's working lives. Childcare policy may be seen as a key lever in the promotion of gender equality – although if so, then needing to tread carefully around presumptions that (for example) work itself is the key measure of gender equality, or that care for one's children is positioned as subsidiary to the overriding social duty to work (Duncan, 2002). It may be that 'gender-blind' approaches to child welfare serve to reinforce existing gender inequalities, and result in policies that serve, for example, to marginalise male carers at the same time as overlooking crucial ways in which children's opportunities for care are themselves shaped by gender dynamics (Featherstone, 2006).

A focus on *family autonomy* will address the family unit as a whole, and the expectations and privileges attached to it. It will interrogate the rightful role of the family in providing childcare, as opposed to the state or other 'outside' agencies; the degree of discretion to be afforded to parents in gauging their children's best interests; and on balancing the value of family life and relationships against other goods and values – for example, equality of opportunity. Such a focus needs to take into account the ways in which parental privileges and the operations of the family, even in the most mundane aspects of care provision and decision-making, work to disrupt the fair distribution of life chances (Archard, 2011, Chapter 5). Thus the implications for childcare of class inequalities, for example, will be exacerbated in various ways by the assumption that parents have a right to promote the interests of their own children, given that families of lower and higher incomes will have different amounts of resources to devote to this (Stewart, 2016). Equally, for critics from the right seeking to defend equality of opportunity for children, family autonomy may provide excessive licence to parents to *harm* the interests of their children – for example, by not actively looking for work.

A focus on *class* will look at the costs of childcare, at how these hit lower earners hardest, and at how they may serve to impede parents from entering into work (Butler and Rutter, 2016). It will look at how the spending gap on childcare and education between lower- and higher-income families has grown in recent decades, along with differentials in time spent by parents on developmental childcare (see Rutter and Stocker, 2014; see also Putnam, 2015, pp 125-30, on trends in the US).

It will consider how efficiently free childcare provision helps families from the most disadvantaged backgrounds (Weale, 2017). It may also address class inflections in different understandings of the care of children and its ultimate purposes – for example, the way parenting styles may have implications for the orientations and expectations of children with regard to school and career (Lareau, 2011), and the ways curriculum, classroom practice and the allocation of school resources may reinforce working-class disadvantage (Reay, 2017, Chapters 3-4). And it may look at how parent-focused family policy serves to 'responsibilise' disadvantaged parents, directing blame their way when their children's outcomes are poorer (Hartas, 2014; Armstrong, 2017).

The distinct role of a child-focused analysis

Given the clear importance of each of those three dimensions, it may seem artificial to separate out children's interests in receiving childcare from those other questions of fairness in which childcare provision is embedded. Child-focused policies have been criticised precisely for decoupling children's interests from those other factors relevant to social justice – and hence, for example, lacking an adequate gender analysis (Featherstone, 2006; Lister, 2006; Ball, 2013). Yet there are various reasons, as part of an overall analysis of childcare as a social justice issue, to bracket those other factors and focus in on the interests of children themselves. Three of these, we might suggest, are particularly compelling.

First, children have independent moral status. The interests and rights of care receivers are in principle distinct from the interests of caregivers – whether parents or otherwise. So while caring is necessarily relational, the parties to that relationship are positioned differently in ways of key importance to questions of justice and fairness. It is by no means guaranteed that their interests will coincide. More specifically: children occupy a distinct position compared to other care receivers. They may – because of their size, stage of development and the ways in which their current treatment impacts on the bulk of the remainder of their expected lifespan – be dependent, vulnerable, subject to influence and in a position to gain from care provision in ways that may in turn make childhood a special case in the wider consideration of the relationship between care and social justice.

Second, what social justice means for children cannot be fully appreciated solely in connection with questions of gender, class or the family, or an aggregate of those three. Thus the question of whether and how children should receive care as a matter of justice is in principle separate from established conventions about how such care is provided – for example, assumptions about gender roles or about the role or composition of the nuclear family. It may be that in exploring the alternatives, and looking at the evidence of how children's interests are best served, we conclude that (for example) something like the nuclear family is the best 'default' model for the care and rearing of children, and so children should be regarded as entitled to the closest approximation to that. But we can't simply *start* from there as an automatic assumption. And any realistic assessment of the meeting of children's care needs will recognise the role to be played by a range of agencies beyond the immediate family. Relatedly, there is a strong case for saying that the interests of care receivers (in this case, children) should be paramount – and if need be, take precedence over those of caregivers.

Third, a fair life chances agenda, in particular, requires that we address childcare in terms of what it does *for children*: the differences that it makes to how their lives go, both as the beings they are in childhood and the adults they become. This aspect of social justice is particularly instructive – partly because it often remains neglected.

The discussion above about yardsticks and destinations pointed to an important lopsidedness in how the care of children features in the life chances agenda. Going by destinations, we will judge the value of childcare retrospectively, in terms of its ultimate effects on the shape of adulthood. We will dwell on its value as an investment – as with a recent report for the Social Market Foundation by Lucy Powell MP, with its stress on 'the wealth of evidence to show that early education and care for young children can boost development and lead to benefits in later life' (Powell, 2017, p 6).[1] An exclusive focus on destinations presumes that the value of, for example, early years experiences cashes out in the quality of our future adult lives: the options open to us, our standard of living, and so on. It presumes that children are best viewed as unfinished adults – with childhood a deficient version of human life, a step on the way to its completion (Gheaus, 2015). It neglects the extent to which children's wellbeing is significant to them at the time, *as children*.

One of the reasons this matters is simply that what contributes to future flourishing may not enhance flourishing in childhood. Sociological studies of dominant middle-class modes of parenting, for example, have been characterised in terms of a certain kind of short-term sacrifice for longer-term goals (Lareau, 2011; Reay, 2017). This applies especially strongly to parental strategies to maximise their children's life chances. Success at school offers rewards that in their most crucial respects are deferred – to be experienced via positioning in the job market, increased confidence, a sense of entitlement, the accumulation of cultural capital or in the form of greater income. Some of the most direct (and exclusive) ways of advantaging children in later life – at least in terms of typical yardsticks of success – may have the most detrimental effects on childhood. 'Hothoused' children, or those sent to boarding schools, may succeed despite the traumatic experiences during the cultivation of their positioning for longer-term advantage (Duffell and Basset, 2016; Renton, 2017). Conversely, what contributes most to flourishing in childhood may in some cases work against later flourishing. Regular shared family mealtimes featuring 'feel-good' but generally unhealthy food may be the source of rich, much-valued experiences at the time, but cause health problems in the longer term.

None of this is to suggest that destinations do not matter, in terms of social justice or of flourishing. It is, however, to suggest that sole or disproportionate emphasis on them, as opposed to the wellbeing of children as children, obscures many of the reasons why childcare matters for social justice. A life chances agenda needs to accommodate the value of a good childhood alongside the value of the achievement of adult success – as well as avoiding one-dimensional yardsticks of that success.

Childcare as a (maldistributed) relationship good

How might that be achieved? How might life chances talk be reset to give due space to the pivotal value of care for flourishing in childhood? Here is a proposal: that we treat childcare as a 'relationship good', and treat its distribution as a core component of social justice.

Care is a form of relationship good, which is to say that it is valuable, that it necessarily involves a relationship, and that its value consists *in* that relationship. The value of care is thus not reducible to individualised metrics. It is valuable for individuals, but in relational terms. Both caregivers and care receivers have a distinct interest in realising these goods – whether the former are parents or otherwise. There are distinct goods, realised in childcare and crucial to human flourishing, which are not available elsewhere, and are valuable *in themselves*. Caregiving is not just work, and care receiving is not just a means to the end of future educational attainment or a higher salary. Whether these relationship goods are secured via domestic arrangements or through outside-family institutions, their availability is a matter of social justice. This poses a question about whether and how we can assess the fairness of their distribution. In their recent work on the ethics of family life, Brighouse and Swift have suggested that we treat what they call 'familial relationship goods' as distribuenda – 'that is, as among the goods that people should have opportunities, perhaps equal opportunities for' (Brighouse and Swift, 2014, p 147).[2] Given the pivotal place of childcare in the wider horizons of children's life chances and of social justice more generally, there are strong grounds for treating it in just this way.

This may strike an odd note. Treating relationship goods as distribuenda strikes some as a reductive move – either because they presume that good relationships are not the kind of thing that we can redistribute, or because they regard relationships as a matter of the politics of recognition (on the side of culture, attitudes and ways of life), rather than that of redistribution (on the side of the allocation of resources) (Fraser, 1997). Yet as we have seen, what report after report on the distribution of childcare reveals is precisely the extent to which it *is* unevenly distributed – and to which aspects of its maldistribution have knock-on affects along the parameters of gender, family autonomy and class. Indeed, what the significance and impacts of childcare highlight is the complex bind between inequalities of resources on the one hand, and good relationships on the other. What it also highlights is the extent to which we assess children's interests as if they were 'unfettered market actors', with the conditions of their flourishing accountable for in individualised terms. As Featherstone et al develop this point:

> To think of a child as a free floating individual denies elemental ties: to the body that gave birth to her, the breast that fed her, the aunt who sneaked her sweets, the streets where she played, the friends she played with. Interdependence is the basis of human interaction and autonomy and independence are about the capacity for self-determination rather than self-sufficiency. (Featherstone et al, 2014, p 32)

We might add to the list of ties the carers, a relationship with whom would be preconditional to the child's flourishing, as a child and as a future adult. Thus a focus on the distinct status of children's flourishing points to the incoherence of an individualist take on life chances. Childhood – like the rest of life but in particular senses – is a relational state.

Conclusion

This chapter has aimed to establish a series of points: the influence and appeal of the 'life chances' agenda, from New Labour through to Theresa May's premiership; the looseness of the elaboration of the notion at the level of policy; the importance of a pluralistic understanding of links between life chances and human flourishing and the avoidance of reductive yardsticks; the centrality of childcare to any adequate understanding of the promotion of fairer life chances; and the value of addressing childcare as a 'relationship good' worthy of protection in its own right, rather than simply as a means to later 'success'. On our working definition of a fair distribution of such goods it would be impossible to predict their distribution at birth based on a ward of babies' race, gender, parental income or neighbourhood of upbringing. Part of the use of that gauge is to reinforce how very far we are from anything like a fair distribution of life chances. Any resumption of a Life Chances Strategy will have its work cut out. Part of that work must include avoiding treating children's flourishing in reductive or instrumental terms.

Notes

[1] Part of Powell's aim in making this point is to show the value of investment in early years care for any proponent of social mobility regardless of party allegiance. She does not claim that the economic dividends are the only ones at stake; there are other social benefits. But those, too, as with the great bulk of equivalent literature, are destination-focused.

[2] As the term 'familial relationship goods' suggests, Brighouse and Swift make a particular case for the unique value of family relationships (for a fuller discussion, see Calder, 2015). This is not part of the case being made here, which may stand independently of that position: that is, that such relationship goods may coherently be considered as distribuenda.

References

Archard, D. (2011) *The family: A liberal defence*, Houndmills: Palgrave Macmillan.

Armstrong, S. (2017) *The new poverty*, London: Verso.

Ball, W. (2013) *Transforming childcare and listening to families: Policy in Wales and beyond*, Cardiff: University of Wales Press.

Brighouse, H. and Swift, A. (2014) *Family values: The ethics of parent–child relationships*, Princeton, NJ: Princeton University Press.

Butler, A. and Rutter, J. (2016) *Creating an anti-poverty childcare system*, York: Joseph Rowntree Foundation.

Calder, G. (2015) 'Brighouse and Swift on the family, ethics and social justice', *European Journal of Political Theory*. doi:10.1177/1474885115587119

Calder, G. (2016a) *How inequality runs in families: Unfair advantage and the limits of social mobility*, Bristol: Policy Press.

Calder, G. (2016b) '*Of course* we do: inequality, the family and the spell of social mobility', *Soundings*, vol 64, pp 117-27.

Calder, G. (2018) 'Social justice, single parents and their children', in R. Nieuwenhuis and L.C. Maldonado (eds) *The triple bind of single-parent families: Resources, employment, and policies to improve well-being*, Bristol: Policy Press, pp 423-39.

Cameron, D. (2016) 'Prime Minister's speech on life chances', 11 January (www.gov.uk/government/speeches/prime-ministers-speech-on-life-chances).

Clegg, N. (2011) 'Foreword by the Deputy Prime Minister', in HM Government, *Opening doors, breaking barriers – A strategy for social mobility*, London: Cabinet Office.

CPAG (Child Poverty Action Group) (2016) *Life chances indicators*, Submission to Child Poverty Unit, London: CPAG.

DSS (Department for Social Security) (1999) *Opportunity for all: Tackling poverty and social exclusion*, London: The Stationery Office.

Duffell, N. and Basset, T. (2016) *Trauma, abandonment and privilege: A guide to therapeutic work with boarding school survivors*, London: Routledge.

Duncan, S. (2002) 'Policy discourses on "reconciling work and life" in the EU', *Social Policy and Society*, vol 1, no 4, pp 305-14.

Eisenstadt, N. (2011) *Sure Start: How government discovered early childhood*, Bristol: Policy Press.

Ellison, N. (2017) 'The whys and wherefores of Brexit', in J. Hudson, C. Needham and E. Heins (eds) *Social Policy Review 29: Analysis and debate in social policy, 2017*, Bristol: Policy Press, pp 3-22.

Fabian Society (2006) *Narrowing the gap: The Fabian Commission on Life Chances and Child Poverty*, London: Fabian Society.

Fawcett, B., Featherstone, B. and Goddard, J. (2004) *Contemporary child care policy and practice*, Houndmills: Palgrave Macmillan.

Featherstone, B. (2006) 'Why gender matters in child welfare and protection', *Critical Social Policy*, vol 26, no 2, pp 294-314.

Featherstone, B. White, S. and Morris, K. (2014) *Re-imagining child protection: Towards humane social work with families*, Bristol: Policy Press.

Fishkin, J. (2016) *Bottlenecks: A new theory of equal opportunity*, Oxford: Oxford University Press.

Flint, C. (2017) 'Childcare', in S. Keeble (ed) *This woman can: 1997, women and Labour*, London: Fabian Society, pp 29-38.

Fraser, N. (1997) 'From redistribution to recognition? Dilemmas of justice in a "post-socialist" age', in N. Fraser, *Justice interruptus: Critical reflections on the 'postsocialist' condition*, New York and London: Routledge, pp 68-93.

Gheaus, A. (2015) 'Unfinished adults and defective children: On the nature and value of childhood', *Journal of Ethics and Social Philosophy*, vol 9, no 1, pp 1-21.

Gillies, V., Edwards, R. and Horsley, N. (2017) *Challenging the politics of early intervention: Who's 'saving' children and why*, Bristol: Policy Press.

Gove, M. (2013) 'The civil rights struggle of our time', 22 November (www.gov.uk/government/speeches/the-civil-rights-struggle-of-our-time).

Guy, C. (2017) 'It will be a disaster if May drops Cameron's life chances plan', Conservative Home, 13 January (www.conservativehome.com/platform/2017/01/christian-guy-it-will-be-a-disaster-if-may-drops-camerons-life-chances-plan.html).

Harding, C., Wheaton, B. and Butler, A. (2017) *Childcare Survey 2017*, London: Family and Childcare Trust.

Harding, L.F. (1996) *Family, state and social policy*, Houndmills: Macmillan.

Hartas, D. (2014) *Parenting, family policy and children's well-being in an unequal society*, Houndmills: Palgrave Macmillan.

Hochschild, A. (2012 [1989]) *The second shift: Working families and the revolution at home*, New York: Penguin.

Holden, C. (2017) 'Confronting Brexit and Trump: Towards a socially progressive globalisation', in J. Hudson, C. Needham and E. Heins (eds) *Social Policy Review 29: Analysis and debate in social policy, 2017*, Bristol: Policy Press, pp 63-82.

Lareau, A. (2011) *Unequal childhoods* (2nd edn), Berkeley, CA: University of California Press.

Lister, R. (2006) 'Children (but not women) first: New Labour, child welfare and gender', *Critical Social Policy*, vol 26, no 2, pp 315-35.

Lister, R. (2016) 'What do we mean by "life chances"?', in J. Tucker (ed) *Improving children's life chances*, London: Child Poverty Action Group.

May, T. (2016) 'Statement from the new Prime Minister Theresa May', 13 July (www.gov.uk/government/speeches/statement-from-the-new-prime-minister-theresa-may).

Osborne, G. (2013) Interview, *The Andrew Marr Show*, BBC1, 1 December (www.youtube.com/watch?v=YObFTW8pH_E).

Powell. L. (2017) *A lost generation: Why social mobility in the early years is set to go backwards*, London: Social Market Foundation.

Puffet. N. (2016a) 'Life chances strategy shelved after Brexit vote', *Children & Young People Now*, 27 June (www.cypnow.co.uk/cyp/news/1157966/life-chances-strategy-shelved-after-brexit-vote).

Puffet, N. (2016b) 'Government confirms life chances strategy has been dropped', *Children & Young People Now*, 20 December (www.cypnow.co.uk/cyp/news/2002923/government-confirms-life-chances-strategy-has-been-dropped).

Putnam, R. (2015) *Our kids: The American dream in crisis*, New York: Simon & Schuster.

Reay, D. (2017) *Miseducation: Inequality, education and the working classes*, Bristol: Policy Press.

Renton, A. (2017) *Stiff upper lip: Secrets, crimes and the schooling of the ruling class*, London: Weidenfeld & Nicholson.

Robinson, N. (2013) 'All infants in England to get free school lunches', BBC News, 17 September (www.bbc.co.uk/news/uk-politics-24132416).

Rutter, J. and Stocker, K. (2014) *Childcare Costs Survey 2014*, London: Family and Childcare Trust.

Savage, M. (2017) 'Theresa May faces new crisis after mass walkout over social policy', *The Observer*, 3 December (www.theguardian.com/politics/2017/dec/02/theresa-may-crisis-mass-walkout-social-policy-alan-milburn).

Shipman, T. (2017) *Fall out: A year of political mayhem*, London: William Collins.

Social Mobility and Child Poverty Commission (2015) *Elitist Britain?*, London: Social Mobility and Child Poverty Commission.

Social Mobility Commission (2017) *State of the nation 2017: Social mobility in Great Britain*, London: Social Mobility Commission.

Stewart, K. (2016) 'Why we can't talk about life chances without talking about income', in J. Tucker (ed) *Improving children's life chances*, London: Child Poverty Action Group.

Stewart, K. and Obolenskaya, P. (2016) 'Young children', in R. Lupton, T. Burchardt, J. Hills, K. Stewart and P. Vizard (eds) *Social policy in a cold climate: Policies and their consequences since the crisis*, Bristol: Policy Press, pp 81-103.

Strategy Unit (2005) *Improving the life chances of disabled people*, London: Cabinet Office.

Weale, S. (2017) 'Free childcare provision could widen gap between rich and poor, says charity', *The Guardian*, 28 September (www.theguardian.com/education/2017/sep/28/free-childcare-extension-could-widen-gap-between-rich-and-poor-says-charity).

FOUR

Outcomes-based approaches and the devolved administrations

Derek Birrell and Ann Marie Gray

Introduction

A relatively new common feature of the devolved administrations has been the emergence of outcome-based frameworks as key components of their policy-making processes. This trend has received comparatively little analysis or comment in academic work on devolved policy-making, and existing work has tended to focus mainly on other policy dimensions (Birrell, 2009; Cairney, 2011; Birrell and Gormley-Heenan, 2016; Cole and Stafford, 2015; Cairney et al, 2016). Coverage in more specialist forms in reports or articles is limited, as is any comparative analysis. There are a range of different outcomes-based models or frameworks (Penna and Williams, 2005) rooted in different methodological positions, including in England specific NHS, adult social care and public health outcomes frameworks. Therefore the use of the generic term 'outcomes-based approaches' in government narratives in all three countries has not helped provide clarity.

In the devolved jurisdictions there has been much attention on the influence of the outcomes- or results-based accountability methodology developed and promoted by Friedman (2005). Based on population measures and indicators, the Friedman model has been used in performance management, particularly in the US. Key features of the approach include working backwards from a set of desired outcomes and the use of three performance categories: 'How much did we do?', 'How well did we do it?' and 'Is anyone better off?' Although not extensively adopted by the Westminster government, the outcomes-based accountability (OBA) approach has been used by some local authorities in England, particularly with regard to children's services and education. This chapter is mainly concerned with the introduction and use of OBA in policy-making in the three devolved administrations where there has been divergence in its use and in the nature and scope of approaches. It examines the emergence of outcomes-based approaches in Scotland, Wales and Northern Ireland, the rationale for their adoption and arguments about benefits and criticisms. Conceptual and definitional issues associated with OBA are considered as are the choice and use of indicators and the policy implications arising from its use.

Development of outcomes-based approaches in the devolved administrations

Scotland led the way in using an outcomes-based approach that has come to be associated with a Scottish approach to public sector performance (Cook, 2017a). The model introduced in Scotland was seen as being primarily based on a system developed for the state government of Virginia in the US (Campbell, 2012). The main manifestation of the outcomes-based approach in Scotland has been through what is known as the National Performance Framework (NPF). Practically, the NPF was instigated by the Scottish Nationalist Party (SNP) in preparing its manifesto in 2007. The overall purpose was expressed as relating to creating a more successful country. Purpose targets were then identified under eight themes linked to economic growth, inequalities, population and sustainability. This was articulated overall in terms of improvement in public services over a 10-year period along with five strategic or general policy objectives: making Scotland wealthier and fairer, healthier, safer and stronger, smarter, and greener. The core of the NPF was a dual matrix consisting of 16 national outcomes and 50 national indicators. The 16 outcomes are written as a vision of what the Scottish Government wishes to achieve covering a range of economic, social, health, environmental and justice issues, such as: 'We have tackled the significant inequalities in Scottish society'; 'We live longer, healthier lives' and 'Our children have the best start in life'. The 50 national indicators are more detailed expressions of desired improvements and are intended to track progress towards the national outcomes and purpose targets. They are expressed in terms of improvement, for example, in children's services or levels of educational achievement or reductions in children's deprivation or the gender pay gap.

The outcomes-based approach as set out in the principles of the NPF was also introduced to local government through a concordat between central and local government. Each of Scotland's 32 councils developed a single outcomes agreement (SOA) with the Scottish Government based on the underpinning national framework. Introduced in 2009, these established a set of local government outcomes taking into account local priorities and covering all local government services. Underpinning the development of SOAs was the need for improvements in performance management and reporting, and a view that local councils should focus SOAs on a manageable and meaningful number of high-level outcomes and supporting indicators (Audit Scotland, 2010). All SOAs had to be developed jointly by community planning partnerships (CPPs), the structure in Scotland by which councils and other public bodies work together with local communities to plan and deliver better services. The Community Empowerment (Scotland) Act 2015 requires CPPs to publish a local outcomes improvement plan setting out priorities and identifying communities with the poorest outcomes, and to publish a locality plan and report on progress.

The Welsh Government also endorsed an outcomes-based approach as a key element of improving public services and delivery. The major pressure for government action on performance came from a Commission on Public Service Governance and Delivery (2014), which had identified the performance of public services in Wales as poor. It recommended a radical overhaul comprising a clear and concise set of outcome measures with milestones and targets; a standard set of measures of overall service performance; and local and organisational indicators of programme effectiveness. Legislation in 2015 required that national indicators be applied for the purpose of measuring progress towards the achievement of wellbeing goals (Seaford, 2015). Five/six headline indicators are underpinned by 34–35 second-tier whole-Wales indicators plus a set of comparative indicators by sub-population and areas of Wales. Examples of national indicators include: health life expectancy, gross disposable income, and percentage of adults with qualifications.

In Northern Ireland an outcomes-based approach and use of indicators was copied from Scotland and Virginia in the US but was directly linked to a Programme for Government (PfG) framework (Northern Ireland Assembly Research and Information Service, 2016) by the newly elected government in 2015. The draft PfG consisted of 14 outcomes and 44 indicators that would measure progress on the outcomes. This draft document emphasised that the PfG was based on Friedman's OBA model and that the government was committed to the use of this model (Northern Ireland Executive, 2016). Despite the declared commitment to OBA, the actual format and presentation of the PfG still appeared to strongly reflect Scotland's NPF. As with Scotland and Wales, the outcomes are broadly defined. For example, the outcome 'We care for others and we help those in need' was accompanied by the following indicators: population with scores signifying possible mental health problem; the number of adults receiving personal care; the percentage of care leavers in education, training or employment; and the percentage of people living in absolute and relative poverty.

In Scotland and Wales the outcomes-based approach was put on a statutory basis. The Community Empowerment Act (Scotland) 2015 placed a duty on Scottish ministers to consult on, develop and publish a set of national outcomes for Scotland. These were linked to devolved functions and were to be used by all organisations that carry out public functions. A requirement of Scottish ministers is that in setting outcomes they must pay regard to the reduction of inequalities that result from social-economic disadvantage, and data for national indicators is broken down by protected equality characteristics and socioeconomic factors. In Wales, under the Wellbeing of Future Generations (Wales) Act 2015, Welsh ministers must publish national indicators for the purpose of measuring progress towards the achievement of wellbeing goals. A national indicator is expressed as a value or characteristic that can be measured quantitatively or qualitatively against a particular outcome, and there are 46 of these (Welsh Government, 2015a). The Act puts in place seven wellbeing goals: a prosperous Wales; a healthy Wales; a more equal Wales; a resilient Wales; a Wales of cohesive communities; a Wales of vibrant culture; and a globally responsive Wales.

Rationale for an outcomes-based approach

Cook (2017b) notes that all three administrations emphasised the important role an outcomes approach plays in signalling what the government is seeking to achieve. In Scotland, as a government-wide policy framework the NPF was developed by the SNP to build a consensus around broad ideas for a 10-year vision for the nation (Arnott and Ozga, 2010). The national outcomes in Scotland have been described as a high-level picture of how Scotland is doing (Tannahill, 2016). There has been an impressive level of buy-in to the principle of an outcomes-based approach and to measuring progress and assessing tangible improvements. Outcomes have been seen as a tool of scrutiny, enabling the government to be held to account and assisting parliamentary scrutiny committees (Conlong, 2016), and securing transparency through the Scotland Performs website that shows the direction of travel – whether performance is improving, worsening or being maintained.

In Wales the introduction of an OBA approach was seen as a way of improving the performance of public services by providing clarity on higher-level outcomes and a transparent framework for measuring the impact on policies and services on outcomes for citizens. In Northern Ireland, the Executive referred to 'a new approach which focuses on major societal outcomes that the Executive wants to achieve' (Northern Ireland Executive, 2016), with a focus on outcomes over a generation. As noted earlier many of the outcomes were somewhat vague and aspirational, perhaps an important consideration in Northern Ireland where politically the outcomes approach facilitated compulsory inter-party power sharing by promoting very general agreed outcomes.

Attraction of an outcomes-based accountability approach

While the OBA approach has attracted international interest, there is a limited empirical basis for its use (Law, 2013; Cook, 2017a). There has been no systematic evaluation of its impact and more limited assessments and analysis have produced mixed results. In Scotland it has been seen as supporting a consistent basis for ministerial strategic direction to public bodies so that they align their performance measurement arrangements (Elvidge, 2011). Work by the Carnegie Trust has suggested that the outcomes-based approach supported by the NPF has helped Scotland achieve a more holistic approach to public sector reform that is not evident in other small countries (Elvidge, 2014). It has also been linked to a stronger performance culture in many services, professions and localities, with closer attention to data and variations in performance (Housden, 2014). The general use of an NPF has been seen as helping align people in the same direction and making a difference to how people talk, think and act (Tannahill, 2016), and reference has been made to the successful impact of NPF as a discursive framework developed by the SNP to build a vision and consensus pointing to an independent Scotland (Arnott and Ozga, 2012).

In Wales the national and local outcomes indicator frameworks have not always been based solely on OBA methodology. The Strategic Improvement Framework for Social Services (Welsh Government, 2013) appeared to use a more traditional model of objectives and standards involving evidence-gathering, drafting priorities, designing plans, delivery and evaluation. However, there was undoubtedly a growing interest in using the OBA methodology with a top level of an outcomes framework and a performance measurement framework underneath at the various levels of governance. Such an approach, for example, was specified within a multi-agency context across aspects of a Local Safeguarding Children's Board. This project claimed to be using the principles of OBA to deliver key performance indicators, measure Board effectiveness and promote participation (Welsh Government, 2015b). The Northern Ireland Executive was willing to see the use of the specific OBA methodology in central and local government, health and social care and the voluntary and community sector. Substantial numbers of staff from the civil service, public bodies and the voluntary sector have undergone training in the basics of OBA provided through a children's charity, the National Children's Bureau (NCB, 2016), which is licenced to provide training on the model (Hansard [NI], 2016).

All three devolved administrations have clearly found aspects of outcomes-based approaches attractive, and despite the existence of a number of different outcomes-based methodologies, it is the OBA methodology that has been most influential. This can be related to a number of factors. A change of emphasis to assessing achievements and performance rather than previous methods of relying on citing inputs, processes and securing detailed targets has had an appeal. This emphasis has suited the predominant policy style in the devolved countries that has been based on strong support for government action and respect for the public sector. The preparation of outcome strategies or objectives has usually been couched in visionary language relating the outcomes to the measure of a successful country and the goal of an improved society. This was particularly important in Scotland with the SNP keen to build a consensus around a vision for the future of Scotland and to translate it into day-to-day policy (Arnott and Ozga, 2012; Mooney and Scott, 2012).

Establishing broad goals and outcomes around which governments can build a consensus for policy development and delivery has also had a strong appeal in Northern Ireland and Wales, supplying a common framework for diverse services that can be readily understood across the country. An attraction of OBA has been the apparent offer of a simple solution to complex problems. This appears to reduce the need for detailed policy analysis to a list of simple statistics or indicators. The methodology provides an easily understood framework to assess the performance of government bodies. The OBA methodology is also presented as a disciplined approach, applicable at all levels from local to national, and for evaluating all kinds of public projects – a uniform approach as opposed to the more ad hoc approach of other methodologies.

The devolved administrations have tended to use the outcomes-based approaches on long-term projections of government achievement. There is an obvious attraction for governments in being able to set more time for producing achievements, for postponing difficult decisions and for avoiding political conflict over policy. Some assessments have stressed the alignment of outcomes with joined-up government for linking social, economic and environmental aspects and avoiding government departments and public bodies acting in silos. In Wales there has been an additional aspect through the use of financial incentives of a pro rata grant if local councils meet outcomes and improvements set out in agreements. These financial rewards have been identified as an important factor in motivating staff and politicians (Law, 2013, p 35).

The adoption of Outcomes Agreements between the Welsh Government and local authorities in 2010 gave a major role to indicators. These are intended to provide an outcome-focused approach to local performance management. They have been seen as an important example of the move towards OBA in Wales. In contrast to Scotland, the Welsh guidance on local authority Outcomes Agreements allows a wide range of data and evidence, including activities as indicators (Law, 2013, p 18). Local authorities in Wales were legally obliged to collect and publish data for each of the indicators that are aligned to one or more of the Welsh Government's strategic priorities. Councils complete an annual monitoring report that is assessed by officials in the Welsh Government. In 2016 the Welsh Government announced its intention to revoke the statutory provisions on local government indicators, although the Welsh Local Government Association continues to collect National Strategic Indicators data on a voluntary basis.

Keating (2010) sees the adoption of the NPF in Scotland as ambitious but with significant challenges in translating this into policy practice, while the Commission on the Future Delivery of Public Services reported evidence that the wider system of governance and organisation of public services did not fully embrace the outcomes-based approach (2011). The Scottish Government is not required to report to Parliament on the information in Scotland Performs; however, in the last three years the Scotland Performs team has produced performance information to assist parliamentary committees in their scrutiny tasks. This information is regarded as particularly significant for the scrutiny of the draft budget, but the Scottish Parliament's Finance Committee reported its surprise that 2011 spending review did not mention the NPF or the five strategic objectives set by the government (Campbell, 2012, p 18).

Assessment and criticisms of the outcomes-based accountability approach

Clearly it is the OBA model that has attracted the most attention and that has proved appealing to devolved government departments and local authorities. It has, however, been subject to criticism at a conceptual level with questions about its validity as a basis for performance management or formulating a PfG. The key elements in OBA that give rise to conceptual difficulty are the meaning of the terms 'outcomes' and 'indicators'; the relationship between indicators and outcomes; selection of data; the particular focus of OBA on a population–service distinction; and basing evaluation of improvement on a key criterion of who is better off.

Concepts and definitions

The term 'outcome' has been seen as a very wide concept, even a vague term susceptible to different interpretations that reflect different situations and disciplinary perspectives (Glendinning et al, 2008). In the OBA framework, outcome is used in a very distinctive way in the sense of 'desired outcome' or 'imagined outcome', not in its more usual meaning of actual outcomes as identified in terms of impact in a retrospective perspective. Desired outcomes have been assessed by Sanderson (2011) as normative statements about what ought to be and not empirical statements of impact. Outcomes can often be conflated to cover a range of performance management terms that have a discrete meaning, including objectives, goals, aims, targets, benchmarks and outputs. A clear distinction is often drawn between outputs and outcomes, for example, that 'outcomes' means the impact of support on a person's life, not the outputs of services (IRISS, 2013). The tendency to compound different meanings in outcomes-based approaches is noted by Petch (2014), who suggests that often outputs and performance measures masquerade as outcomes. It has been argued that the distinction between outcomes and outputs is very important but is often confused, and that outcomes as the objectives of government policy should be different from operational outputs (Centre for Social Justice, 2015). The Northern Ireland Assembly's research unit has published two short papers, both of which briefly raise some concerns about the lack of specificity in terms of outcomes, and also the quality, availability and timeliness of related data. Cook (2017a, p 18) has argued that there is a danger of 'outcomes' becoming a term '… that means all things to all people and is therefore rendered meaningless.'

A common criticism of the meaning of outcomes as used in the desired outcomes narratives adopted by the devolved governments addresses the generality and vagueness of many of the outcome statements. Sanderson (2011, p 70) views many of the outcome statements as unintelligent, lacking clear meaning and therefore unmeasurable. A common outcome put forward in all three administrations, for example, is 'improving children's services', but this raises a range of issues about availability of services, the scope of services, and quality and entitlement. The language used to express outcomes is also often unclear about the degree of change that is desired, and without clear timetables for achievement or specific targets.

Outcomes and indicators

Problems in the translation of the outcomes into precise indicators in Scotland have been identified by Keating (2010), with additional criticism of the lack of transparency about the methods used to draw up the list of outcomes and indicators (Campbell, 2012, p 15). Also noted has been the limited opportunity for those outside government, the public sector and wider public to influence the development of the NPF through any process of deliberative dialogue (Royal Society of Edinburgh, 2013). In Wales, the Commission on Public Service Governance and Delivery (2014) has drawn attention to the way the proliferation of indicators may produce complex systems that do not drive improvement. In Northern Ireland there has been criticism that that the OBA approach is attempting to reduce policy-making to a technical and problem-solving exercise, with little recognition that indicators are inevitably value-laden (Lowe and Wilson, 2015). Another concern emerging from the draft Northern Ireland PfG consultation is that many of the indicators used do not capture the complexities of policy issues (Housing Rights, 2016). The most comprehensive critique of outcomes-based approaches in Wales focuses on local authority outcomes agreements, with Law (2013) arguing that in practice a large proportion of indicators measured activities rather than outcomes, with the timescale for achieving outcomes varying considerably. She also attributes confusion regarding the concept of outcomes to some Welsh departments going off on an 'outcome based frolic' (2013, p 25), but with managers sometimes confused by the complexities of the OBA approach. Ultimately the report found limited evidence that particular processes and outputs would lead to desired outcomes due to the difficulty establishing causality between actions and their effect on high-level outcomes, the use of gaming in the choice of indicators, manipulation of data and output distortion.

As a consequence of the complexity in measuring expressed outcomes there has been a tendency for outcome-based methodologies to turn to proxy indicators with a focus on information that substitutes for the outcome with a set of data that is simple to collect. OBA has been said to use simple, easy-to-collect data as a proxy for genuine outcome information, for example, BMI (body mass index) as a proxy measure for obesity (Lowe and Wilson, 2015, p 9), leading to limited information on outcomes. This approach can also reflect an exaggerated respect for hard quantitative data, leading to a form of tunnel vision (Pidd, 2005), resulting in too great a focus on numbers and entering data into a computer with the quality and nature of client or user contact declining (Keevers et al, 2012). There have been calls for more weight to be given to qualitative data to provide a more accurate and balanced picture than can be gained through mere statistically orientated proxy indicators (Inspiring Impact NI, 2016). The emphasis on statistical indicators may also contribute to a view that indicators are simply descriptors or detailed definitions of outcomes, implying no significant difference in meaning. An analysis of lists of indicators will reveal that they incorporate value positions and implicit statements about what ought to be achieved. It can be noted that the Welsh Government overall was not as strongly committed to the measurement of outcomes as in Scotland, and inclined to accept a range of evidence.

The relationship between outcomes and indicators is of key importance. The OBA methodology of working backwards from the desired outcomes has been seen as assuming a direct and linear relationship, step by step, from desired outcomes to indicators to activities. Thus the four or five indicators must generate a set of hypotheses to be tested on a cause-and-effect spectrum. Bovaird (2014) sees such outcomes-based approaches as placing too much confidence in narrow, under-specified cause-and-effect chain models, and a misguided attempt to use these models in policy areas where behaviours are better modelled as complex adaptive systems. Tannahill (2016), writing on the Scottish experience, acknowledges that outcomes emerge from complex systems, but Lowe (Pelan, 2016) argues that rather than seeing outcomes as emergent properties of complex systems, OBA conceptualises them as products of a simple linear model rather than non-linear complex attribution patterns. Attention has also been drawn to the difficulties of measuring outcomes. Lowe and Wilson (2015, p 8) view measuring outcomes as a complicated resource-intensive business that can involve surveys and interviews, control groups and longitudinal follow-up, necessary to understand the impact of social policy interventions. Social policy interventions and their outcomes can be seen as only understandable in the context of people's perceptions and evaluation of the impact on their lives. But Bovaird (2014, p 19) has argued that lists of outcomes have been paraded as providing a rationale for government policies, without any convincing attempt to show how they relate to actual interventions.

The second part of the OBA framework relates to accountability and a distinction between population and performance accountability (Friedman, 2005). Population outcomes are outcomes for a whole population, whether for a country or region, and performance accountability relates to the performance of a service for those who receive the service. The validity of this distinction can be questioned, and in more traditional outcome-based models a distinction was often made between macro, meso and micro levels, with the micro usually the individual or group. The performance of a service was described in terms of the impact of a sub-set of the population with certain characteristics. Few social policy interventions are aimed at a whole population. A question also arises concerning the meaning of the word 'accountability' in this context and its different meaning from public or political accountability. The OBA methodology includes examination of performance measurement categories 'quantity' and 'quality', and asks 'is anyone better off?', but interpretations and calculation of this can vary and, in practice, government policies may not be not intended to make people better off but have other objectives including reducing expenditure, achieving fairness or making people less dependent.

Policy implications

National outcomes in each country are expressed as high-level statements. General in content and scope they can be seen as fulfilling an important political purpose in securing cross-party and cross-sectoral agreement. The more specific the outcomes, the more likely there is to be disagreement and conflict. This dimension has particular but not dissimilar importance in each country. In 2006 the SNP had adopted the NPF in its manifesto as part of its strategy of building a national policy consensus and even to achieve consensus within the different sectors of the SNP. High-level or very general outcomes are also important in Northern Ireland to facilitate agreement between the two main political parties that are divided on many issues. The need to reach a consensus may be better explained by regarding the outcomes for the PfG as a lowest common denominator approach, as the outcomes reflect expressions of policy generality that the parties can support (Gray and Birrell, 2012). Inter-party agreement would soon disappear when the discussion moved to more detailed policy, and the difficulty in finding agreement in the nuts and bolts of delivery and implementation of the outcomes becomes apparent. In Wales devolution has operated with the requirement for a coalition government in most periods, and national outcome indicators can be seen as '… framework integrating decision making at national and local level' (Law, 2013, p 4). The production of outcomes and indicators has also been helpful in Wales and in Scotland in providing a good working relationship between central and local governments through outcomes-based agreements.

A further assessment of the possible policy impact of the outcomes-based approach relates to the programmes for government that are renewed annually. In Scotland these reveal little reference to the NPF, with the presentation following traditional lines of a vision statement, setting out policies and strategies, a listing of proposed legislation and general funding commitments. The PfG for 2015/16 devotes only a few lines to the NPF (Scottish Government, 2015), and in the PfG 2016/17 there is only a brief section in an 86-page document on the NPF (Scottish Government, 2016). While the PfG sees the NPF as intended to record progress achieved, it pays more attention to the UN Sustainable Development Goals and Scotland's National Action Plan for Human Rights, throwing doubts on the view that in Scotland a distinctive approach to policy was marked by the NPF and Scotland Performs (Coutts and Brotchie, 2016).

Midwinter (2009, p 68), with reference to the outcomes-based approach in Scotland, has written of 'inflated performance rhetoric', pointing to problems of methodology and measurement. The Scottish Parliament Finance Committee (2013, para 19) has also been critical of the idea of national outcomes, seeing them as covering too broad a range of policies and delivery models and being open to different interpretations. The Infrastructure and Capital Investment Committee suggested that the NPF should be used to scrutinise Scottish Government interventions (Scottish Parliament Infrastructure and Capital Investment Committee, 2013), and recommended the use of a logic model. This is a more traditional outcomes methodology consisting of priorities, inputs, outputs and outcomes or impact covering short-, medium- and long-term perspectives (Burnside, 2014), and has been described as measuring the right outcomes at the right time (Evaluation Support Scotland, 2017). In 2016 Parliament's Finance Committee concluded that despite the new performance-based approach there has been little change in the nature of the budget process (Scottish Parliament Finance Committee, 2016). The relationship of spending to outcomes also became an issue with the government report on progress with the NPF making no direct link between spending allocations and performance. This led to calls for the NPF to be integrated into the Scottish Government's spending plans and the budget setting process (Royal Society of Edinburgh, 2013).

In Northern Ireland in response to government consultations there has been a tendency to support outcomes-based approaches but without defining what this may mean or whether it means the OBA model. The OBA agenda has been planned for rather than been implemented as the production of a final PfG agreed by the Northern Ireland Executive was halted by the political crisis that led to the collapse of the Executive, an election and negotiations on the basis for restoring the Executive. The position of the Democratic Unionist Party (DUP) and Sinn Féin as dominating government is likely to continue in any new government with the implication of an eventual OBA-based PfG. In the event of no local agreement and a return to Direct Rule, it is likely that the Northern Ireland Civil Service would exert influence to implement an OBA-based PfG. In the local government sphere the key development of community planning has been strongly influenced by the requirements of OBA. Community planning was largely copied from Scotland despite the limited functions of local councils in Northern Ireland. It had the original aim of assessing local needs, joining up the delivery of services between agencies, and achieving major public participation. Many of the draft community plans developed by the 11 local councils have been guided to follow the OBA methodology, some very precisely, resulting in a list of general outcomes for a 13- to 15-year period, and with each outcome having four or five indicators/statistical measures – but often no policies or delivery plan. A strong dissenting voice on Northern Ireland's outcomes-based approach has been produced by Lowe (Pelan, 2016), who argued that it was shocking that a Northern Ireland Government was choosing to adopt a version of OBA in the face of critical evidence. He suggests that the use of OBA will undermine effective practice, questions whether it will improve outcomes and criticises the waste of public money on consultants and training.

Conclusions

Outcomes-based approaches have developed as a common feature of strategies to improve social conditions. They have facilitated the monitoring of the performance of devolved governments, assisted with public transparency and accountability, and helped develop a shared set of priorities. In the devolved administrations the specific methodology of outcomes- or results-based accountability has had a major influence on the NPF in Scotland and National Indicators in Wales, supported by legislation. In Northern Ireland OBA is used in the PfG framework and content, and its use has been encouraged by many public bodies and local councils. OBA has the attraction of apparent simplicity in a formula that can be readily taught and applied using basic statistical data. The promotion and use of OBA has seen the emergence of theoretical criticisms of the principles and the value of this particular methodology. These criticisms have focused on four aspects of OBA: definition of outcomes; attempt to simplify the task of measuring outcomes; limitations of using easy-to-collect data as indicators; and the underlying assumption of a simple cause-and-effect chain. OBA has some distinctive characteristics, the most significant of which is 'working backwards' from the specified desired outcomes to the interventions that created them. This distinguishes OBA from alternative outcome approaches and suggests OBA is incompatible with them. This would apply particularly to what is known as the 'logic model' of objectives-inputs-processes-outputs and short- and long-term outcomes and also the Outcomes Framework models used in England and now Wales for the NHS, social care and public health, which focus on users' experience and impact on quality of life. While OBA originally had a major influence on the production of outcomes and indicators in Scotland and Wales, it is no longer suggested in these jurisdictions that OBA is the only accepted methodology and other outcomes approaches are used. Northern Ireland is more enthusiastic in turning to rely totally on OBA as a basis for a PfG.

The wider literature on performance indicators has traditionally and effectively (Flynn, 2012) drawn attention to the dangers of distortion on the three main grounds of: difficulty in reaching agreement on outcomes and indicators; the likelihood of data manipulation or stripping the context from data to produce the desired results; and the problem of attribution. The weight of these criticisms did lead to considerable discrediting of the use of performance indicators. Although there has been an impressive buy-in to the principle of an outcomes-based approach in the devolved countries, there is little evidence that outcomes-based approaches at national level have improved performance in Scotland or explained changes in performance data (Wimbush, 2011). In Scotland the use of the NPF has thrown up a dispute about data manipulation, for example, with statistics on educational achievement. Scotland and Wales have emphasised the monitoring value of an outcomes approach rather than applying OBA precisely. The evidence that has been produced suggests that the benefits of OBA have tended to relate to small-scale localised projects. OBA appears more possible for use under a limited range of conditions where attribution can follow a simple linear progression and what people experience is easily measured. This may explain achievements claimed for OBA in local council projects. Cook (2017a) has acknowledged some benefits from a focus on intended outcomes in providing a focus for activity, collecting specific statistics providing information on how programmes are doing in encouraging long-term thinking. However, the outcome of social policy interventions is more complex than collating a few statistics or always applying an off-the-shelf formula. The OBA methodology has not produced any robust evidence regarding the impact on policy-making, and the limited numbers of outcomes or indicators proposed reveal little about the policy intervention that would be justified or required.

References

Arnott, M. and Ozga, J. (2010) 'Nationalism, governance and policymaking in Scotland: The Scottish National Party (SNP) in power', *Public Money and Management*, vol 30, no 2, pp 91-8.

Arnott, M. and Ozga, J. (2012) 'Education policy and social justice', in G. Mooney and G. Scott (eds) *Social justice and social policy in Scotland*, Bristol: Policy Press, pp 147-64.

Audit Scotland (2010) *An overview of local government in Scotland 2009*, Edinburgh: Audit Scotland.

Birrell, D. (2009) *The impact of devolution on social policy*, Bristol: Policy Press.

Birrell, D. and Gormley Heenan, C. (2016) *Multi-level governance and Northern Ireland*, Basingstoke: Palgrave Macmillan.

Bovaird, T. (2014) 'Attributing outcomes to social policy interventions – "gold standard" or "fool's gold" in public policy and management?', *Social Policy & Administration*, vol 48, no 1, pp 1-23.

Burnside, R. (2014) *Budget Scrutiny 2015-16*, Briefing 14/23, Edinburgh: Scottish Parliament Information Centre.

Cairney, P. (2011) *The Scottish political system since devolution*, Exeter: Imprint Academic.

Cairney, P., Russell, S. and St Denny, E. (2016) 'The "Scottish approach" to policy and policymaking: what issues are territorial and what are universal?', *Policy & Politics*, vol 44, no 3, pp 333-50.

Campbell, A. (2012) *The National Performance Framework and Scotland Performs*, Briefing 12/12, Edinburgh: Scottish Parliament Information Centre.

Centre for Social Justice (2015) *Outcome based government: How to improve spending decisions across government* (www.centreforsocialjustice.org.uk/library/outcome-based-government-improve-spending-decisions-across-government).

Cole, A. and Stafford, I. (2015) 'Wales and the challenges of multi-level governance in A. Cole and I. Stafford (eds) *Devolution and governance: Wales between capacity and constraint*, London: Palgrave Pivot, pp 84-115.

Commission on the Future Delivery of Public Services (2011) *Report on the future delivery of public services by the commission chaired by Dr Campbell Christie* (Christie Report), Edinburgh: Scottish Government.

Commission on Public Service Governance and Delivery (2014) *The report of the Commission on Public Service Governance and Delivery* (Williams Report), Cardiff: Welsh Government.

Conlong, A.M. (2016) Email communication with author, Head of Scotland Performs, June 2016.

Cook, A. (2017a) *Outcomes based approaches in public service reform: Position Paper*, Edinburgh: What Works Scotland.

Cook, A. (2017b) *Delivering change, defining outcomes and capturing evidence*, London: Alliance for Useful Evidence.

Coutts, P. and Brotchie, J. (2016) *The Scottish approach to evidence: A discussion paper*, Dunfermline: The Carnegie Trust.

Elvidge, J. (2011) *Northern exposure: Lessons from the first twelve years of devolved government in Scotland*, London: Institute for Government.

Elvidge, J. (2014) *A route map to an enabling state*: Dunfermline: The Carnegie Trust.

Evaluation Support Scotland (2017) *Developing a logic model support guide*, Edinburgh: Evaluation Support Scotland.

Flynn, N. (2012) *Public sector management*, London: Sage Publications.

Friedman, M. (2005) *Trying hard is not good enough: How to produce measurable improvements for customers and communities*, Bloomington, IN: Trafford Publishing.

Glendinning, C., Clarke, S., Hare, P., Maddison, J. and Newbronner, L. (2008) 'Progress and problems in developing outcomes-focused social care services for older people in England', *Health & Social Care in the Community*, vol 16, pp 54-63.

Gray, A.M. and Birrell, D. (2012) 'Coalition Government in Northern Ireland: Social policy and the lowest common denominator thesis', *Social Policy and Society*, vol 11, no 1, pp 15-25.

Hansard (NI) (2016) *Committee for the Executive Office: Outcomes-based approach to Government*, Official report (http://data.niassembly.gov.uk/HansardXml/committee-19251.pdf).

Housden, P. (2014) 'This is us: a perspective on public services in Scotland', *Public Policy and Administration*, vol 29, no 1, pp 64-74.

Housing Rights (2016) 'Housing Rights responds to Programme for Government consultation', 6 January (www.housingrights.org.uk/news/policy-housing-rights-responds-programme-government-consultation).

Inspiring Impact NI (2016) *Response to NI Programme for Government Consultation* (https://inspiringimpactni.org/2016/12/21/response-to-ni-programme-for-government-consultation).

IRISS (Institute for Research and Innovation in Social Services) (2013) *Leading for outcomes: Integrated working*, Edinburgh: Institute for Research and Innovation in Social Services.

Keating, M. (2010) *The government of Scotland: Public policy making after devolution*, Edinburgh: Edinburgh University Press.

Keevers, L., Treleaven, L., Sykes, C. and Darcy, M. (2012) 'Made to measure: taming practices with results-based accountability', *Organization Studies*, vol 33, pp 97-120.

Law, J. (2013) *Do outcomes based approaches to service delivery work? Local authority outcome agreements in Wales*, University of South Wales: Centre for Advanced Studies in Public Policy.

Pelan, B. (2016) 'Dr Toby Lowe: A dissenting voice on outcomes-based approach', View Digital, 1 July (http://viewdigital.org/2016/07/01/dr-toby-lowe-dissenting-voice-outcomes-based-approach/).

Lowe, T. and Wilson, R. (2015) 'Playing the game of outcomes-based performance management. Is gamesmanship inevitable? Evidence from theory and practice', *Social Policy & Administration*, doi:10.1111/spol.12205

Midwinter, A. (2009) 'New development: Scotland's concordat – An assessment of the new financial frameworks in central–local relations', *Public Money and Management*, vol 29, no 1, pp 65-70.

Mooney, G. and Scott, G. (eds) (2012) *Social justice and social policy in Scotland*, Bristol: Policy Press.

NCB (National Children's Bureau) (2016) *Outcomes-based accountability: What is OBA and how can NCB help you with it?* (www.ncb.org.uk/northern-ireland/outcomes-based-accountability).

Northern Ireland Assembly Research and Information Service (2016) *Outcomes-based government: Scrutiny of outcomes*, Research and Information Series, Briefing Paper 54/16, Belfast: Northern Ireland Assembly.

Northern Ireland Executive (2016) *Draft Programme for Government Framework*, Belfast: Northern Ireland Executive.

Penna, R. and Williams, W. (2005) *Outcomes frameworks: An overview for practitioners*, Albany, NY: Fort Orange Press.

Petch, A. (2014) *Delivering integrated care and support*, Glasgow: Institute for Research and Innovation in Social Services (IRISS).

Pidd, M. (2005) 'Perversity in public service performance measurement', *International Journal of Productivity and Performance Management*, vol 54, no 5/6, pp 482-93.

Royal Society of Edinburgh (2013) *The Scottish Government's National Performance Framework, Advice Paper 13-08* (www.rse.org.uk/wp-content/uploads/2016/09/AP13_08.pdf).

Sanderson, I. (2011) 'Evidence-based policy or policy-based evidence? Reflections on Scottish experience', *Evidence & Policy*, vol 7, no 1, pp 54-76.

Scottish Government (2015) *Programme for Government 2015–16*, Edinburgh: Scottish Government.

Scottish Government (2016) *A plan for Scotland: The Scottish Government's Programme for Scotland 2016–17*, Edinburgh: Scottish Government.

Scottish Parliament Finance Committee (2013) *Report on Draft Budget 2014–15*, SP Paper 341 (www.parliament.scot/S4_EconomyEnergyandTourismCommittee/Reports/eer-13-DraftReportw.pdf).

Scottish Parliament Infrastructure and Capital Investment Committee (2013) *Report on Draft Budget 2014–15* (www.parliament.scot/S4_InfrastructureandCapitalInvestmentCommittee/Reports/trR13-BudgetReport.pdf).

Seaford, C. (2015) *Measuring progress on well-being: The development of national indicators*, Cardiff: Public Policy Institute for Wales.

Tannahill, C. (2016) *Ten years of outcomes in Scotland. Does it make a difference?*, Carnegie UK Trust Conference Presentation, Belfast, 28 September.

Welsh Government (2013) *Sustainable social services for Wales: An approach to social services improvement 2013–14*, Cardiff: Welsh Government.

Welsh Government (2015a) *How to measure a nation's progress? National indicators for Wales*, Cardiff: Welsh Government.

Welsh Government (2015b) *Sustainable social services for Wales: A framework for action*, Cardiff: Welsh Government.

Wimbush, E. (2011) 'Implementing an outcomes approach to public management and accountability in the UK – are we learning the lessons?', *Public Money and Management*, vol 3, pp 211-18.

Part Two
Contributions from the Social Policy
Association Conference 2017

Elke Heins

This section of *Social Policy Review 30* assembles some of the highlights of the annual conference of the Social Policy Association held in Durham in July 2017. Although perhaps not as momentous as the previous year, 2017 was undoubtedly an eventful political period, both in the UK and across the globe, as the timely contributions in this section remind us. To name but a few select events, we witnessed a snap UK General Election with surprising results that significantly weakened the Prime Minister and had important repercussions for her (social) policy agenda. It was also the first year in office of an explicitly populist US President, and themes of far-right populism dominated elections and debates in many European countries. Social inequality, the conference's leading theme, continued to be a dominant political issue. At a local level, the extent of inequality became perhaps most painfully visible through the Grenfell Tower fire, as already discussed in Chapter One by Stuart Hodkinson. Yet, further intriguing insights into the global scale of tax evasion and avoidance with important implications for inequality were also revealed through the leak of the Paradise Papers. The use of offshore tax havens by a global elite has massive implications for our welfare systems through lost taxes and for the extent of income inequality. Both taxes and benefits form the backbone of the welfare state, but the British media and public are notoriously obsessed with stories about the benefits side of the welfare system, with a particular focus on 'benefit cheats'. In contrast, the revelations of the Panama Papers in 2016, followed by the Paradise Papers in 2017, moved the spotlight, at least for a while, onto issues of tax avoidance and evasion.

While the leak of these papers in mainstream newspapers reveals secrets of the world's elite's hidden wealth, there is another 'hidden world' of the tax system that demands our attention, as Adrian Sinfield argues in Chapter Five. The tax reliefs and related subsidies of fiscal welfare in the UK contribute significantly but virtually invisibly to maintaining and reinforcing inequality. In his chapter Sinfield examines how tax reliefs support those benefiting from occupational and personal pensions, the largest area of social spending through the tax and National Insurance systems. The benefits go to less than half the working-age population and disproportionately to those paying higher rates of tax, their employers and the pensions industry. It is a major example of 'means-enhancing' redistribution as opposed to the means testing of much welfare state provision. The considerable value of National Insurance exemptions deserves far more attention than government or independent analysts have given it. Sinfield concludes that official statistics need to integrate fiscal with public spending and include the impact of fiscal welfare in their distributional analyses. Democratic policy-making needs to take account of it in tackling and reducing inequality across the whole society.

Without explicitly analysing what measures the UK government might adopt to respond to the revelations about the hidden world of taxation, Chapter Six by Robert Page takes a specific social policy angle on the current UK Prime Minister, including her views on social inequality. This chapter explores Theresa May's brand of Conservatism and her approach towards the welfare state since she unexpectedly became Prime Minister in June 2016. It is argued that her self-ascription as a 'good solid' conservative accurately captures her 'non-ideological' doctrine and her pragmatic approach to social policy. However, May's desire to create a 'fairer' society is unlikely to come to fruition given the pressing need to deliver a 'successful' Brexit and maintain party unity, as Page argues.

In 2017, the UK government's controversial flagship welfare-to-work programme (the Work Programme) stopped taking new participants as of April that year. In Chapter Seven, Eleanor Carter compares the Work Programme with the parallel-running programme Work Choice, which focused on individuals with health and disability-related support needs. Both programmes are grounded in the same commissioning strategy, but demonstrate important differences in the degree to which they embrace highly marketised provider-directed governance arrangements. While evaluations of social policy programmes are often difficult, the twin-track approach of the two programmes provides a powerful opportunity to consider potential differences in employment outcomes through a quasi-experimental design, facilitated by unique access to participant-level administrative data. Carter demonstrates that among matched programme participants with health conditions and disabilities, the Work Programme is performing significantly worse than Work Choice. The Work Choice arrangement counterpoises provider dominance through an enhanced role for the state in stipulating activity and regulating service quality and by furnishing service users with at least a limited degree of choice. Work Choice retains important elements of both a state-directed and user-responsive arrangement. These results have important policy design implications as they make a strong case for greater public regulation of quasi-marketised welfare services.

Extending the scope of social policy analysis from the UK to the case of Sweden, Chapter Eight by Markus Ketola and Johan Nordensvard investigates the relationship between far-right populism and social policy. The authors argue that an approach anchored in framing and policy narratives will yield new understandings of how far-right populist discourses have come to challenge social democratic and neoliberal welfare narrative. This new narrative challenges and denigrates the economic and political elite as self-serving and corrupt, claiming to represent the interest of the 'people' instead. In defining 'people', the interests of certain societal groups are prioritised on the bases of culture or ethnicity. Importantly for social policy in this, universal social rights and social citizenship are reframed in ethno-nationalist and welfare chauvinist terms.

We conclude this section with some introspection into our own academic practice. As every social policy researcher employed in UK academia is acutely aware, the next round of assessing the quality of research in UK higher education institutions is fast approaching. Since the publication of this volume falls exactly halfway through the 2014 and 2021 Research Excellence Frameworks (REFs), this is an opportune moment to scrutinise more closely the specific yardsticks by which the performance of UK higher education research is assessed. Of particular interest here is the first-time inclusion of research impact in the last REF. As Tina Haux notes in Chapter Nine, this focus on impact was greeted with scepticism by the academic community, not least to the challenges of defining and measuring the nature and significance of impact of social policy research. A new analytical framework of the nature of impact is developed by Haux that distinguishes between policy creation, direction, discourse and practice. This framework is then applied to the top-ranked impact case studies in the REF2014 from the Social Work and Social Policy sub-panel as well as the ESRC Early Career Impact prizewinners in order to assess impact across the life course of academics.

FIVE

Fiscal welfare and its contribution to inequality

Adrian Sinfield

Introduction

When governments spend the funds they have collected, this shows in the national accounts. When they choose not to collect revenue but to use some special relief or exemption, these decisions and their impact nearly always remain invisible and so unaccountable. Fiscal welfare is the social spending part of this 'hidden' world of tax reliefs and related subsidies (Greve, 1994; Howard, 1997). It reduces the revenue that we are told is needed to sustain the welfare state and reduce poverty.

The term 'fiscal welfare' was first used by Richard Titmuss in his essay, 'The social division of welfare: Some reflections on the search for equity', where he demonstrated that the welfare state was not the only way in which resources could be redistributed (Titmuss, 1958, first presented in 1955, reprinted with some omissions in Alcock et al, 2001). Including reliefs for taxes and National Insurance (NI), *fiscal* welfare allocates resources alongside *public* welfare, as Titmuss called the welfare state, and *occupational* welfare that fiscal welfare often supports and encourages (Sinfield, 1978).

'Simultaneously enlarging and consolidating the area of social inequality' (Titmuss, 1958, p 55), the social division of welfare has the effect of 'reinforcing sectoral advantage, nurturing privilege and contributing to exclusion and marginalisation' with 'the demoralising effect of cumulative social rejection' (Titmuss, 1958, quoted in Alcock et al, 2001, p 145).

At a time when public spending is subject to greater cuts and controls, with a particular impact on lower-income groups, the visibility and accountability of fiscal welfare becomes all the more important since the distribution of benefits through tax and related reliefs contributes to maintaining, if not widening, inequality. Even the International

Monetary Fund (IMF) now recognises the importance of tackling inequality: progressive taxes can help, and they need not inhibit growth (IMF, 2017).

The ways in which tax systems and tax havens can be exploited have been made more visible through the Panama and Paradise Papers (ICIJ, 2017). While fiscal welfare is no more immune to such treatment than other reliefs (as Titmuss showed in 1962, Appendix E), the analysis in this chapter concentrates on its uses for the purposes set out by governments.

This chapter focuses on fiscal welfare in pensions after indicating the main elements of fiscal social spending. The tax reliefs and NI exemptions for pensions are probably the largest area, although it is still remarkably little-known and researched. The limited published evidence on the size of these tax benefits and the even scantier official analysis of their distribution is examined. Particular attention is given to NI reliefs because of their much neglected role in subsidising private welfare – an especially fine example of the 'individualisation of the social' (Ferge, 1997). How fiscal welfare might be made more visible and open to discussion in, for example, tackling the problems of inequality, is discussed in the final sections of the chapter.

Discovery of the greater scale of tax reliefs

Fiscal welfare remains a largely hidden area of activity, although some changes have attracted attention: the merger of public welfare family allowances with fiscal welfare child tax allowances into child benefit in the 1970s; the phasing out of mortgage interest relief and married couples' allowances in the 1990s; and currently the replacement of child and working tax credits by Universal Credit.

In 2016–17 social spending through income tax reliefs alone totalled £30 billion. They were equivalent to some 16 per cent of the income tax actually collected, making up over three-quarters of the cost of income tax reliefs published by Her Majesty's Revenue & Customs (HMRC) (2016, excluding personal allowances). In addition, NI exemptions for pensions cost another £16 billion and capital gains tax relief on selling one's only or main residence £28 billion. The £2 billion relief on charities might also be considered as a subsidy to service provision as well as to the original donors.

The overall administration of the area of fiscal welfare has remained virtually unchanged for a very long time. HMRC (until 2005, the Inland Revenue [IR]) is responsible for administering tax reliefs once they have been introduced, usually in Finance Acts following annual budgets. This is a large, 'non-ministerial Department with qualified, but not full, independence from Government' (Treasury Committee, 2016, para 9), but the number of staff managing tax and NI reliefs is small.

Little has been reported on the scrutiny and control of tax reliefs. HMRC sees its role as ensuring that reliefs are properly administered and denies any responsibility for policy, an issue that its staff have repeatedly argued over with the Public Accounts Committee (PAC) (see, for example, PAC, 2015, 9 September, oral evidence, question 141 on). What higher control there is rests with the Chancellor of the Exchequer and the Treasury that has long 'reserved its sole proprietorship of "budget" matters such as tax expenditures and national insurance contributions' (Deakin and Parry, 2000, p 47).

In 2011 evidence emerged of a world of tax reliefs that has long been very much greater than officially reported. The Office of Tax Simplification (OTS), set up by the Coalition government to reduce the burdens of red tape and bureaucracy on business, began by compiling a list of tax reliefs: it found 1,042 across all taxes and NI reliefs (OTS, 2011). Their list revealed a rise to 1,156 by 2015, despite the removal of some reliefs OTS recommended for abolition (OTS, 2015). Yet HMRC has listed no more than 400 for many years. Many reliefs are technical, defining the scope of a tax, and some result from international agreements to avoid, for example, double taxation. However, OTS classified half of their much longer list as special cases for special interest groups, targeted to influence behaviour and/or establishing thresholds for exemptions: many constitute fiscal welfare.

The new evidence led the National Audit Office (NAO) to examine the management of tax reliefs (NAO, 2014a, b). There was strong opposition from the Chancellor of the Exchequer and the Treasury to NAO even investigating tax reliefs on the grounds that they did not constitute public spending. The NAO analysis was very critical, arguing that regulation had been at best patchy and often inadequate. This was followed by some vigorous hearings by the PAC, already pushing HMRC to be more accountable on tax reliefs (PAC, 2015; Hodge, 2016, Chapter 9).

HMRC has been tackling some of the issues raised, setting out 'best practice guidance', commissioning some research and consulting on proposals in some areas long neglected. So far the PAC has not been satisfied: 'We remain concerned that HMRC does not scrutinise effectively whether tax reliefs are being used as intended.... *Despite our repeated recommendations, HMRC still does not make tax reliefs sufficiently visible to support parliamentary scrutiny and public debate about areas where the UK chooses not to collect tax*' (PAC, 2016, summary, second main conclusion; original emphasis; see also paras 17-22). NAO has also continued its criticisms in reviewing the HMRC annual report and accounts (NAO, 2016). While resistance from the Treasury and HMRC reportedly continues, the world of tax reliefs is receiving more parliamentary and public attention, and this is extending beyond reactions to the exploitation revealed in the Panama and Paradise Papers.

The cost of all these reliefs remains little known. HMRC continues to provide estimated costs for some 200 reliefs, half its list, and barely one-sixth of the OTS one. Long-established ones occasionally emerge, some at a cost well above the £50 million threshold of the main list. The latest lists in December 2016 show data over five years for the first time rather than the two previously provided, and HMRC appears to be revising past figures more regularly (HMRC, 2016).

How many more resources are effectively re-allocated through tax and related spending is still uncertain in marked contrast to public spending, where virtually all items are identified, together with the cost and number receiving. How much value the taxpayer gets from public welfare services is much discussed, but not fiscal welfare. Some areas seem to pass unnoticed for years at a time, if mentioned at all.

How these reliefs affect the redistribution of resources across society is still more neglected, even by NAO and PAC. Who gets what in fiscal welfare is virtually undocumented – no regular data, only occasional answers to PQs (Parliamentary Questions) and even rarer mentions in official papers. The distributions of mortgage interest tax relief and housing benefit appeared regularly until the former was abolished in the 1990s.

'Pre-distribution' is the term introduced by Jacob Hacker to describe activities before government spending (Hacker, 2011, p 35; see also Chwalisz and Diamond, 2015). However, the term also fits fiscal welfare because its transfer takes place before governments decide on budgetary allocations to spending departments.

Fiscal welfare for pensions

In the 1950s and 1960s Titmuss examined the separate world of non-state pensions, contrasting its predominantly occupational welfare form supported by increasing fiscal welfare with the limited state pension (Titmuss, 1958, Chapter 3; 1962, Chapter 7 and Appendices D and E). Today the differences persist with less than half the working-age population (43 per cent) able to take any advantage from fiscal welfare in pensions (DWP, 2017a, p 11 and Table 6.5).

In 2015–16 62 per cent of UK employees between the age of 22 and state pension age were building up occupational pensions, a marked rise from 50 per cent in 2012 when automatic enrolment began (DWP, 2017a, p 11). The great majority were in defined contributions schemes with an average contribution rate of 4.2 per cent – 1.0 per cent members and 3.2 per cent employers – due to increase to a total of 8.0 per cent from April 2019 (ONS, 2017, Section 8, p 12). Defined benefit pensions for the half million in the private sector still in these schemes was substantially larger, 22.7 per cent of pensionable earnings, 5.8 per cent for members and 16.9 per cent for employers. Among self-employed workers, only 17 per cent were contributing to personal pensions. While many more women were contributing than in the past, the proportion was still lower (41 per cent) than for men (45 per cent), and women were much less likely to receive higher salaries with their greater benefits from fiscal welfare (DWP, 2017a, p 11 and Table 6.5; see also Ginn, 2001).

Pension contributions by both employee and employer are free of income tax, bringing taxable income down, so saving tax and often reducing the top rate of tax the individual has to pay. If the generally much larger employer's contribution were treated as taxable income, this would take many more into higher tax rates, but this is little noted. The investment income of pension funds is also mostly untaxed. Pensions are taxed on receipt but not the tax-free lump sum generally worth one-quarter of the pension.

The current system of taxing pensions was implemented in 2006 with annual and lifetime limits to the tax allowances. Since 2011 the annual limit has been brought down from £255,000 to £40,000 and the lifetime from £1.8 million to £1 million. This has restricted tax benefits at the very top and probably increasingly the better-off as well: the annual allowance takes account of the full change in the value of the defined benefit pension in the year (PPI, 2013, 2016).

In addition, there are two NI contribution exemptions. Employees have already paid NI at 12 per cent (2 per cent above the upper earnings limit of £45,000) on their gross salary, and that includes their own contribution to their pension. However, no employer NI contributions at 13.8 per cent are levied on the employers' occupational pension contributions. In addition, employees are not required to contribute NI on that extra support of the employers' contribution. These additional NI exemptions are scarcely ever mentioned, although the advantage to those with higher pay and greater pension contributions are significant and have not been restricted like the income tax reliefs.

Many, if not most, large employers also take advantage of 'salary sacrifice', generally making it the default arrangement with savings to both them and their employees. Staff 'sacrifice' that part of their salary they would have paid into their pension, and the employer pays it in instead. The resulting reduction in salary saves NI contributions for both employee and employer. Yet as far as bonuses, mortgages applications, pay rates given to potential employers and indeed earnings-related pensions, it is the original, higher, salary that is taken into account, to the advantage of the employee.

Taking up income tax reliefs can even maintain receipt of the public welfare child benefit that has been subject to tax for individual incomes over £50,000 since April 2014. Since that threshold is taxable, not gross, income, and tax reliefs reduce taxable income, a substantial pension contribution can maintain access to the full child benefit of £1,076.40 for the first and £712.40 for second and subsequent children for the year. This adds that benefit to the advantages of tax reliefs plus the tax saved by the tax-free child benefit of £215, or £430 if taxed at the higher rate. With pension tax reliefs, childcare vouchers, the cycle-to-work scheme and a small additional voluntary pension contribution, someone paid £60,000 a year can carry on receiving full child benefits. How much this costs and how many people gain is not known.

Costs and distribution of fiscal welfare for pensions

The pension reliefs resulted in an estimated total subsidy of £40.6 billion to private pensions in 2015–16 – an Income Tax cost of £24.9 billion net (after deducting income tax of £13.4 billion collected on pensions in payment) and a further £15.7 billion for NI (HMRC, 2017a; see Table 5.1 below). This total is more than six times Pension Credit, the means-tested benefit for those over working age on low incomes: it is equivalent to 45 per cent of the spending on contributory state pensions (DWP, 2016, Table 1a). These estimates of the revenue losses do not include tax relief on capital gains from the funds 'because of estimation difficulties' (HMRC, 2017a, footnote 1). The published cost has increased faster than spending on the contributory state pension since 2001-02, despite the reductions in the lifetime and annual allowances.

Any examination of the ways in which inequality is preserved and reinforced in the UK should take account of these subsidies that are 'means-enhancing' in contrast to means-testing. They not only benefit

Table 5.1: Cost of Income Tax and NI reliefs on occupational, personal and self-employed pensions, 2015–16, £ million

No Income Tax on contributions by individuals	7,600
No Income Tax on contributions by employers	22,800
Investment income from pension fund mostly untaxed	7,900
No NI contributions by employers on payments in, nor by individuals on, those payments	15,700
Less Income Tax on pensions in payment	13,400
Total net	**40,600**

Source: Adapted from HMRC (2017a): 'The figures are based on HMRC administrative data and information compiled from a variety of sources by the Office for National Statistics (ONS). Costs are subject to large revisions and have a particularly wide margin of error.... The cost of the tax relief is calculated as the tax that would be paid on contributions to registered pension schemes presuming they were not registered and the payments were subject to the normal tax rules applying to individuals' remuneration. The estimates do not represent the yield from withdrawing tax relief as there would be significant changes in taxpayers' behaviour' (HMRC, 2017a, notes 1 and 2).

those who can take advantage of them by obtaining higher pensions in later life; they also allow people on good salaries to keep their take-home pay higher than it would be if they were having to put the same amount into their pensions without these reliefs. This benefit during working life deserves closer attention from analysts of inequality.

Understandably, the reliefs are vigorously defended by business and the pensions industry (Lawson, 1992). However, despite their scale, 'tax incentives have not been successful in encouraging overall saving for retirement' (NAO, 2013, para 13; see also Hughes, 2000; PPI, 2013). Yet this lack of 'value for money' from such large subsidies has received little attention.

Given the unequal impact, one would expect regular and careful monitoring of the distribution of the £40 billion of pension subsidies instead of the limited and occasional data available. The latest evidence comes from an answer to a PQ in December 2014 (*Hansard*, 2014; see Table 5.2 below). This only takes account of the contributions made by employees, employers and the self-employed, but not the tax relief on the investment income of pension funds, totalling another £7.9 billion in 2015–16 (HMRC, 2017a). The distribution of the NI contribution exemptions, well over one-third of the estimated subsidy, is not analysed.

In recent years the proportion of the tax benefit going to the top group (£150,000 or more) has dropped greatly, from 20 per cent to 7 per cent, as the ceilings for the lifetime and annual allowances for tax-free

Table 5.2: Distribution of some of tax benefits for non-state pensions

Income bands	% of cost of Income Tax relief on pension contributions					
	2009–10	2010–11	2011–12	2012–13	2013–14	2014–15
Up to £19,999	8	6	5	6	5	5
£20,000-£44,999	31	32	35	37	37	36
£45,000-£74,999	25	26	28	32	33	34
£75,000-£99,999	7	8	8	10	10	10
£100,000-£149,999	8	9	9	7	8	8
£150,000 or more	20	18	14	8	7	7
All	100	100	100	100	100	100

Source: Written answer to PQ from Steve Doughty by David Gauke, 10 December 2014:
'Estimates are based on Surveys of Personal Incomes with projections for 2012-13 onwards.
Historical estimates have been updated to take into account the latest outturn data and
updated projections' (*Hansard*, 2014).

contributions have been brought down, probably reducing much of their use for tax avoidance rather than savings. However, some three-fifths of the cost continues to go to those paying above the basic rate of tax, or who would be if the pensions tax relief did not bring them below the higher level. The proportion going to those at the bottom has also fallen, from 8 per cent to 5 per cent, as the tax threshold has risen and not all pension schemes give the relief automatically.

The increasing proportion of workers in insecure and low-paid jobs is very unlikely to be able to take advantage of these reliefs to build up private pensions. Currently only seven out of ten pensioners receive any income from private pensions (occupational and personal). The median for those in receipt is £145, and it is widely distributed. While nearly one in eight receive over £500 a week (13 per cent), nearly two-fifths (38 per cent) receive less than £100 (DWP, 2017b, p 8 and Data Table 6.6, for pensioner benefit units including couples and any income from dependent children in the unit). Although pensioner poverty has fallen, one in six were living in poverty in 2015-16. By contrast, 7.6 per cent of households held almost half (47 per cent) of all pension wealth in the UK in 2012–14 (ONS, 2015, Chapter 6).

The total savings from tax and NI reliefs can be considerable, but it is not at all clear who should be regarded as the beneficiaries of the different elements. How far the contributors benefit from all these subsidies deserves further examination than I have been able to give. Defined benefit schemes, for example, do not allocate directly to the individual as defined contribution ones (PPI, 2013, p 12). It is not clear to what extent the benefits go to subsidise employers and pension funds.

Pre-distribution in National Insurance

The NI subsidy is estimated at £15.7 billion in 2015–16 via NI contribution relief on employer contributions (including employee contribution relief on this extra amount; see HMRC, 2017a, note 3). This is equal to 41 per cent of the gross income tax relief cost and 63 per cent of the net amount. It is surprising that amounts of this scale are seldom included in discussions of incentives to invest in pensions.

NAO and various select committees that have considered the management and administration of tax and other reliefs have repeatedly criticised the failure to regularly monitor, report and assess any changes including in costs. NI exemptions appear to have received even less attention from political or official bodies than income tax reliefs. These reliefs only warrant a memorandum item in the one HMRC table on the cost of registered pension scheme tax relief (HMRC, 2017a). They are not included in the annual accounts of the NI Fund, although subsidies to the redundancy payments scheme are (HMRC, 2017b, p 12). Funded by the NI Fund since 1991, the latter have cost only some £0.25 billion for many years (net, after taking account of small payments in).

The much larger subsidies of NI reliefs to private pensions may be seen as worth reporting in the NI Fund accounts. The Treasury Grant that comes from the general revenue to maintain the level of the Fund when necessary does appear in the accounts. So far in this century only two annual payments in 2014–16, totalling £14.2 billion, have been made from the Treasury Grant to the NI Fund: the tripartite arrangements of 1911 and 1948 with contributions from employee, employer and government have long been ended (Cracknell, 2014; HMRC, 2017a). By contrast NI exemptions to non-state pensions have continued year after year but are not shown in the NI accounts. Over the five years to March 2016 this cost £72.7 billion, an annual average of £14.5 billion compared with an average of £2.4 billion from the Treasury Grant to the NI Fund over the same period. Over the past five years the public accounts show Treasury Grants to the NI Fund of 3 per cent while effectively an unaccounted-for 16.6 per cent grant has been going from the NI Fund to support private pension arrangements.

NI contributors are now receiving very little occasional support from the general revenue, and are not told that they regularly provide considerable support to the private pensions of a minority, some of whom are doing extremely well from their hidden subsidy (TUC, 2015). This represents a significant effective transfer from NI to the private pensions industry, reinforcing the questions about power and control that Richard Titmuss posed in 1959 in *The irresponsible society* (reprinted in Alcock et al, 2001).

This is not to argue that such support should necessarily be reduced or removed, but to challenge the convention that such exemptions should not be made more visible and accountable. As a result they are very unlikely to be used to inform any discussion of policy-making and the allocation of resources for retirement, or for any other purpose that governments might want to take action on. While recognition that inequality is a major problem increases, the ways in which these significant subsidies are supporting a largely more privileged group and so maintaining inequalities is not visible and therefore not part of the debate.

Apparently NI has never been levied on employers' contributions to private pensions. Initially there was a ceiling on both employees and employers' NI contributions. When employers were required to pay NI against the whole pay range in 1985, 'a substantial industry developed in NIC avoidance planning', as Archy Kirkwood MP had warned in the debate (quoted in Sandler, 1993, p 11). In 1991 the employers' NI contribution ceiling was removed for company cars and fuel for private motoring with the introduction of Class 1A contributions; by 2001 most benefits in-kind were included but not pensions.

Certainly the tax industry was well aware and taking advantage of this. For example, Nick Braun, founder of Taxcafe in 1999 and author of seven editions of *Pension magic: How to make the taxman pay for your retirement* (2017), wrote:

A recent article in The Times reported that Gordon Brown has decided NOT to clamp down on what is described as the "tax dodge of the decade", which allows employers and employees to avoid paying hundreds of millions of pounds in national insurance (NI) each year.... If the arrangement is structured correctly neither the employer nor the employee will be worse off – only the taxman loses out! (Braun, no date)

The 'taxman' is, of course, the rest of the community whose resources are effectively reduced.

The only consideration of the costs of NI exemptions in any official or parliamentary discussion I have been able to find was by the Social Security (now Work and Pensions) Select Committee when I was asked to present a paper on the tax welfare state, but this issue was not followed up in the report (Sinfield, 1998).

NAO have acknowledged that exemptions from NI contributions constitute an incentive to non-state pensions (NAO, 2013). However, they did not venture into the pension area in examining the management of tax reliefs because the scale of this set of reliefs could have dominated the wider enquiry (NAO, 2014a, b).

HM Treasury and HMRC Green Papers on the costs of pensions tax relief have rarely mentioned the NI subsidy although the one in 2015 did include it in listing the total support (HM Treasury, 2015). It was not presented as a possible option for achieving a fairer distribution. The report on responses and the government reaction mentioned NI subsidies cryptically: 'Suggestions for how the government might continue to incentivise employer contributions focused on National Insurance contributions relief ...' (HM Treasury, 2016, para 240). Apparently this included restricting NI exemptions.

Some independent analysts have referred to NI exemptions, often in relation to merging income tax and NI, but rarely the wider policy implications of amounts exempted and their distribution. The discussion and proposals in the Mirrlees Review (2011, Chapter 14, especially pp 338-40, curiously not indexed) have led to more consideration from the Institute for Fiscal Studies (IFS) (see, for example, Emmerson, 2014) and the Centre for Policy Studies (Johnson, 2012, 2016).

The general neglect of NI exemptions results in only limited listing of their costs – for example, employment allowance £2 billion and employer-supported childcare including workplace nurseries £410 million (HMRC, 2016). The basic allowances (not levying contributions below the primary threshold for employees, the secondary threshold for employers and the Lower Profits Limit for the self-employed) cost £53.7 billion. How much removing the upper earnings and profits limits would cost is not published, although IFS estimated £8.3 billion in 2003 (Adam and Reed, 2003, p 61). Unlisted NI contribution exemptions such as the one for termination payments are rarely mentioned, let alone costed, although a PQ elicited the cost of not collecting NIC from people in employment but over pensionable age at £1.1 billion in 2014–15 (*Hansard*, 2017).

How can fiscal welfare be made more visible and accountable?

Given the scale and importance of these concealed multipliers of inequality, more account needs to be taken of the impact of what has been called 'off-the-books', 'off-budget' or 'backdoor' spending. Social policy has traditionally debated the merits of universal and selective means-tested provision, but the 'means-enhancing' selective operation of most fiscal welfare also affects the final distribution of resources, and so needs to be included in the analysis.

Public spending totals include many items but not tax spending, despite its similar impact on balancing the budget. Revenue is less when tax spending is greater: it is simply 'an accounting convenience', as Richard Titmuss pointed out over 60 years ago (1958, pp 44-5; see also Alcock et al, 2001, p 65). Its inclusion alongside conventional public spending would enable fuller debate of the use of scarce resources under 'austerity' regimes. What should be included in tax spending including fiscal welfare, and how it should be reported, deserves more analysis and wider discussion. Should costs and their distribution be reported whenever income or capital is treated differently from the basic tax framework? Should this include the costs of basic personal tax allowances and the lower rate of NI for higher incomes? And who really benefits and how?

Fiscal welfare could be routinely shown in official statistics such as *The effects of taxes and benefits on household income*, the detailed annual analysis by the Office for National Statistics (ONS) and its forerunners for nearly half a century. This shows that the total tax system has not been progressive but basically proportionate; indeed, there has long been a continuing slightly higher incidence of total taxes on the quintile with the least money. In 2015–16 the bottom quintile of households paid 35 per cent of their gross income in all taxes, higher than the average (33.4 per cent) and even the top quintile (34.1 per cent) (Tonkin, 2017, Table 22 in the accompanying dataset). This is, at least in part, because those with lower incomes have fewer resources to exploit the range of fiscal welfare. This pattern is greatly at odds with the public perception focused on income tax alone by many politicians and media. The large proportion of income tax paid by the top few per cent is because their income has become so large, but this is rarely mentioned. Tax and NI contribution reliefs should be shown alongside state benefits to reveal the extent to which fiscal welfare affects the distribution of resources across society.

Chapter 4 of the same ONS survey is headed 'Half of households in the UK receive more in benefits than they paid in taxes' (Tonkin, 2017, Chapter 4: 50.5 per cent, non-retired households, 37.2 per cent, retired 88.0 per cent). That point is frequently quoted in ONS press releases and in the media where it is argued that the better-off have to bear the 'burden of the welfare state' as part of the 'burden' of taxation. If tax reliefs were treated as the subsidies they are and were taken into account in these calculations, public and policy debates would be differently, and better, informed.

Power and the pre-distribution that reinforces inequality

Those who benefit from the status quo have little incentive to deal with inequality-enhancing fiscal welfare. Its form of pre-distribution is not even considered by those who are setting up the policy-making agenda. It lingers on in the dark area that Bachrach and Baratz (1970) called 'non-decision-making'. 'Inequality in the distribution of benefits and privileges tends to persist through time ... power may be, and often is, exercised by confining the scope of decision-making to relatively "safe" issues' (Bachrach and Baratz, 1970, pp 105, 106).

It is the very routine nature of most pre-distribution through fiscal welfare that renders them so normal and invisible that it does not occur to analysts to include them in the arithmetic of inequality and poverty. Yet, given the 'heavy distributional skew' of fiscal welfare that reinforces inequality, it 'cannot be treated as an analytic afterthought. It must be placed at the heart of any explanation of the distinctive political dynamics' (Hacker, 2002, p 39). This point, originally made about the US, applies strongly to the UK and many other countries too (see Hughes and Sinfield, 2004, on pensions).

International agencies and multinational bodies are now taking more account of tax expenditures and have even included suggestions for action. The 2003 World Bank note, 'Why worry about tax expenditures?', recognised that tax expenditure 'violates' both vertical and horizontal equity (The World Bank, 2003, p 2). A 2010 OECD (Organisation for Economic Co-operation and Development) study acknowledged: 'this incentive pattern might be judged absolutely perverse – giving the most inducement to those who need the inducement least – and yet it is the common practice in at least some countries' (OECD, 2010, p 28). Its comment on governments' lack of action was more scathing than the usual international discourse: 'Though evaluation of tax expenditures may be difficult, a more serious problem may be the failure to try....

An out-of-sight, out-of-mind attitude can arise and continue to insulate inefficiencies from scrutiny for periods of years' (OECD, 2010, p 29). This neglect also serves to insulate inequalities from scrutiny, not just inefficiencies.

In 2014 the European Commission drew attention to the growing use of tax expenditures. Since then European Union (EU) member states have been required to publish regular reports of tax expenditure; up to then they did so in 'very diverse' forms and varying 'a lot in presentation, deepness and coverage', 'often fragmented and not fully transparent' (EC, 2014, pp 19-20).

A 2016 OECD working paper, *Tax design for inclusive economic growth*, was unusually specific about the strategies that governments should be adopting: 'tax bases should be broadened first by removing or reducing tax expenditures that disproportionately benefit high income groups' to promote inclusive growth. 'Scaling back tax expenditures that are not well-targeted at redistributive objectives may help achieve both greater efficiency and a narrower distribution of disposable income' (Brys et al, 2016, p 51). Research or working papers from these powerful organisations may not constitute policy recommendations, but they still bring tax expenditures on to the agenda, with more data being collected.

Independent analyses are also bringing hidden elements of tax spending into the light. The Fiscal Welfare Network is examining the political economy of fiscal welfare policies across Europe (Morel et al, 2016, and see also their website, fiscalwelfare.eu). This initiative provides a major opportunity to pursue many of these issues on a comparative basis. More analysis is needed, for example, to ensure that all elements of fiscal welfare appear in official tax expenditures and in the OECD's TBSPs, 'tax benefits for social purposes' (Adema et al, 2014; Sinfield, 2013, pp 21-3).

Richard Murphy and colleagues at the Tax Justice Network are pursuing questions integral to issues of inequality nationally and internationally (see, for example, Murphy, 2012, 2016). Fiscal welfare needs to be linked more closely with the corporate welfare identified by Kevin Farnsworth (Farnsworth, 2012, 2015). Benefits, including fiscal ones, may be largely or wholly directed through the company to employers and certain staff, supporting and reinforcing inequalities.

Conclusion

Analysis of fiscal welfare support for pensions through taxes and NI confirms Titmuss's warning of the simultaneous enlargement and consolidation of inequality over 60 years ago (quoted at the start of this chapter). It demonstrates the ways in which inequalities can be maintained and even reinforced through the hidden 'tax welfare state', means-enhancing and separate from the much-debated welfare state that is becoming increasingly means-tested: 'Power is at its most effective when least observable' (Lukes, 2005, p 1).

'The problem for the future is to refuse to tolerate two standards of social value and to apply one: to see how the privileges of the few can be transferred to the many.' This challenge was set out by Peter Townsend in his essay, 'A society for people', as long ago as 1958. 'We have hardly begun to understand how to abandon the double standard of values in the social services and treat people as we would ourselves like to be treated' (Townsend, 1958 [2009], pp 114, 115).

The single standard requires, for example, official statistics to integrate fiscal with public spending and include the impact of fiscal welfare in their distributional analyses. Democratic policy-making needs to take account of means-enhancing fiscal measures in tackling and reducing inequality across the whole society.

When the privileges of fiscal welfare are not even visible in the current accounting of UK resources and their allocation through government actions, the inequalities that their separate standards foster remain outside public debate. Public examination might support some elements more than others, but while they remain unseen, they continue invisibly and unconsidered. Policy debate, let alone change, is kept off the agenda. The inequalities that they reinforce continue and even grow as 'the level playing field' of current public accounts is tilted unregarded to reward quietly, but significantly, those who benefit from these arrangements.

The hidden world of fiscal welfare was nicely caught by Jacob Hacker in his study of American healthcare and pensions: 'subterranean politics ... allow policies to pass that would not survive if subjected to the bright light of political scrutiny or the cold calculations of accurate budgeting' (Hacker, 2002, pp 43-4; see also Greve, 1994; Howard, 1997, 2007). Stanley Surrey, the American lawyer who introduced the term 'tax expenditure' in deliberate contrast to 'public expenditure', made the same point in explaining 'upside-down' benefits (1973, p 37) (McDaniel and Surrey, 1985, pp 72-82). It is difficult to believe that a Secretary of State would stand up in Parliament and explicitly lay out the details of a scheme that had the regressive effect of most fiscal welfare.

As David Byrne and Sally Ruane observe, 'The tax system functions as a whole with the effect of preserving the financial advantage enjoyed by those in households with the highest incomes' (Byrne and Ruane,

2017, p 80). Given how much the main writers on fiscal welfare have constantly stressed the implications for inequality and the evidence they have assembled, the continuing failure to obtain much better, more accessible and more visible routine analysis of who gets what from fiscal welfare deserves further examination and greater policy attention.

Acknowledgements

I am grateful to Jon Aldous at HMRC, Fran Bennett, Andy Morrison at NAO, Lynne Robertson-Rose, Sue Ward, the editors of *Social Policy Review* and, once again, Dorothy Sinfield for their help and advice. None of them are, of course, responsible for any of my errors or omissions.

References

Adam, S. and Reed, H. (2003) 'Income tax and National Insurance contributions', in *IFS Green Budget 2003*, London: Institute for Fiscal Studies.

Adema, W., Fron, P. and Ladaique, M. (2014) 'How much do OECD countries spend on social protection and how redistributive are their tax/benefit systems?', *International Social Security Review*, vol 67, p 1.

Alcock, P., Glennerster, H., Oakley, A. and Sinfield, A. (eds) (2001) *Welfare and wellbeing: Richard Titmuss's contribution to social policy*, Bristol: Policy Press.

Bachrach, P. and Baratz, M.S. (1971) *Power and poverty: Theory and practice*, New York: Oxford University Press.

Braun, N. (2017) *Pension magic: How to make the taxman pay for your retirement* (7th edn), London: Taxcafe UK.

Braun, N. (no date) 'How employees can reduce National Insurance' (www.taxcafe.co.uk/resources/employeesnatinsurance.html).

Brys, B., Perret, S., Thomas, A. and O'Reilly, P. (2016) *Tax design for inclusive economic growth*, OECD Taxation Working Papers 26, Paris: Organisation for Economic Co-operation and Development.

Byrne, D. and Ruane, S. (2017) *Paying for the welfare state in the 21st century: Tax and spending in post-industrial societies*, Bristol: Policy Press.

Chwalisz, C. and Diamond, P. (2015) *The predistribution agenda: Tackling inequality and supporting sustainable growth*, London: Tauris.

Cracknell, R. (2014) *National Insurance Fund accounts 1975–2014*, House of Commons Library, Standard Note 797, 20 May.

Deakin, N. and Parry, R. (2000) *The Treasury and social policy: The contest for control of welfare strategy*, Basingstoke: Palgrave Macmillan.

DWP (Department for Work and Pensions) (2016) 'Benefit expenditure and caseload tables 2016', April (www.gov.uk/government/publications/benefit-expenditure-and-caseload-tables-2016).

DWP (2017a) *Family Resources Survey 2015/16*, London: DWP, March.

DWP (2017b) *Pensioners' income series: An analysis of trends in pensioners' income series 1994/95-2015/16*, London: DWP, March.

EC (European Commission) (2014) *Tax expenditures in direct taxation in EU Member States*, Occasional Papers 207, Brussels, Belgium: EC.

Emmerson, C. (2014) 'Taxation of private pensions', in *IFS Green Budget 2014*, London: Institute for Fiscal Studies.

Farnsworth, K. (2012) *Social versus corporate welfare: Competing needs and interests within the welfare state*, London: Palgrave.

Farnsworth, K. (2015) *The British corporate welfare state: Public provision for private businesses*, SPERI Paper No 24, Sheffield: Sheffield Political Economy Research Institute (SPERI), University of Sheffield (http://speri.dept.shef.ac.uk/wp-content/uploads/2015/07/SPERI-Paper-24-The-British-Corporate-Welfare-State.pdf).

Ferge, Z. (1997) 'The changed welfare paradigm: The individualisation of the social', *Social Policy and Administration*, vol 31, no 1, pp 20-44.

Ginn, J., Street, D. and Arber, S. (eds) (2001) *Women, work and pensions: International issues and prospects*, Buckingham: Open University Press.

Greve, B. (1994) 'The hidden welfare state: Tax expenditure and social policy', *Scandinavian Journal of Social Welfare*, vol 3, no 4, pp 203-11.

Hacker, J.S. (2002) *The divided welfare state: The battle over public and private social benefits in the United States*, Cambridge: Cambridge University Press.

Hacker, J.S. (2011) 'The institutional foundations of middle-class democracy', *Policy Network*, 6 May (www.policy-network.net/pno_detail.aspx?ID=3998&title=The+institutional+foundations+of+middle-class+democracy).

Hansard (2014) Written answer to Parliamentary Question from Steve Doughty, 10 December.

Hansard (2017) Written answer to Parliamentary Question from Jon Trickett, 18 April (www.taxation.co.uk/Articles/2017/02/21/336058/what-does-simplifying-national-insurance-mean-practice).

HMRC (Her Majesty's Revenue & Customs) (2016) *Estimated costs of tax reliefs*, KAI Data Policy and Coordination, 31 December (www.gov.uk/government/uploads/system/uploads/attachment_data/file/579720/Dec_16_Main_Reliefs_Final.pdf).

HMRC (2017a) 'PEN 6 Cost of Registered Pension Scheme Tax Relief', February (http://webarchive.nationalarchives.gov.uk/20170421185348/https://www.gov.uk/government/statistics/registered-pension-schemes-cost-of-tax-relief).

HMRC (2017b) *National Insurance Fund Account for the year ended 31 March 2017*, 17 October (www.gov.uk/government/uploads/system/uploads/attachment_data/file/652655/National_Insurance_Fund_Accounts__Great_Britain__-_2016_to_2017.pdf).

HM Treasury (2015) *Strengthening the incentive to save: A consultation on pensions tax relief*, Cm 9102, July.

HM Treasury (2016) *Strengthening the incentive to save: Summary of responses to the consultation on pensions tax relief*, March.

Hodge, M. (2016) *Called to account*, London: Little, Brown.

Howard, C. (1997) *The hidden welfare state: Tax expenditures and social policy in the United States*, Princeton, NJ: Princeton University Press.

Howard, C. (2007) *The welfare state nobody knows: Debunking myths about US social policy*, Princeton, NJ: Princeton University Press.

Hughes, G. (2000) 'Pension financing, the substitution effect and national savings', in G. Hughes and J. Stewart (eds) *Pensions in the European Union*, Dordrecht: Kluwer, pp 45-61.

Hughes, G. and Sinfield, A. (2004) 'Financing pensions by stealth', in G. Hughes and J. Stewart (eds) *Reforming pensions in Europe: Evolution of pension financing and sources of retirement income*, Cheltenham: Edward Elgar, pp 163-92.

ICIJ (International Consortium of Investigative Journalists) (2017) 'The long twilight struggle against offshore secrecy' (www.icij.org/investigations/paradise-papers).

IMF (International Monetary Fund) (2017) 'Tracking inequality', IMF Fiscal Monitor, October (www.imf.org/en/Publications/FM/Issues/2017/10/05/fiscal-monitor-october-2017).

Johnson, M. (2012) *Costly and ineffective: Why pension tax reliefs should be reformed*, London: Centre for Policy Studies, November.

Johnson, M. (2016) *2016 Budget: Pensions*, London: Centre for Policy Studies, 18 February.

Lawson, N. (1992) *The view from No 11*, London: Bantam.

Lukes, S. (2005) *Power: A radical view* (2nd edn), Basingstoke: Palgrave Macmillan.

McDaniel, P.R. and Surrey, S.S. (1985) *International aspects of tax expenditures: A comparative study*, Deventer, Netherlands: Kluwer.

Mirrlees, J., Adam, S. Besley, T., Blundell, R., Bond, S., Chote, R. et al (2011) *Tax by design*, London: Institute for Fiscal Studies.

Morel, N., Touzet, C. and Zemmour, M. (2016) *Fiscal welfare and welfare state reform: A research agenda*, LIEPP Working Paper 45, February, Paris: Laboratory for Interdisciplinary Evaluation of Public Policies (LIEPP).

Murphy, R. (2012) *Is 50/50 fair?*, London: Trades Union Congress, March.

Murphy, R. (2016) 'Wealth taxation for the UK', Tax Research Network (www.taxresearch.org.uk/Blog/wp-content/uploads/2016/08/WealthtaxUK816.pdf).

NAO (National Audit Office) (2013) *Government interventions to support retirement incomes*, Department for Work and Pensions and HM Treasury, HC 536, Session 2013-14, 12 July.

NAO (2014a) *Tax reliefs*, HC 1256, Session 2013-14, 7 April.

NAO (2014b) *The effective management of tax reliefs*, HC 785, Session 2014-15, 7 November.

NAO (2016) *Report by the Comptroller and Auditor General*, in HMRC, *Annual report and accounts 2015-2016*, London: HMRC, pp R1-90.

OECD (Office for Economic Co-operation and Development) (2010) *Tax expenditures in OECD countries*, Paris: OECD.

ONS (Office of National Statistics) (2015) *Wealth in Great Britain Wave 4: 2012 to 2014*, Newport: ONS.

ONS (2017) *Occupational Pension Schemes Survey, UK: 2016*, Statistical Bulletin, 28 September.

OTS (Office of Tax Simplification) (2011) *Review of tax reliefs: Final report*, London: OTS, March.

OTS (2015) *Finance Act 2015: New tax reliefs* (https://taxsimplificationblog.wordpress.com/category/tax-reliefs-2/).

PAC (Public Accounts Committee) (2015) *HMRC's performance in 2014–15*, HC 393, September.

PAC (2016) *HMRC's performance in 2015-16*, HC 712, December.

PPI (Pensions Policy Institute) (2013) *Tax relief for pension saving in the UK*, London: PPI, July.

PPI (2016) *The new pensions landscape*, London: PPI, November.

Sandler, D. (1993) *Harmonising the fringes of National Insurance and Income Tax*, London: Institute for Fiscal Studies, March.

Sinfield, A. (1978) 'Analyses in the social division of welfare', *Journal of Social Policy*, vol 7, no 2, pp 129-56.

Sinfield, A. (1998) 'Social security through tax benefits: How some are helped to become securer than others', Tax and Benefits, Minutes of Evidence, House of Commons Paper HC 423-iv, Session 1997-98, pp 62-7.

Sinfield, A. (2013) 'Fiscal welfare', in B. Greve (ed) *The Routledge handbook of the welfare state*, London: Routledge, pp 20-9.

Surrey, S.S. (1973) *Pathways to tax reform*, Cambridge, MA: Harvard University Press.

Titmuss, R.M. (1958) *Essays on 'The welfare state'*, London: Allen & Unwin.

Titmuss, R.M. (1962) *Income distribution and social change*, London: Allen & Unwin.

Tonkin, R. (2017) *The effects of taxes and benefits on household income: Financial year ending 2016*, London: Office for National Statistics, April.

Townsend, P. (1958 [2009]) 'A society for people', in N. Mackenzie (ed) *Conviction*, London: Mackibbon and Kee [and in the shorter *New Statesman* version, reprinted in *Social Policy and Society*, April].

Treasury Committee (2016) *Appointment of Edward Troup as Executive Chair of HMRC*, Third Report of Session 2016-17, HC 498.

TUC (Trade Unions Congress) (2015) *Pensionswatch2015: An analysis of director and staff pensions*, London: TUC (www.tuc.org.uk/sites/default/files/PensionsWatch2015.pdf).

World Bank, The (2003) 'Why worry about tax expenditures?', *PREMnotes*, Economic Policy, no 77, January.

SIX

'Good solid Conservatism': Theresa May's 'doctrine' and her approach to the welfare state

Robert M. Page

Theresa May has endured an eventful 18 months (June 2017–December 2018) since unexpectedly becoming both leader of the Conservative Party and Prime Minister following David Cameron's sudden departure in the wake of the referendum vote to leave the EU in June 2016. In the initial phase of her premiership, May appeared to exude the 'decisive' form of leadership previously associated with Margaret Thatcher by declaring her intention to pursue an effective Brexit policy and to create a 'fairer' society. However, her decision to call a General Election in June 2017 in an effort to secure a larger majority to smooth the path of Brexit backfired, and since then her position as Prime Minister has become precarious.

The focus of this chapter is to explore May's strand of Conservatism and how this influences her approach to the welfare state. In response to a question from BBC Two *Newsnight*'s political editor Nick Watt, at the launch of the Conservative Party's (2017) General Election manifesto on 18 May 2017, Theresa May declared that there was no such thing as 'Mayism'. She contended that she was merely pursuing a 'good solid' form of Conservatism. Since becoming a senior figure within the party, May has been keen to stress that she is not an 'ideological' Conservative in the mould of Margaret Thatcher but rather, a dutiful public servant seeking to serve her country as best she can. May's preference for 'pragmatism' was emphasised in the party's manifesto of 2017, which stated that the party must 'reject the ideological templates provided by the socialist left and the libertarian right' (Conservative and Unionist Party, 2017, p 7). Under Theresa May, 'ideological crusades' were to become a thing of the past (Conservative and Unionist Party, 2017, p 7). As she made clear,

True Conservatism means a commitment to country and community; a belief not just in society but in the good that government can do; a respect for the local and national institutions that bind us together; an insight that change is inevitable and change can be good, but that change should be shaped, through strong leadership and clear principles, for the common good. (Conservative and Unionist Party, 2017, p 9)

Before examining Theresa May's 'doctrine' and her approach to the welfare state in more detail, it is useful to provide an overview of her background and political career.

Theresa May's background and political career

Born in Eastbourne, East Sussex, in 1956 Theresa May was a 'child of the vicarage' (Prince, 2017, Chapter II): her father served as a Church of England cleric in Oxfordshire. She attended the local state primary school before enrolling at St Juliana's – a fee-paying Roman Catholic secondary convent school. She subsequently studied at a state grammar school for girls that acquired comprehensive status towards the end of her school days. The young Theresa Brasier became active in the Conservative Party from an early age and aspired to be the first female Prime Minister while still a sixth former (Prince, 2017, p 27). May read Geography at St Hugh's College Oxford, graduating in 1977 (see Paxman, 2017). She became a graduate trainee at the Bank of England before becoming a junior analyst, then member, of the Bank's Monetary Policy Group. She went on to work at the Association for Payment Clearing Services (APCS), becoming manager of the European Affairs Unit.

May's political career began in Wimbledon, South West London. She was elected as a Conservative councillor for the Durnsford ward in the London Borough of Merton in 1986, becoming deputy leader and chair of the Education Committee two years later. She stood unsuccessfully as a parliamentary candidate in North West Durham in the 1992 General Election and in the Barking by-election of 1994, where she finished a distant third to Labour's Margaret Hodge. She was then selected (ahead of over 300 other applicants, including Philip Hammond and David Cameron) to contest, and win, the relatively safe seat of Maidenhead in the 1997 General Election (see Prince, 2017, Chapter V). With little more than a year's experience in the Commons, the then Party leader William Hague appointed May as a member of the Shadow Education and Employment team, subsequently promoting her to Shadow Secretary in 1999. She was also chosen to be the Party's spokesperson for Women.

After the Conservatives' defeat in the 2001 General Election, May was appointed Shadow Secretary of State for Transport, Local Government and the Regions by Hague's successor, Iain Duncan Smith. In 2002 May was the first woman to be appointed as Party Chair. In her first major speech in that role, she attracted considerable media attention after telling delegates that many voters still viewed the Conservatives as the 'nasty' party.[1] May was replaced as Party Chair following Michael Howard's unopposed election as the Party's new leader in 2001. She became Shadow Secretary for Transport and the Environment and subsequently Shadow Secretary of State for the Family. When David Cameron succeeded Howard as Conservative leader in 2005, following the party's third consecutive General Election defeat, May was appointed Shadow Leader of the House. The portfolio for Women and Equalities was added in 2007. In 2009 May was appointed Shadow Secretary for Work and Pensions. In 2010, after the Conservatives finally returned to government (in coalition with the Liberal Democrats), May was appointed Home Secretary. She remained in this post until she succeeded David Cameron as Prime Minister in 2016.

Evolution of the May 'doctrine'

May's family background, education and early career have clearly influenced her political beliefs. In a speech to the party's annual conference in 2002, May set out the broad parameters of her pragmatic Conservative political philosophy. She contended that 'Our party is at its best when it takes Conservative principles and applies them to the modern world. It is at its worst when it tries to create a bygone age. We cannot bring back the past. We can work together to make today and tomorrow's world a better place' (May, 2002; see also Gray, 2009, pp 137-8). Like many Conservatives, Theresa May's Conservatism derives from inclinations and dispositions that are 'honed by maturity and experience of life' (Ball, 2013, p 2) rather than by deep ideological fervour. As Scruton (2001) reminds us, this is not an uncommon position: many Conservatives find it difficult to give a detailed account of their political beliefs. Indeed, it is often left to scholars and commentators to piece together the precise elements of Conservative doctrine (see, for example, Hickson, 2005 and Dorey, 2011). This involves explorations into the party's approach to the nation, the family, the role of the state and the free market. Such exercises tend to uncover varying degrees of commitment to some or all of these elements. Significantly, opinions can change subtly over time. Moreover, as Ewart Green (2002) has pointed out, it is not uncommon for Conservatives to combine authoritarian, liberal and paternalistic rationales when discussing topical economic and social issues.

May's strand of Conservatism has proved difficult to compartmentalise in part because of her enigmatic persona (see Bagehot, 2017a; Prince, 2017). In addition, the fact that she was catapulted, effectively unopposed, into the leadership of both her party and the country, without even contesting a General Election, led to a situation in which the May 'doctrine' had to be discerned *after* 'key' political developments rather than before. As a consequence, it is not surprising that May has been described as a Christian Democrat (*The Observer*, 2017), a One Nation Tory (Bagehot, 2017b; *New Statesman*, 2017; *The Sunday Times*, 2017), a middle or Third Way Conservative (Forsyth, 2017; Goodhart, 2017; Nelson, 2017b), an ethical or puritanical Conservative (Gimson, 2016; Goodman, 2016), a red Tory (Shipman, 2017; see also Blond, 2010) and a 'modern' or 'new model' Conservative (Cowley, 2017; Grice, 2017). Similarities have also been detected between May and a number of former Prime Ministers such as Stanley Baldwin (see *The Sunday Times*), Clement Attlee (Young, 2017), Edward Heath (Gimson, 2016) and Margaret Thatcher (Johnson, 2016; Glover, 2017).

In exploring the key themes of Theresa May's self-proclaimed 'pragmatic' brand of Conservatism, it is apparent how much of her thinking has been influenced by her family background and political experiences. For example, in contrast to politicians such as Tony Crosland who rebelled against their religious upbringing (see Jefferys, 1999, Chapter 1), Theresa May has retained a strong personal commitment to her family's faith (see Ridley-Smith, 2017; Sandbrook, 2017). She is a regular church goer and has demonstrated a willingness to speak out in support of her religious beliefs.[2] Her father's Anglo-Catholic, Christian socialist-influenced training, which led to an emphasis on virtue (underpinning the revival of 'character' education),[3] and on community rather than individual salvation, seems to have been transmitted from father to daughter. For May, a career in politics is a vocation, not simply an occupation. Her commitment to public service is reflected in her desire to combat divisive forms of unfairness in society. This has proved to be a key theme of her Premiership to date. In her first Prime Ministerial speech outside 10 Downing Street in July 2016 she detailed a number of burning injustices she wished to tackle, including the lower life expectancy of those born into poverty, the harsh treatment afforded to black citizens within the criminal justice system and 'the despicable stigma and inadequate help for those with mental health conditions' (May, 2016a). She also made it clear that she intended to govern in a way that supported the ordinary citizens (the 'just about managing') who, despite being virtuous, hard-working and modestly ambitious, were experiencing everyday 'injustices' such as job insecurity, poor quality schooling for their children and an inadequate share of the nation's resources and opportunities (May 2016a; see also May, 2017a, b).

Tackling 'unfairness' both within her party and in the wider society has been a key feature of May's political philosophy. In terms of the former, for example, she made a concerted attempt in the early 2000s to ensure that the Conservative Party reflected the diverse nature of the wider community. The under-representation of women in the parliamentary party was one injustice that May was particularly keen to address.[4] In her first Conference speech as Party Chair in 2002 she drew attention to the fact that only one of 38 new Tory MPs who were successful in the 2001 General Election had been a woman, declaring this to be a 'travesty' that will 'never be allowed to happen again'.[5]

She co-founded (with Anne Jenkin) an internal campaign group Women2Win in 2005, which offered practical help to aspiring female candidates and lobbied for changes in local party selection procedures. This initiative bore fruit after David Cameron became Party leader in 2005. One of Cameron's first decisions was to instruct the party's candidates committee to compile a register (the so-called 'A list') of the 100 prospective Conservative MPs that merited preferment, of which at least 50 per cent should be women. In all target seats and constituencies where a sitting Conservative MP was due to retire, local associations were instructed to choose a candidate from this list unless there were exceptional circumstances for an alternative course of action (Bale, 2016, p 271).

May has also been willing to voice her concern about broader economic and social problems. She has been critical of those elements of the corporate sector that indulge in unethical or harmful practices. In cases where commercial activity can be shown to have had damaging impacts on the rest of society, May has indicated that she will act quickly to remedy this. She has pledged, for example, to confront international companies that treat their tax obligations as an 'optional extra' as well as to hold those company directors to account when they take out 'massive dividends' while knowing the company pension scheme 'is about to go bust' (May, 2016b). She has also sought to tackle growing inter-generational inequalities (Willetts, 2011). In her 2016 Leader's speech she made it clear that the gap between the 'prosperous' older generation, particularly those living in London with substantial assets, and a struggling younger generation, who were finding it hard to get on to the property ladder, needed to be addressed (May, 2016b).

While May has a strong sense of patriotism and is supportive of the Monarchy, the Church and the armed services (May, 2016b), she has been highly critical of privileged elites (the so-called 'chumocracy'; see Mosbacher, 2013; Gray, 2015; Lawson, 2016) that continue to enjoy disproportionate and unmerited access to influential positions in fields such as politics, the media and the professions. She rejects the traditional Tory belief that self-selecting elites of this kind have an inalienable and inherent right to govern or legislate on the basis of some assumed social and intellectual superiority.

Although the Conservatives have gradually accepted that some of the upper echelons of society should be replenished on the basis of merit rather than lineage, as the party's choice of some recent party leaders demonstrates (see Major, 2000; Ziegler, 2010; Moore, 2013), the pace of change has proved painfully slow for meritocrats like May. May has been particularly critical of the way in which so many well-connected men from elite public schools and Oxbridge colleges, such as David Cameron, George Osborne and Boris Johnson, have been able to secure safe parliamentary seats and ascend rapidly to influential positions within the Conservative Party with little, if any, perceivable effort, while other, equally talented, individuals from less privileged backgrounds (like herself) have had to strive far harder to succeed (see Runciman, 2017).

May's desire to establish a socially just hierarchy based on merit rather than privilege owes much to her own grammar school life course, which she shares with one of her most trusted and influential long-term advisers, Nick Timothy,[6] who is a devotee of the municipal 'socialist' statesman Joseph Chamberlain (Timothy, 2016). Given that both May and Timothy credit their own 'meritocratic' success to publicly funded selective education, it was not surprising that one of the new Prime Minister's first policy pronouncements was to signal her desire to overturn the ban on the establishment of new grammar schools.

Although May was by all accounts delighted to have finally been offered one of the great offices of state (the Home Office) by David Cameron in 2010 (see Prince 2017, Chapter XII), her relationship with many of the 'Notting Hill', cosmopolitan Conservatives, particularly George Osborne at the Treasury, came under increasing strain during her six-year tenure in the role at Marsham Street (see Davies, 2016). It has been argued that the social and political divide that developed between May and members of the 'Notting Hill set' was exacerbated by the contrasting political cultures of the socially protective, communitarian Home Office and the outward, economically liberal ethos of the Treasury. As Davies (2016, p 3) notes, 'Home secretaries see the world in Hobbesian terms, as a dangerous and frightening place, in which vulnerable people are robbed, murdered and blown up, and these things happen because the state has failed them.' For Davies, May was a perfect choice for the position of Home Secretary because the underlying ethos of the Department dovetailed with her own belief that state power needed to be exercised in order to protect less well educated and culturally marginalised ordinary citizens from threats to their personal safety and from economically exploitative forms of immigration. May continued to adhere to this approach when she became Prime Minister. Her more positive approach to government intervention differed from the more sceptical inclinations of both Thatcher and, albeit to a lesser extent, Cameron.

The role of government and the welfare state

May's 'pro-statist' sympathies might lead one to the premature conclusion that May should be seen as the latest incarnation of the interventionist strand of 'One Nation' Conservatism (see Walsha, 2000, 2003; Seawright, 2010; Carr, 2014), which has a lineage stretching back to former Prime Ministers such as Benjamin Disraeli (1868 and 1874–80), Stanley Baldwin (1923–24, 1924–29 and 1935–37) and arguably reaching its apogee under Harold Macmillan (1957–63). While she certainly concurs with their general concern for improving the wellbeing and life chances of less advantaged citizens, curbing excessive inequalities, supporting a managed form of capitalism, establishing effective industrial partnerships and supporting (albeit in a qualified way) the welfare state, she does not, crucially, share the deeper enthusiasm for state intervention displayed by post-1945 luminaries such as Rab Butler, Iain Macleod and Harold Macmillan (see Dorey, 2011; Carr, 2014).

Unlike her predecessor, David Cameron, who in his 'progressive' pre-austerity phase as Party leader attempted to demonstrate his compassionate Conservative credentials by standing up for the very poorest members of society and for the rights of minority groups (see Cameron, 2010; Page, 2010, 2015), May believes that collective action should be focused more specifically on the economic hardships endured by those deemed to be 'just about managing'. Although this has not involved the full blooded embrace of the 'blue collar' Conservative' approach espoused by former deputy Party Chair and Skills Minister, Robert Halfon (who has even suggested that the Party should re-badge itself as the 'Workers' Party'; see Halfon, 2017; see also Elgot, 2017), it was intended to demonstrate May's acceptance that the Conservatives had neglected this key cohort of the electorate, and that future policies must prioritise their needs.

May's support for state intervention is reflected in her approach to contemporary economic issues. She has expressed reservations about doctrinal neoliberal claims that privatisation, global free markets, light regulation and low taxes have been wholly beneficial for British society. While supportive of business and enterprise, May believes government should act to ensure that corporations operate according to a common set of rules, and that free market activity is compatible with the broader public interest (May, 2017b). May also believes that government has a vital role to play in developing a modern industrial strategy. This will not necessitate propping up failed industries or even rejuvenating older companies but rather, providing strategic forms of support such as investing in infrastructure and enhancing the skills sets of workers in successful sectors of the economy such as financial services, life sciences and the creative industries.

In a similar way, May believes that government has a positive role in the field of social policy. May has no doctrinal objection to what she regards as settled aspects of the postwar welfare state, most notably the National Health Service (NHS) (see *New Statesman*, 2017). Although she has stipulated her intention to 'revolutionise' some spheres of social policy, this should not, as noted previously, be equated with an embrace of the more positive interventionist policy agendas pursued by One Nation Conservative governments in the 1950s and 1960s. For May, social service improvements in 21st-century Britain are always more likely to be achieved through administrative reform rather than higher spending.

May's approach towards the welfare state was set out in the Party's 2017 General Election manifesto (Conservative and Unionist Party, 2017) following her surprise announcement on 8 June 2017 that she would be seeking a fresh electoral mandate. Her frequently stated political goals of improving opportunities for more disadvantaged citizens, enhancing inter-generational justice and remedying specific long-standing inequities underpinned a wide range of manifesto pledges.

Educational reforms were seen, for example, as the key way of equalising opportunities and establishing a 'great meritocracy'. Increased numbers of 'good and outstanding schools' were planned to ensure that all children will have 'a fair chance to go as far as their talent and their hard work will allow' (Conservative and Unionist Party, 2017, p 49). Some 100 new free schools were to be opened each year, while those local authority schools deemed by Ofsted to be either inadequate or in need of improvement would be prevented from increasing their pupil numbers. New funds were to be provided for the creation of a specialist maths school in every major English city, while universities seeking approval to charge maximum tuition fees would be expected to sponsor an academy or establish a free school. The ban on new selective schools was to be lifted in an effort to promote social mobility for working-class pupils. The schools budget was also to be increased, and plans for a 'fairer' funding formula for schools developed. The pupil premium, introduced by the Coalition government in 2011 to support disadvantaged children, was to be retained (Conservative and Unionist Party, 2017, p 51). In order to fund these commitments, universal free school lunches for primary pupils (during their first three years at school) were to be withdrawn (with exemptions for poorer children) and replaced with a universal free school breakfast, available for the entire period of a child's primary education.

Major reforms in both the funding and qualification frameworks for technical education were planned. New 'T-levels', covering 15 'career' routes in areas such as construction, engineering and manufacturing, were to be created to replace the plethora of existing technical qualifications.

Concerns about inter-generational injustice underpinned pronouncements across a wide range of social policy areas. In the sphere of housing, ambitious plans were proposed in the manifesto to ensure that ordinary working families would be able to buy their own home or meet the costs of renting. The 'dysfunctional' housing market was to be overhauled with a million more homes scheduled to be built by 2020 and a further 500,000 by 2022. Councils committed to creating 'high-quality, sustainable' and 'integrated communities' would be given access to low-cost capital by central government to build more social housing.

Reforms were proposed in the areas of social security and social care in an effort to tackle inter-generational injustices. While increased longevity was welcomed, it was acknowledged that this would give rise to higher levels of pension expenditure. To ensure that the cost of this demographic 'shift' did not fall disproportionately on younger age groups, the manifesto outlined changes to the triple lock on pensions and to Winter Fuel Payments. In terms of the former, it was announced that one element of the pensions lock (the 2.5 per cent guaranteed increase) would be withdrawn in 2020 and that a 'fairer', although less generous, 'double lock', based on either the rise in earnings or prices (whichever is the highest), would be introduced. Universal Winter Fuel Payments would also be withdrawn and replaced with a new selective scheme targeted at the 'least well-off pensioners most at risk of fuel poverty' (Conservative and Unionist Party, 2017, p 66; see also Nelson, 2017a). The proposed savings arising from this change in the eligibility rules would be used to bolster the health and social care budget.

Inter-generational justice also underpinned the party's social care reforms for older people. In an effort to find additional resources for social care provision without placing an extra burden on the younger generations of taxpayers, the manifesto proposed to introduce a 'fairer' funding system. Under this new scheme, wealthier pensioners with sizeable assets would be expected to meet any residential or domiciliary social care costs in excess of £100,000 from the proceeds of their estate. It was envisaged that this new measure would reassure older people that any care cost liabilities they might incur would not necessitate the sale of their family home during their lifetime. Those facing charges were assured that they would still be able to pass on what the then Department for Work and Pensions (DWP) Minister Damian Green (2017) was to describe as a 'decent' inheritance (£100,000 of protected assets) to their beneficiaries.

The manifesto also reflected May's determination to tackle 'entrenched injustices' based on gender, race and disability. In terms of gender, for example, companies with more than 250 employees were to be required to publish data on remuneration as a way of closing the gender pay gap (Conservative and Unionist Party, 2017, p 56). The Conservatives would also seek to ensure that there was greater gender parity in relation to public appointments, and that greater numbers of women were recruited to company boards. In the case of racial inequalities, greater enforcement of equalities legislation to prevent discriminatory practices by landlords and businesses was promised. Police 'Stop and Search' practices would continue to be monitored, and the 'disproportionate use of force against Black, Asian and ethnic minority people' in the criminal justice system would be reduced. People with disabilities would be helped to find flexible paid work and their access to 'licenced premises, parking and housing' (Conservative and Unionist Party, 2017, p 57) would be improved.

Reforms in two areas where May has shown a particularly keen interest, namely, mental health and domestic violence, was also proposed in the manifesto. In the case of the former, concerted efforts would be made over the longer term to ensure that those requiring mental ill health services were given parity of esteem within the NHS. Increased spending on such services would be complemented by legislative changes to 'out-dated' mental health laws. Some one million volunteers would be recruited to provide mental health awareness advice in an effort to tackle the long-standing stigma attached to this form of ill health. In terms of domestic violence, new legislation was planned 'to consolidate all civil and criminal prevention and protection orders and provide for a new aggravated offence if behaviour is directed towards a child' (Conservative and Unionist Party, 2017, p 58).

The 2017 General Election and the aftermath

With a convincing lead in the opinion polls and an Opposition leader, Jeremy Corbyn, who appeared unelectable and who even lacked majority support among his fellow Labour MPs, the stage seemed set for a convincing Conservative General Election victory. With an enhanced majority, May hoped that she would have the opportunity to oversee a 'smoother' withdrawal from the European Union (EU) before the time of the next scheduled General Election in 2022. This proved to be a miscalculation. Although the Conservatives were returned as the largest party with 318 seats (including 12 gains in Scotland) and 42.4 per cent of the popular vote, the slender overall majority inherited from David Cameron evaporated as Labour performed far better than anticipated (securing 262 seats and 40 per cent of the popular vote).

The Conservatives' disappointing performance in the election has been attributed to various factors. First, the party's decision to run a 'presidential-style' campaign, focusing on the strength and stability of the leader and the delivery of a 'hard' Brexit, misfired (see Crace, 2017; May, 2017c). May's confident performances when facing Jeremy Corbyn across the despatch box in the House of Commons were not replicated in the campaign, where she appeared uneasy at being in the spotlight – a perception that was reinforced by her decision to absent herself from the televised, seven-way, leaders' debate. Second, the Conservatives under-estimated the potential appeal of the Labour opposition. With an optimistic, anti-austerity message delivered to well-publicised mass gatherings of enthusiastic supporters across the country and with a detailed 'fully costed' manifesto, Labour was able to appeal to traditional supporters, younger voters (not least through effective messaging on social media; see Peston, 2017) as well as floating 'Remain' voters who were attracted to the party's softer stance on Brexit (see Fieldhouse and Prosser, 2017). Third, although the Conservative Party manifesto was designed to appeal to the 'just about managing' group, the decision to include controversial pledges relating to social care funding and Winter Fuel Payments appeared to alienate some of the party's older, core supporters (*The Economist*, 2017; Lewis, 2017). Fourth, the decision to target working-class 'Leave' voting, United Kingdom Independence Party (UKIP) and Labour supporters had limited success. Notable Conservative victories in seats such as Mansfield, Walsall North and Middlesbrough South & Cleveland East were cancelled out by Labour triumphs in what were previously seen as unwinnable seats in London (Kensington and Chelsea) and the South East (Canterbury) (see Hinsliff, 2017).

Following the unexpected shock of losing its overall parliamentary majority, the Conservatives set about forming a new government and maintaining party unity. May remained in post but was forced to part company with her controversial joint Chiefs of Staff, Nick Timothy (who had co-authored the manifesto with Ben Gummer) and Fiona Hill, on the grounds that they had exercised too much control over the direction of policy and the election strategy (see Palmer, 2017; Rayner, 2017). They were replaced by Gavin Barwell, the former Housing Minister, who was a much more popular figure within the Party. The emollient Damian Green, a close ally and long-standing friend of the Prime Minister, was appointed as First Secretary of State and Minister for the Cabinet Office. Another significant ministerial change was the decision to recall the controversial former leadership candidate, Michael Gove, as Secretary of State for the Environment (see Riddick, 2017).

To shore up her precarious political position in the newly elected House of Commons, May entered into a controversial, formal agreement with the Democratic Unionist Party (DUP; the Party only fields candidates in Northern Ireland) to establish a workable parliamentary majority. Following protracted negotiations, the DUP agreed to support the Conservative government on all motions of confidence, budgetary matters as well as legislation relating to Britain's exit from the EU. To secure DUP support, May was forced to withdraw some key elements of her 'progressive' inter-generational agenda such as means testing the Winter Fuel Payment and the ending of the triple lock on prospective pension payments because these contravened the DUP's manifesto commitments (DUP, 2017). As part of this agreement, the DUP was also able to secure significant funds from the government to enhance health, education and infrastructure in Northern Ireland.

May's plans for creating a 'fairer' society were modified in the Queen's Speech delivered to Parliament on 21 June 2017. Plans to reintroduce selective grammar schools and to withdraw universal school lunches were shelved. In addition, the funding reforms for social care were jettisoned although a further consultation was proposed. The government reaffirmed its intention, however, to press ahead with improving technical education, and promised to increase the number of so called 'good' school places. Commitments to increase house building and curb unfair tenant fees were retained. In addition, prospective legislative commitments to afford greater protection to the victims of domestic abuse and to reform out-dated mental health laws were to be carried forward, not least because it was thought that such measures would attract cross-party support. The desire to assist those 'just about managing' was reflected in a proposed increase in the National Minimum Wage and commitments to tackle high energy prices and unacceptable corporate practices.

The successful passage of the Queen's Speech did little to quell speculation about May's long-term political future, with former Chancellor George Osborne declaring that the Prime Minister was 'a dead woman walking'.[7] Nevertheless, the Prime Minister signalled her willingness to defy her critics and continue in office for as long as the party deemed appropriate.

In her 2017 annual party conference speech in Manchester,[8] the Prime Minister responded to those who had accused her of being too hostile to business interests during the election campaign by mounting a more upbeat defence of capitalism (May, 2017c). This proved insufficient, however, to appease some of her right-wing critics (on this issue, see May 2017d; see also Heath, 2017). She also declared her intention to uphold the 'British dream' that enables younger citizens, whatever their background, to develop their talents and aspire to living standards that exceed those enjoyed by their parents. Following a spirited defence of the 'Conservative' government's record since 2010, May declared that she intended to pursue a more ambitious and interventionist agenda than her predecessor. She reiterated her desire to root out specific injustices, promote social mobility and ensure that the 'economy and society work for everyone in the country not just the privileged few' (May 2017d). In particular, May was keen to persuade younger citizens that her government would seek to address their concerns, not least in gaining a foothold on the housing ladder.

Conclusion: Theresa May, a good solid Conservative?

As noted earlier, Theresa May has described herself as a 'good solid Conservative'. This phrase does seem to capture the essence of May's Conservatism and underpin her approach to the welfare state. Since becoming Prime Minister, May has been at pains to stress that she is not an ideological or programmatic Conservative. Rather, she portrays herself as a public servant who is respectful of long-standing social institutions and traditions and who seeks to tackle the pressing problems of the age in a pragmatic way. She is not opposed to using the power of the state to correct perceived injustices where private or voluntary action has proved ineffective, but will remain alive to the possibility that government action can prove costly and ineffective and as such, must be subjected to constant scrutiny. From this perspective, it is not surprising that some commentators have likened May to the statecraft of the earlier 20th-century Conservative leader Stanley Baldwin (see Williamson, 1999; Lexden, 2017; Perkins, 2017a, b). May is patriotic and shares Baldwin's strong Christian convictions. Like Baldwin, she has proved willing to sanction a greater role for the state in social and economic policy provided that such action is undertaken as a *pragmatic* response to changing economic and social conditions rather than an abandonment of other core party values.

Although a number of May's former advisers have called on her to persevere with the 'radical' social policy reform agenda she articulated on the steps of Downing Street in 2016 (see D'Ancona, 2017; Tanner, 2017; Timothy, 2017a, b, c), it seems unlikely that she will be able to make much headway in this regard given the intricacies of the Brexit negotiations, her precarious parliamentary majority and gloomy economic prospects in terms of growth and productivity (OBR, 2017). Unless May can continue as Prime Minister for a second term (which is improbable given her disappointing performance in the 2017 General Election campaign[9] and the reluctance of influential Party donors to support her candidature[10]), her ambition to bring about 'positive' remedial changes in the field of social policy are unlikely to come to fruition. In the interim May's energies are likely to be devoted to the Herculean task of securing a 'successful' Brexit, avoiding a 'snap' general election, seeing off potential leadership rivals and keeping her party 'united' rather than laying down foundation stones for a 'fairer' society.

Notes

[1] It should be noted that May went on to say, 'I know that's unfair but it's the people out there we need to convince – and we can only do that by avoiding behaviour and attitudes that play into the hands of our opponents. No more glib moralising, no more hypocritical finger wagging. We need to reach out to all areas of our society' (see May, 2002).

[2] In April 2017 May criticised the National Trust for its 'ridiculous' decision to omit the word 'Easter' from its annual egg hunt so that the event would appeal to 'people from all faiths and none' (*Catholic Herald*, 2017).

[3] For example, with financial support from the John Templeton Foundation, The Jubilee Centre for Character and Values was established at the University of Birmingham in 2012 to 'promote, build and strengthen character virtues in the context of the family, school, community, university, professions, voluntary organisations and the wider workforce' (see www.jubileecentre.ac.uk).

[4] In her 2002 conference speech, May contended that, 'Our associations cherish their independence, but with independence comes responsibility. When selecting a candidate you aren't simply choosing someone to represent your association or your area. Your candidate becomes the face of the Conservative party. So don't ask yourself whether you would be happy to have a drink with this person on a Sunday morning, ask instead what this person says about us' (May, 2002).

[5] Although May was photographed wearing a black t-shirt with the inscription 'This is what a feminist looks like' in 2006, she has proved reticent about describing herself as a feminist when pressed by interviewers to do so, arguably because she opposes positive forms of discrimination (see Wood, 2017). Her decision to seek a Confidence and Supply Agreement with the Democratic Unionist Party (DUP) (who oppose abortion and gay marriage on religious grounds) following the 2017 General Election occasioned a stinging rebuke from one newspaper columnist; see Moore (2017).

[6] Timothy was an adviser to Theresa May when she was Shadow Secretary of State in 2006 and a special adviser during her tenure at the Home Office from 2010 to 2015. He returned to government in 2016 as May's joint Chief of Staff but left in 2017 following the 'lacklustre' Conservative General Election campaign in June 2017. See Grice (2016); Spence and Mctague (2016); Shipman (2017); Timothy (2017a).

⁷ This comment was made on *The Andrew Marr Show*, BBC One, 11 June 2017. In a subsequent *Evening Standard* editorial, Osborne suggested that May's Premiership was 'like the living dead in a second-rate horror film'. See Osborne (2017). See also Parris (2017).

⁸ This speech was described by *The Times* as 'shambolic' because of the Prime Minister's 'repeated coughing fits', an interruption by a serial prankster and a faulty backdrop (see Elliott, 2017).

⁹ The leading Conservative historian Andrew Roberts (2017) has, however, suggested that Theresa May could become one of the nation's longest-serving Prime Ministers.

¹⁰ One influential Conservative donor, Lord Harris of Peckham, has been one of May's harshest critics. See Khan (2017).

References

Bagehot (2017a) 'Theresa May, Tory of Tories', *The Economist*, 22-28 April, p 28.

Bagehot (2017b) 'One nation under May', *The Economist*, 6-12 May, p 28.

Bale, T. (2016) *The Conservative Party from Thatcher to Cameron* (2nd edn), Cambridge: Polity.

Ball, S. (2013) *Portrait of a party. The Conservative Party in Britain 1918–1945*, Oxford: Oxford University Press.

Blond, P. (2010) *Red Tory*, London: Faber & Faber.

Cameron, D. (2010) 'Labour are now the reactionaries, we are the radicals as this promise shows', *The Guardian*, 9 April, p 34.

Carr, R. (2014) *One Nation Britain*, Aldershot: Ashgate.

Catholic Herald (2017) 'Theresa May criticises National Trust over "ridiculous" decision to drop "Easter" from egg hunt', 4 April 2017.

Conservative and Unionist Party (2017) *Forward together: The Conservative manifesto. Our plan for a stronger Britain and a prosperous future*, London: The Conservative Party.

Cowley, J. (2017) 'May's method', *New Statesman*, 10-16 February, pp 22-8.

Crace, J. (2017) *I, Maybot*, London: *The Guardian*/Faber.

D'Ancona, M. (2017) 'The Tory party must change hard, and change now', *The Guardian*, 7 August, p 23.

Davies, W. (2016) 'Home Office rules', *London Review of Books*, 3 November (www.lrb.co.uk/v38/n21/william-davies/home-office-rules).

Dorey, P. (2011) *British Conservatism*, London: I.B. Tauris.

DUP (Democratic Unionist Party) (2017) *Standing strong for Northern Ireland: DUP Manifesto for the 2017 Westminster Election*, Belfast: DUP.

Economist, The (2017) 'The four-day manifesto', 27 May-2 June, p 26.

Elgot, J. (2017) '"Tarnished" Tories must undergo radical change, says former minister', *The Guardian*, 10 October.

Elliott, F. (2017) 'Tory dismay as PM falls victim to prank, coughing fits and faulty set', *The Times*, 5 October, p 1.

Fieldhouse, E. and Prosser, C. (2017) 'General Election 2017: Brexit dominated voters' thoughts', BBC Politics (www.bbc.co.uk/news/uk-politics-40630242).

Forsyth, J. (2017) 'The new third way', *The Spectator*, 25 February, pp 10-11.

Gimson, A. (2016) 'Hail the new puritans', *New Statesman*, 30 September–6 October, pp 25, 27.

Glover, S. (2017) 'Theresa May emerges from Thatcher's shadow', *Standpoint*, vol 90, April, pp 22-5.

Goodhart, D. (2017) 'Middle way', *The Spectator*, 20 May, pp 12-13.

Goodman, P. (2016) 'Mother Theresa', *conservativehome*, 5 October.

Gray, J. (2009) *Gray's anatomy*, London: Allen Lane.

Gray, J. (2015) 'The neo-Georgian Prime Minister', *New Statesman*, 22 October.

Green, D. (2017) 'Interview' on *The Andrew Marr Show*, BBC One, 21 May.

Green, E.H.H. (2002) *Ideologies of Conservatism*, Oxford: Oxford University Press.

Grice, A. (2016) 'Nick Timothy: Who is Theresa May's "muse" with great influence at the heart of government,' *The Independent*, 4 October.

Grice, A. (2017) 'A thoroughly modern Tory', *The i*, 19 May, p 17.

Halfon, R. (2017) 'The right's lost for words', *Standpoint,* September.

Heath, A. (2017) 'This was a new incarnation of wet, statist Tory thinking: It must stop', *The Daily Telegraph*, 5 October, p 18.

Hickson, K. (ed) (2005) *The political history of the Conservative Party*, Basingstoke: Palgrave Macmillan.

Hinsliff, G. (2017) 'Welcome to the red shires', *Prospect*, December, pp 35-7.

Jefferys, K. (1999) *Anthony Crosland*, London: Richard Cohen.

Johnson, D. (2016) 'Is Theresa May the true heir to Mrs Thatcher?', *Standpoint*, November.

Khan, S. (2017) 'Theresa May is a hopeless leader of a weak government', *The Independent*, 9 September (www.independent.co.uk/news/uk/politics/theresa-may-tories-uk-pm-leader-hopeless-attack-lord-harris-a7937381.html).

Lawson, D. (2016) 'After the May revolution, the chumocracy is dead. Long live the chumocracy', *The Sunday Times*, 17 July.

Lewis, H. (2017) 'Out of the ordinary', *New Statesman*, 24-30 November, p 22.

Lexden, Lord (2017) 'Stanley Baldwin in a year of anniversaries', Lecture given at the Carlton Club, London, 29 March.

Major, J. (2000) *John Major: The autobiography*, London: HarperCollins.

May, T. (2002) Speech to the Annual Conference of the Conservative Party, Bournemouth, 7 October.

May, T. (2016a) First Prime Ministerial Speech outside 10 Downing Street, 7 July.

May, T. (2016b) Speech to the Annual Conference of the Conservative Party, Birmingham, 5 October (www.independent.co.uk/news/uk/politics/theresa-may-speech-tory-conference-2016-in-full-transcript-a7346171.html).

May, T. (2017a) 'I'm determined to build the shared society for all', *The Sunday Telegraph*, 8 January, p 17.

May, T. (2017b) 'The shared society', Speech at the Annual Meeting of the Charity Commission, London, 9 January.

May, T. (2017c) Speech to the Annual Conference of the Conservative Party, Manchester, 4 October.

May, T. (2017d) 'For Britain's sake, it's time to tackle the unacceptable face of capitalism', *The Mail on Sunday*, 27 August, p 29.

Moore, C. (2013) *Margaret Thatcher: The authorised biography, Volume One, Not for turning*, London: Allen Lane.

Moore, S. (2017) 'The Tories are bartering with women's bodies to keep power. It's disgusting', *The Guardian*, 12 June.

Mosbacher, M. (2013) 'The myth of Cameron's Etonian "chumocracy"', *Standpoint*, June.

Nelson, F. (2017a) 'Tory manifesto takes the first steps towards intergenerational fairness', *The Daily Telegraph*, 19 May, p 18.

Nelson, F. (2017b) 'What are the Tories for?', *The Spectator*, 24 June, pp 10-11.

New Statesman (2017) 'Q&A: Theresa May on Jane Austen, late nights and original sin', 10-15 February, p 29.

OBR (Office for Budget Responsibility) (2017) 'Overview of the November 2017 Economic and fiscal outlook' (http://obr.uk/overview-of-the-november-2017-economic-and-fiscal-outlook/)

Observer, The (2017) 'Editorial: Will Brexit menace progressive Mayism?', 21 May.

Osborne, G. (2017) Evening Standard Comment: 'Britain deserves better than this horror show', Evening Standard, 31 August (www.standard.co.uk/comment/comment/evening-standard-comment-Britain-deserves-better-than-this-horror-show-a3623806.html).

Page, R.M. (2010) 'David Cameron's modern Conservative approach to poverty and social justice: Towards one nation or two?', Journal of Poverty and Social Justice, vol 18, no 2, pp 147-60.

Page, R.M. (2015) Clear blue water? The Conservative Party and the welfare state since 1940, Bristol: Policy Press.

Palmer, A. (2017) 'A decent woman betrayed by her gruesome twosome', Standpoint, July/August, pp 22-5.

Parris, M. (2017) 'Tories are trapped in a zombie apocalypse', The Times, 30 September, p 25.

Paxman, J. (2017) 'The politicians we deserve: Nervous geography student vs avuncular lecturer', FT Weekend, 3 June/4 June, p 12.

Perkins, A. (2017a) 'Theresa May's paralysis on the big issues has echoes in history', The Guardian, 2 August.

Perkins, A. (2017b) 'Stanley Baldwin', in C. Clarke, T.S. James, T. Bale and P. Diamond (eds) British Conservative leaders, London: Biteback, Chapter 11.

Peston, R. (2017) 'Corbyn 2.0', The Spectator, 18 November, pp 12-13.

Prince, R. (2017) Theresa May – The enigmatic Prime Minister, London: Biteback.

Queen's Speech (2017), 21 June (www.gov.uk/government/speeches/queens-speech-2017).

Rayner, G. (2017) '"We didn't get the election campaign we intended … I didn't challenge it", Interview with Nick Timothy', The Daily Telegraph, 5 August, pp 4-5.

Riddick, G. (2017) 'Tories refuse to deny Rupert Murdoch role in Michael Gove's cabinet return', The Guardian, 18 July.

Ridley-Smith, B. (2017) 'Exclusive interview with Theresa May', The Sunday Telegraph, 21 May, p 4.

Roberts, A. (2017) 'If her party keeps its nerve, Mrs May could be one of our longest-serving PMs', The Daily Telegraph, 5 August, p 16.

Runciman, D. (2017) 'Do your homework', London Review of Books, 16 March, pp 5-8.

Sandbrook, D. (2017) 'Enter the era of the vicar's daughter', *The Daily Mail,* 19 May, p 17.

Scruton, R. (2001) *The meaning of Conservatism* (3rd edn), Basingstoke: Palgrave Macmillan.

Seawright, D. (2010) *The British Conservative Party and One Nation politics,* London: Continuum.

Shipman, T. (2017) 'The class warrior turning May red', *The Sunday Times,* 21 May, p 18.

Spence, A. and Mctague, T. (2016) 'The man who is really running Britain', *Politico,* 10 April.

Sunday Times, The (2017) 'Editorial', 21 May, p 2.

Tanner, W. (2017) 'I saw Theresa May at work: a new message is vital to avoid defeat', *The Observer,* 6 August, p 34.

Timothy, N. (2016) *Our Joe: Joseph Chamberlain's Conservative legacy* (2nd edn), London: Conservative History Group.

Timothy, N. (2017a) 'Diary', The *Spectator,* 17 June, p 9.

Timothy, N. (2017b) 'Tories cannot be free-market fundamentalists', *The Daily Telegraph,* 10 August, p 15.

Timothy, N. (2017c) 'The PM sees her future in Britain's common ground', *Daily Telegraph,* 31 August, p 17.

Walsha, R. (2000) 'The One Nation group: A Tory approach to backbench politics and organisation, 1950-55', *Twentieth Century British History,* vol 11, no 2, pp 183-214.

Walsha, R. (2003) 'The One Nation Group and One Nation Conservatism, 1950–2002', *Contemporary British History,* vol 17, no 2, pp 69-120.

Willetts, D. (2011) *The pinch: How the baby boomers took their children's future – And why they should give it back,* London: Atlantic.

Williamson, P. (1999) *Stanley Baldwin,* Cambridge: Cambridge University Press.

Wood, G. (2017) 'May Day', *Vogue,* American edition, April, pp 204-7, 257.

Young, T. (2017) 'Fraternity, solidarity and the spirit of 1945', *The Spectator,* 27 May, p 84.

Ziegler, P. (2010) *Edward Heath,* London: Harper Press.

SEVEN

Making markets in employment support: does the variety of quasi-market matter for people with disabilities and health conditions?

Eleanor Carter

In common with other developed economies the UK has, over the past 15 years, sought a marked shift in the function of social security away from 'passive' benefits to an 'activating' welfare system where access to social security for working-age people is linked to the responsibility to seek paid work (Bonoli, 2013). In parallel with this 'activation turn' (Bonoli, 2010), reforms to the institutional arrangements of welfare-to-work services have introduced quasi-markets by separating the roles of those purchasing and providing services. Importantly, marketisation captures a diverse set of processes (Greener, 2008) and the actual form that the quasi-market takes can vary substantially depending on how policy-makers structure the intersection of competition and choice (Wiggan, 2015a). The UK is generally understood as a committed marketiser (Wiggan, 2015a, p 119), and the scope and experimentation involved in its marketising efforts position it at the bleeding edge of international reform experiences.

With the application of highly marketised welfare-to-work provision in the UK there has been a large and persistent gulf in the employment outcomes for those participants who have a limiting health condition or who report a disability and those others who do not. This jars against the ambition of the large-scale, nationwide Work Programme to 'ensure that providers have strong incentives to help *all* of their customers', and close the performance gap between the easiest- and hardest-to-help (DWP, 2012, p 6; emphasis added). The gulf in outcomes now also sits uncomfortably against the government's manifesto commitment to tackle the disability employment gap and 'get 1 million more people with disabilities into employment over the next ten years' (Conservative Party, 2017, p 57). Voluntary sector organisations and think tanks have been united in arguing that the ambition for such high levels of employment cannot be reached on the basis of the current performance of welfare-to-work programmes (Purvis et al, 2014; Oakley, 2015; Disability Rights UK, 2016).

Somewhat peculiarly, given policy-makers' confidence that the 'universal' Work Programme can effectively and simultaneously serve a large cohort of participants with a highly diverse set of characteristics, work experiences and employment support needs (DWP, 2012; WPSC, 2013), there is a parallel programme, Work Choice. Work Choice is a voluntary programme focused on those individuals whose health and disability-related support needs mean that standard Jobcentre Plus support is unlikely to be appropriate. Work Programme and Work Choice are grounded in the same commissioning strategy, but demonstrate important differences in the degree to which they embrace highly marketised provider-directed governance arrangements (Jantz et al, 2015), and particularly the extent to which they implement payment-by-results principles. Given the mixed findings from studies of marketised outcome-based commissioning across policy fields, but particularly in the area of welfare-to-work, the twin-track approach of the Work Programme and Work Choice provides a powerful opportunity to consider potential differences in the impacts of the two marketised service configurations. This chapter implements a novel quasi-experimental analysis to investigate the implications of the alternate market formulations for the shape of the provider landscape, and consequent associations with the support experience of participants and employment outcomes.

Before considering any disparity in programme impacts the chapter begins by drawing on and extending in key ways the conceptual framework for unpacking *variation* in the formulation of quasi-markets as advanced by Gingrich (2011). Central is a consideration of how the marketised relationships are structured, since 'depending on how information, contracts, and demand are shaped, the incentives that producers face in the delivery of services may promote attention to the buyer, or to the user, or even give new producers the scope to follow their own interests' (Gingrich, 2011, p 9). This discussion extends from the fruitful typology of quasi markets (Gingrich, 2011), at the heart of which is a consideration of variation on two dimensions – how access to services is *allocated* (capturing financing and regulation of service provision) and how they are *produced* (referring to the structure of competition and choice in the market). Based on these dimensions Gingrich identifies three broad categories of state-, user- or provider-driven markets that essentially identify 'who is the "piper calling the tune"' (Powell, 2015, p 110; see also Figure 7.3). The value in expanding from this framework is in seeking to understand any pertinent variation across Work Programme and Work Choice in terms of the *form* of quasi-market adopted through each scheme (if these are indeed different), and considering the implications for programme structure in terms of which party's preferences and interests are being prioritised or marginalised as a consequence.

A differential view of markets: the dimensions of variation in public service quasi-markets

As a route to unpack the specific market configurations advanced under each programme, a key contribution of this chapter is the development of an analytic device that extends Gingrich's (2011) framework by more comprehensively mapping and illustrating the dimensions that underpin the varieties of public service markets on offer. In essence, this is a tool for understanding the particular flavour of quasi-marketisation advanced in any given context.

The analytical device begins by considering the allocation dimension (as illustrated in Figure 7.1), which relates to the financing and regulation of service provision (Gingrich, 2011). The first component relates to whether services are collectively financed by society (that is, provision costs are publicly funded through general taxation) or whether provision relies, in full or in part, on private resources of individuals (co-payments, means testing or incentives for private consumption). The second allocation component captures the degree and strength of regulation for provider activity, with an axis that spans from extensive state-directed auditing and service assurance through to a light-touch regulation framework. A high level of state-led regulation 'ostensibly promotes equitable access to services and underpins quality' (Wiggan, 2015b, p 155), whereas weak regulation enables providers to pursue profits by targeting the most lucrative service users and reducing costs by scaling back the quality of provision or reducing services for riskier and/or poorer populations (Gingrich, 2011; Wiggan, 2015a). Figure 7.1 expands on previous work by visualising the underlying concept as a graduated dimension with 'more market-like' arrangements as the right-most options on the spectrum, while the left-hand side is further from the market and actively seeks to mediate the pure market lever. In sum, the allocation dimension captures 'whether price and selection mechanisms are used to allocate services, or whether services preserve a strong collective guarantee of access and funding' (Gingrich, 2011, p 10). Figure 7.1 additionally plots the respective positions of the two programmes under consideration here, marked 'WP' for Work Programme and 'WC' for Work Choice. The positioning of these markers is discussed further on page 139.

Figure 7.1: Visualising the allocation dimension in public service markets

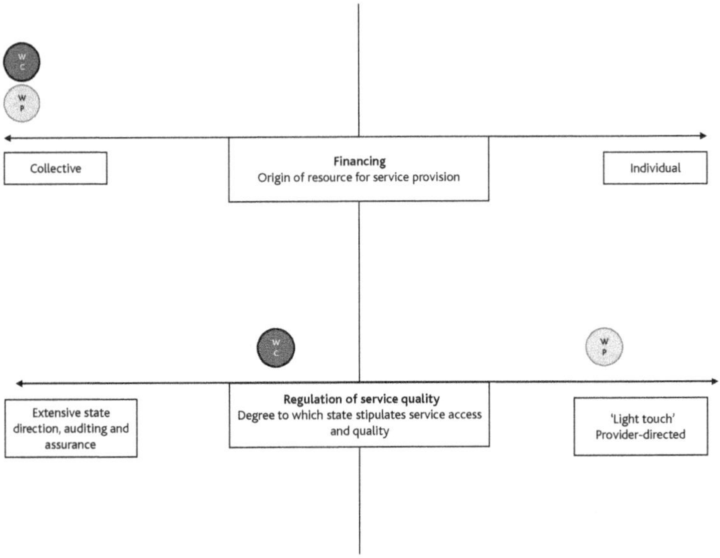

Source: An original illustration informed by and extending from Gingrich (2011) and Wiggan (2015a, b)

The production dimension covers choice and competition – the way that a service is 'produced' within the quasi-market. In his application of Gingrich's framework, Wiggan has argued that different combinations of competition/choice will influence the priorities of service production. Depending on the configuration of provider competition, commissioner control and choice function services will be differently responsive to the needs and (dis)empowerment of either the state, service users or providers (Wiggan, 2015b). Figure 7.2 expands and visualises the discussion offered by Gingrich (2011) and Wiggan (2015a, b). The first sub-component (upper portion of Figure 7.2) relates to how 'open' the market is to new provider entrants, and captures the degree to which the quasi-market arrangements service the hegemony of specific or incumbent providers. This spans from an open, highly contestable and accessible market (far left) to a situation where access is constrained or limited (and therefore appears as an oligopoly), be that through restrictions on the size or sector of 'eligible' providers or other facets (contract duration, likely sanctions for failing to meet contractual obligations etc). The second axis captures the control apportioned to the state (vis-à-vis service providers) in the design and stipulation of provider activity. At the left-most extent there is a high degree of public sector control over provider activity, since payment to providers is explicitly tied to the delivery of fixed service components. Shifting rightwards, the dimension portrays an increasingly outcomes-led approach, whereby service providers are afforded the freedom to innovate and design flexible services geared to pursuing specified outcomes, but where the public sector takes a position of agnosticism on the *means* of securing these outcomes.

The final axis in the lower portion of Figure 7.2 captures the function of user choice and voice within service production. Here, the left-most portion of the axis conveys a situation where service users are powerful agents and where the choice and/or voice of those citizens who use a service provide a powerful steering mechanism to the behaviour of providers. By contrast, at the right-hand extent service users have limited if any 'choice', and their perspectives therefore have no traction for service provider behaviour. For each axis within Figure 7.2 a position closer to the extreme right-hand side reflects a stronger provider position, be that through minimal competition (upper axis), minimal state control (middle axis) or minimal responsiveness to user preferences (lower axis). As with Figure 7.1, a fuller discussion of the relative positioning of Work Programme and Work Choice is offered below.

For Gingrich (2011), the destination for the allocation and production dimensions is a hard classification of six types of markets (Figure 7.3). Although Gingrich acknowledges these as 'ideal' types, her argument and the 'boxing in' of distinct types of quasi-markets in her classification is limiting in two important ways. First, the classification is not particularly strong on identification strategies. In a line-up of different quasi-marketised configurations, what are the key traits that flag a marketised programme or policy domain as exemplifying one particular form or another? For example, how strong does user choice and voice need to be before a market becomes classified as 'consumer-controlled'? Essentially, for each of the quasi-market types in Figure 7.3, *how do we know it when we see it?* A second pertinent limitation of Gingrich's discussion is that of boxing in and marking binary distinctions between particular forms of quasi-market. To some degree in any heuristic device, this scalpel-sharp cleanliness of separation between different forms is needed for conceptual clarity, and aids in conveying a new argument. Importantly, however, what Gingrich's framework misses is the degree to which there may be hybridity and a degree of fuzziness at the edges of each 'type'. This chapter then responds directly to weaknesses in the forerunner framework, first, by offering a clearer articulation of the underlying dimensions and the traits that align with particular quasi-market types (by developing the labelled axes in Figures 7.1 and 7.2) and second, by conceiving and visualising these axes as continua such that the framework can be more alive to subtle variations in the variety of quasi-market under study.

Figure 7.2: Visualising the production dimension in public service markets

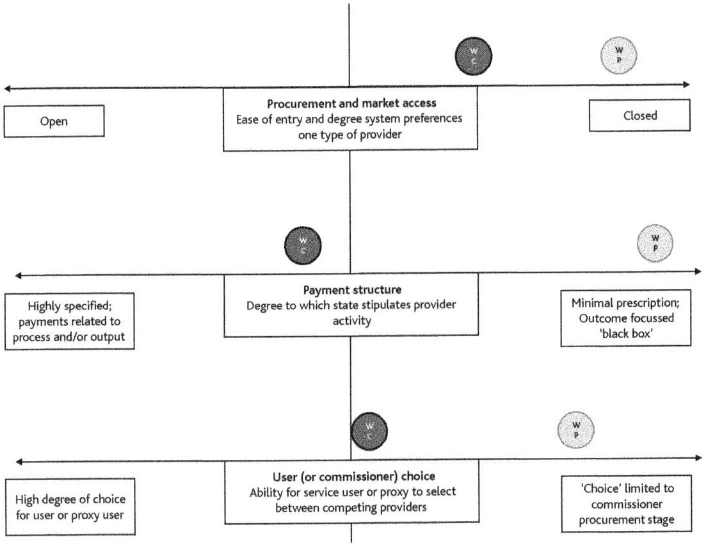

Source: An original illustration informed by and extending from Gingrich (2011) and Wiggan (2015a, b)

By unpacking and expanding the dimensions informing Gingrich's (2011) typology, Figures 7.1 and 7.2 reveal the potential for *gradients* to exist between particular forms of quasi-market configuration. They also open up and expose the possibility for quasi-markets in practice to contain elements compatible with each of the overarching market types simultaneously (that is, a given quasi-marketised arrangement in practice may contain design features and practices that variously point to state-, user- and provider-directed forms). Gingrich hypothesises that quasi-market variation 'is based on partisan control (left and right) and existing programme structure (residual; universal fragmented benefit structure; and universal uniform benefit structure)' (quoted in Powell, 2015, p 111), and therefore sets out a clear reform agenda that will be adopted by different political parties in different operating contexts. Powell contests this, however, and uses the messiness of marketisation reforms in the English NHS to suggest that (i) it may sometimes be difficult to determine a single clear quasi-market 'typology' for a given programme (at a given point in time) and (ii) partisan differences may be less sharp than claimed (Powell, 2015).

Figure 7.3: Gingrich's six quasi-market types

		Production dimension: who has effective control?		
		State-driven 'Efficiency aims'	User-driven: 'Quality aims'	Producer-driven: 'Profits and rents'
Allocation dimension: responsibility for access	Collective	Managed Market (recent English contracting in education)	Consumer-controlled Market (Swedish healthcare market in the early 1990s)	Pork Barrel Market (English elderly care market in the 1980s)
	Individual	Austerity Market (Dutch healthcare markets)	Two-tiered Market (English education market)	Private Power Market (English elderly care market since the mid-1990s)

Source: Gingrich's six quasi-market types (2011: 12)

The dimensions advanced here helpfully respond to the implications flowing from both Powell and Gingrich – that markets vary but that it may require detailed analytical work to understand the subtleties underlying the practical implementation of marketised forms and that inconsistencies and ambiguities need to be walked through explicitly. Such work is particularly pertinent in the case of British welfare-to-work provision as – on paper – all main political parties have signed up to the same reform agenda (that articulated by Freud, 2007; Rees et al, 2014). It is to the task of opening up and examining the specific market forms constituted in the Work Programme and Work Choice that this chapter now turns.

Particularities of the quasi-market configuration embodied by the Work Programme and Work Choice

Both the Work Programme and Work Choice were commissioned subsequent to the Department for Work and Pensions (DWP) 2008 commissioning strategy, which was heavily informed by the work of David (now Lord) Freud, a leading adviser to the Labour Party, who subsequently became Minister for Welfare Reform in the Conservative-Liberal Democrat Coalition government. Freud (2007) strongly advocated for provider-directed market arrangements, suggesting that competition, outcome-based payments and 'black box' delivery models would unlock innovation. Freud also advocated the use of large-scale provider contracts in the belief that large, multinational enterprises 'and their management capabilities, are more likely to provide the conditions in which innovation can take place and quality be assured' (2007, p 62).

Although the procurement process for Work Choice was conducted prior to the 2010 General Election (Mason, 2010), the Coalition government (elected in June 2010) signed off the contracts (DWP, 2010). The establishment of the Coalition led to the cancellation of the Flexible New Deal – the mainstream quasi-marketised employment support programme that the preceding Labour administration had intended to implement – but the underlying DWP commissioning strategy was not altered. The four key principles of the 2008 DWP commissioning strategy are:

- *The Prime provider model*, whereby the DWP only contracts with large 'Prime' providers, that in turn manage a supply chain of 'sub' providers to deliver services.
- *Payment-by-results*, outcome-based funding for contracted employment provision, whereby providers are paid a proportion of their fee on the basis of the sustained job outcomes they achieve.
- *Minimum service prescription*, enabling providers to be flexible in designing interventions and encouraging tailored, personalised support and innovation in service delivery.
- *Larger, longer contracts*, longer contract lengths are intended to produce market stability and encourage investment in delivery structures and innovation.

Despite being commissioned according to the same overarching strategy, however, there are important variations in the design and consequent quasi-market configuration of the two schemes.

Dimensions of variation between Work Programme and Work Choice: allocation

There is no variation between the two programmes in terms of the formal financing component of the allocation dimension. As with all UK employment support programmes these two schemes are both collectively funded – hence the stacked position of the programme markers at the left-hand side of the top axis in Figure 7.1. The Work Programme has implemented an innovative funding arrangement that draws from both the fixed Departmental Expenditure Limit and the Annually Managed Expenditure from which benefit payments are made (known as the DEL-AME switch), but in practice this does not shift the arrangement away from collectively financed provision. The key driver of variation across the allocation dimension in UK activation programmes is therefore the regulation of service quality (Wiggan, 2015a).

Under the Work Programme service quality is intended to be held up by 'minimum service guarantees' (MSGs), which are designed and published by Prime providers themselves. These service guarantees therefore vary from provider to provider, with no common floor standard specified by the DWP. There are also questions as to how clearly these minimum expectations have been communicated to programme participants, and there are concerns as to whether people participating in the Work Programme are aware of these service obligations (Whitworth, 2013). As I have argued elsewhere, 'weaknesses in the substance, consistency and, in some cases, even the possible enforceability of providers' minimum service guarantees render these a far less useful and reliable protection than they could be' (Carter and Whitworth, 2015, p 281). The National Audit Office (NAO) has criticised the variability of MSGs and has suggested that in practice this system provides only limited safeguards for participants who may receive few services or experience 'improper practice' (NAO, 2012; see also Finn, 2012).

By contrast, in Work Choice there is a high degree of clarity over contractual service minima. The invitation to tender (DWP, 2009) set out a contractual requirement for providers to devote a minimum number of support hours per week to each participant across the different service modules (for example, a minimum of eight hours pre-employment support per week to each Module One participant). Programme evaluation material suggests that the minimum contractual requirements appear to have set high expectations in terms of provision, that frontline staff are highly aware of these support commitments, and that providers appear to adhere to the high levels of structured support (Purvis et al, 2013).

The lower axis of Figure 7.1 conveys this divergence between the programmes by positioning a considerable distance between the Work Programme – which sits at the provider-directed, light-touch end of the service regulation spectrum – and Work Choice – which is more congruent with state-directed standards and more robust quality assurance.

Variation on the production dimension

Turning to the production dimension, on the first component – that of market access – both Work Programme and Work Choice were procured through variants of a 'Prime contractor' model, which limits the direct contractual relationship between the DWP to a relatively small number of top-tier 'Prime' providers that are then responsible for managing supply chains of provision (DWP, 2008; Armstrong et al, 2010). There are, however, distinctions between the programmes in the degree to which particular forms and sizes of provider have a stronghold over provision as Prime contractors. Despite its smaller size, Work Choice has a greater number of contract package areas (CPAs) and contracts were awarded to Primes in 28 CPAs compared to Work Programme's 18. Where Scotland operates as a single CPA in the Work Programme, provision is divided across four CPAs in Work Choice. This means that contracts are much smaller both in terms of value and geographical extent.

The size and stipulations associated with Prime contracts has implications for the types of providers involved. Of the eight organisations that successfully became Work Choice Prime providers, four are from the private sector and four are from the voluntary sector.[1] When considering the number of contracts held by these Primes, over 70 per cent of provision is led by voluntary sector providers (Post-tender discussion documentation, quoted in Thompson et al, 2011). For the Work Programme there were considerably tighter requirements for bidding as the DWP sought to ensure that Prime contracts were held by organisations capable of financing upfront investment in services and shouldering the pressures of back-ended outcomes payments. The DWP stipulated that potential Work Programme Prime organisations had to demonstrate an annual turnover of at least £20 million and be accepted on to the Employment-Related Support Services (ERSS) Framework (Wiggan, 2015a). This created a pool of high-value 'preferred suppliers' exclusively entitled to bid for Work Programme contracts (Gash et al, 2013), and resulted in many organisations being unable to compete. Some stakeholders raised concerns about the creation of 'mono-cultures' or 'hyper-Primes' in the delivery of employment services (Fuertes et al, 2014, p 80).

The Work Programme is therefore positioned as comparatively more 'closed' on the market access dimension (see the upper portion of Figure 7.2), since tendering requirements reduced competition for contracts and situate existing private sector providers (and those on the ERSS Framework) in a dominant position to tender for future contracts. Work Choice is comparatively more open, although the long contracting periods do inculcate some degree of 'lock in'.

Both programmes implement outcome-based funding arrangements for providers, but there are key differences in the payment models for the two programmes, most notably in the extent to which payment-by-results dominates the payment profile. Work Choice providers receive a monthly service fee equivalent to 70 per cent of their contract price and only 30 per cent of programme funding is contingent on outcomes (Thompson et al, 2011). Purvis et al (2013) note that in Work Choice there is a tension between the commissioning strategy principle of minimum service prescription intended to facilitate a flexible and personalised approach and the need to guarantee robust minimum levels of service delivery, which is seen as the quid pro quo for the substantial service fee element of the programme. Under this scheme the commissioning Department has established a highly specified set of modular components that offer a high level of structured contact between participants and service providers while aiming to ensure progression towards the ultimate goal of unsupported employment (where this is appropriate) (DWP, 2009; see also Work Choice provider guidance). This balance between prescribed components and provider discretion can be considered a 'grey box'.

The Work Programme holds a much more extreme position on this dimension due to its full embrace of the 'black box' delivery model, whereby Primes have almost complete discretion over the nature and extent of their intervention and where provider payments are based almost entirely on job outcome results (Rees et al, 2014). To counter tendencies for providers to neglect those participants whose barriers to work are greater (that is, where payable job outcomes are less likely to be forthcoming), the DWP relies on a differential payment structure with nine payment groups, each with different payment levels for providers. Outcomes for 'harder-to-help' groups are paid at higher rates than those for groups closer to the labour market, but there have been concerns about the effectiveness of these payment groups as they are based simplistically on participants' prior benefit type (Carter and Whitworth, 2015). In the Work Programme, over the course of the contract the ratio of sustained job outcome fees to attachment fees is intended to be 80:20 (Wiggan, 2015a). Importantly, however, the fixed attachment fee reduces to zero across the early years of the programme, so since 2014 the Work Programme has effectively been operating under 'pure' payment by results, where no portion of provider payment is guaranteed. Correspondingly, the Work Programme is positioned at the most extreme right-hand position on the middle axis of Figure 7.2, while Work Choice sits in a softened, hybrid position.

On the final dimension, relating to the function of choice, there is again deviation between the two programmes. For service users, Work Choice is a voluntary programme while the majority of Work Programme participants are 'mandated' to engage as a condition for their ongoing receipt of unemployment benefits (although importantly, people with long-term health conditions who are understood to be distant from the labour market may be afforded the option of voluntary participation). In the main, choice in terms of programme exit is not an option if people wish to protect their income. User choice within the market *between* providers has been almost non-existent as a feature in UK welfare-to-work provision (Wiggan, 2015a). Under the Work Programme participants are randomly allocated to a Prime provider. Under Work Choice, participants do have a 'choice' between Remploy provision and the single contracted Prime provider in their region, although the official programme evaluation suggests that Jobcentre Plus Disability Employment Advisers will be involved in this process, and it is not clear that user choice exerts influence on provider practice. In neither scheme is user choice/voice likely to be exerting a particularly potent influence on the shape of service provision. Wiggan (2015a) suggests that the 'customer' in the Work Programme market is the DWP (as opposed to programme participants), since the Department, through 'market share shift', reallocates a portion of the provider caseload to better performing providers – and therefore animates the market according to a preference for efficiency. In practice, however, assessment from the OECD (Organisation for Economic Co-operation and Development) (2014) suggests that ongoing competition between providers is unlikely to have been a major driver of performance.

Pure provider-directed or hybrid forms of quasi-market?

Along these dimensions, then, the Work Programme clearly sits as the embodiment of the provider-directed market (sitting as it does at the right-hand edge of each of the axes in Figure 7.2). Within this particular marketised formulation the state has 'relinquished its role in stipulating programme content and reduced its control over service quality in favour of greater freedom for providers to decide what services should be provided, how they should be provided and to who they should be provided...' (Wiggan, 2015a, p 127). The consequence is that *provider* preferences are the dominant set of interests shaping the functioning of this market. Implicitly, service user desires for quality and state ambitions for efficiency are subsumed beneath a provider logic that seeks to maximise profit from job outcomes within a system that gives a high degree of discretion in pursuing this aim. The consequence is a strong tendency towards – and general lack of effective prevention against – the 'creaming' of easier-to-serve claimants who are prioritised while those understood to face more substantial barriers to work are deliberately denied the time, energy or resources of providers and are effectively 'parked' (Struyven and Steurs, 2005; Considine et al, 2011; PAC, 2012; Carter and Whitworth, 2015). Evidence collected through the official programme evaluation (Newton et al, 2012; Lane et al, 2013) and from government select committees (WPSC, 2011, 2013; PAC, 2012, 2013) indicates that the profiling of participants (identifying those for prioritisation) and the targeting of resources on the easier-to-help are serious problems within the Work Programme (Rees et al, 2014).

Contrastingly, although Work Choice was also commissioned according to Freud's guiding principles (described on page 138), it adopts a softer, less extreme position as a 'provider-led' market formulation. Across the allocation dimensions, Work Choice bolsters the state's power to regulate service quality (a preference of service users). Within the production axes, Work Choice leans *towards* a provider-directed configuration. The Prime provider model, outcomes-related payment and grey box specification all point to a strong position for providers, and yet it fails to sit squarely at the 'provider-directed' right-hand portion of these axes. The state has a much stronger role in stipulating activity and service users have *some* degree of choice (a double choice) as to (i) whether to participate and (ii) which of two service providers to work with. This configuration therefore adopts something of a hybridised position – it seems appropriate to position this as a *provider-directed* system but it is a *softer* formulation (that is,

Freud-lite), where provider prerogatives are mediated by bolstering *both* the state and user preferences. It is a hybridised form and does not neatly sit within the brackets of Gingrich's framework.

Intriguingly, although we cannot attribute *causation* to this softer form of provider direction in the Work Choice configuration, concerns in relation to service quality, creaming and parking of clients and market stability have not dogged Work Choice in the same way that they have plagued the Work Programme.

Given the known failings of the Work Programme in its support of participants understood to experience health conditions and disabilities or who may be further from the labour market (Newton et al, 2012; WPSC, 2013; Carter and Whitworth, 2015), the parallel operation of Work Choice offers something of a quasi-experiment through which to assess whether the softening of provider-directed marketisation levers can be seen to have led to differing experiences for participants as illustrated by the patterning of employment outcomes. The key empirical question informing the remainder of this chapter is whether these two programmes (embodying Freud-inspired provider-directed marketised regimes to different degrees) are differently effective for participants who providers may view as 'harder to help' because of their disabilities or limiting health conditions.

Empirical exploration of different quasi-market configurations for employment and earning outcomes

The implication of the distinct quasi-marketised configurations that are implemented within Work Choice and the Work Programme is that these alternate formulations may exert different pressures and incentives on the allocation and production of services. Although both schemes have the same overarching objective – to move those who are currently out of work into sustained paid employment – there may be different tensions and imperatives running across each programme because of their differing quasi-market configurations. The crucial inference is that service provision responds to particular market imperatives and that by shifting services offered, the consequent outcomes achieved by programme participants may also vary. This chapter, for the first time, presents a quasi-experiment comparing the employment outcomes achieved by those participating in these two distinct quasi-market formulations.

The comparison of Work Choice and Work Programme can be understood as a natural experiment, since although *on paper* the programmes targeted different cohorts of service users, in *practice* ambiguities and tensions in the referral processes for the two programmes mean that participants in each scheme are much more similar in terms of their disability-related employment challenges than when the programmes were initially conceived (see Figure 7.4 for a summary of programme characteristics and eligibility criteria). Many Work Programme participants are facing multiple and complex barriers to employment, including significant disability-related support needs (Newton et al, 2012; Purvis et al, 2013). The official Work Choice evaluation has identified 'a number of situations where disabled people with complex support needs, who might have been suitable for Work Choice support, were being referred to the Work Programme' (Purvis et al, 2013, p 145). In parallel, there has been slippage in the degree to which Work Choice participation has been targeted at those with the most profound disability-related employment support needs: the majority of Work Choice participants are claiming Jobseeker's Allowance rather than a specialist, disability-related benefit. The degree to which each of these programmes has experienced stretch and tension in relation to referral routes and eligibility criteria leads to a situation where there is marked overlap in terms of the characteristics displayed by participants attending each of the schemes. There is a group of people who are claiming out of work benefits, have health and disability-related barriers to entering the labour market, but who could have been referred to either scheme.

This partial overlap of participants with similar characteristics at the intersection of the two programmes unlocks the potential for quasi-experimental analysis and specifically raises the ability to use propensity score matching for the construction of an artificial comparator group. Considering the Work Choice participants as the 'treated' individuals, matching is used to find a non-participant from the control group of Work Programme participants with the most similar observed characteristics possible (Gertler et al, 2016): 'By comparing how outcomes differ for participants relative to observationally similar nonparticipants, it is possible to estimate the effects of the intervention' (Heinrich et al, 2010, p 3). This method has been used widely in the evaluation of British welfare-to-work policies (Bryson et al, 2002); has an intuitive appeal arising from the way it mimics random assignment through the construction of a control group post hoc (Bryson et al, 2002), and is based on fewer assumptions than conventional regression-based approaches.

Figure 7.4: High-level programmatic comparison of Work Programme and Work Choice

Dimension	Work Programme	Work Choice
Size (participants)	c. 1 million in year 1	c. 20,000 per year
Eligible participants (on paper)	All long-term unemployed people or those at risk of becoming so including those with disabilities and long-term conditions	People with disabilities who cannot be effectively supported into work through mainstream employment programmes or Jobcentre Plus provision
Participants (in practice)	As above, sizeable Jobseeker's Allowance population who self-identify as having a disability	Restrictions on referral numbers and less focused on those with 'most significant needs'; majority of participants are claiming Jobseeker's Allowance
Compulsion	Largely mandatory, sanction backed	Voluntary, although potential for some participants to opt for Work Choice in light of upcoming Work Programme mandation
Outcomes and objectives	'Sustained' job outcomes (13/26 weeks) with monthly sustainment payments	Sustained, 'unsupported' job outcomes

There are three requirements for this to be a viable method:

- some degree of blurring and randomness as to which participant ends up on which programme (that is, common support requirements are met as people with the same characteristics could end up on either scheme);
- detailed participant information that can be used to identify people who are similar in terms of their observable characteristics (which correlate both with treatment and outcome) are available;
- a standardised outcome measure is available for individuals in both treatment and control group.

Access to participant-level administrative data held by the DWP has uniquely facilitated the analysis presented here. The evaluation uses administrative data for all individuals attached to the Work Programme and to Work Choice from April 2013 to September 2014. The participant-level information is based on National Benefit Data records coupled with the specific administrative datasets for each of the programmes. P45/P60 records are used to construct pre-programme employment histories. This delivers a rich set of matching covariates including pre-programme benefit claim detail and employment durations, fixed individual demographic characteristics and time-coded programme attachment details, used to ensure that participants in both treatment and control groups are experiencing interventions in a shared macroeconomic climate. These variables are used to model propensity scores and the full set of covariates is provided in the Appendix at the end of this chapter.

The final requirement for a standardised outcome metric for treatment and control participants is facilitated through the author's unique academic access to HM Revenue & Customs' (HMRC) Real Time Information (RTI) that provides immediate, regular data on employee earnings (Tarr and Finn, 2012). For the Work Programme and Work Choice participants this data holds a record of gross earnings received by each participant, each month, for 15 months following attachment to their respective programmes.

Historically an 'off-benefit' measure has been used within DWP programme evaluations, but the earnings data presented here offer a more subtle analysis that more closely proxies programme objectives. For both Work Choice and Work Programme the overarching intent is to secure stable employment for participants that endures for the long term, and this objective occurs in a wider policy context that aspires to shift the UK to a 'higher wage, lower welfare economy' (Oakley, 2015, p 4). Hence paid employment that is both more stable and higher paying is the desirable, universal policy outcome. Both the number of months with earnings (where a greater number of months with recorded earnings is the preferable outcome) and earnings value (where greater income levels are seen as superior) serve as appropriate metrics to capture programme 'effect' in a comparable manner across the two interventions.

After data cleaning, the preparation of standardised variables and the removal of those Work Choice participants who were in supported employment, there were 405,417 Work Programme cases and 23,916 Work Choice cases available for analysis. The 1 : 1 nearest neighbour match with replacement is implemented using the PSmatch2 programme (Leuven and Sianesi, 2003) in Stata. Following convention, those treatment cases that have propensity scores falling beyond the maximum extent of corresponding propensity scores for the comparator group are discarded. This results in the removal of 53 cases from the analysis. This constitutes a low level of rejection (as other studies have removed close to one-third of treated cases), and is unlikely to compromise the representativeness of the results.

Employment and earning effects across the two programmes

The estimated employment and earning effect of Work Choice compared to Work Programme participation is presented in Figure 7.5. There are two outcome variables: the number of months, on average, individuals are in paid employment within the 15-month tracking window and the average value of employment income earned within the same time frame. Prior to the propensity score matching process, the average earnings of Work Choice participants and the *full* Work Programme cohort are fairly similar. Work Choice participants on average earned around £250 more than Work Programme participants over the tracking period. For the *unmatched* cohorts, that is, comparing Work Choice participants to the full Work Programme cohort, there is only a very small difference in the average number of months in paid work between the two groups. Work Choice participants are on average in paid work for 1.3 more days than the full Work Programme population. When considering the employment performance for the programme populations *as a whole* – all Work Choice compared to the full Work Programme – there is little to separate the two interventions in terms of the employment effects achieved by participants.

Comparing the performance of the two schemes in aggregate, however, is not appropriate given what is known about the Work Programme's highly diverse participant population, and the scheme's known abilities to support those 'mainstream' jobseekers who are closer to the labour market. The real question is the degree to which these alternate programmes and quasi-market configurations have been successful in supporting those with longer-term health conditions and disabilities. Comparing the employment effects of the two programmes *after* matching, a markedly different picture emerges. When the analysis is focused on those who are similar in terms of their employment histories and health-related characteristics (as per the full list of variables given at the end of this chapter in the Appendix) the value of average earnings and the amount of time in employment for Work Choice participants within common support is significantly higher than that demonstrated by their matched Work Programme counterparts. Work Choice participants, on average, earn £1,287 *more* than the matched Work Programme control group within the 15-month tracking window. Since average earnings for the matched Work Programme population are only £1,558 (within the 15-month window,) this is a sizeable effect. The earnings level of Work Choice participants is 183 per cent of the typical earnings for the Work Programme matched control group.

On average, those participating in Work Choice spend more than an additional month (1.22 months) in paid employment than the matched comparator group. This is a sizeable effect in a context where evaluations of activating labour market policies typically find small impacts (Filges et al, 2015). On both of the outcome metrics – value of earnings and time in employment – the Work Choice programme considerably outperforms the Work Programme for those participants who are matched in terms of their disability-related and wider demographic characteristics.

Figure 7.5: Employment effect of Work Choice compared to Work Programme

Variable	Sample	Treated	Controls	Difference	SE	T-stat
	Unmatched	2848.57	2511.69	336.88	30.97	10.88
Earnings (£)	ATT	2846.17	1558.66	1287.51	60.68	21.22
employment	Unmatched	3.71	3.56	0.15	0.03	4.28
(months)	ATT	3.70	2.48	1.22	0.07	17.55

Given such considerable differences in the average employment effects experienced by Work Choice participants, questions are immediately raised as to the manner by which these improved employment outcomes are achieved. We can begin to consider this by exploring the four potential routes through which aggregate outcomes can be raised: is this through a greater proportion of Work Choice participants entering employment? Speedier transitions into employment? Different earning levels within work? More stable employment trajectories? Or any combination of these features?

Informed by the growing sequence analysis literature (Brzinsky-Fay, 2007; Quintini and Manfredi, 2009; Dorsett and Lucchino, 2012), the analysis begins to trace individual unemployment-earning trajectories and classify them into several transition pathways. This approach seeks to unpack the entire employment and earning trajectory experienced by each matched programme participant following attachment to the programme – including the nature of each month's labour market status and the ordering of spells within the wider transition pattern. A pragmatic, policy-informed approach is taken to constructing the distinct monthly labour market status types, shown in Figure 7.6.

Figure 7.6: Definition of distinct labour market elements within participant employment trajectories

Figure 7.7 presents the matched Work Programme and Work Choice samples through sequence index plots. This representation plots entire individual earning trajectories horizontally, that is, each horizontal stripe when read from left to right represents the 15 monthly activity statuses experienced by one individual. Five shades are used to denote the different element types, and each change in colour corresponds to a change in status.

Figure 7.7: Graphical representation of earning trajectories for matched Work Programme and Work Choice participants

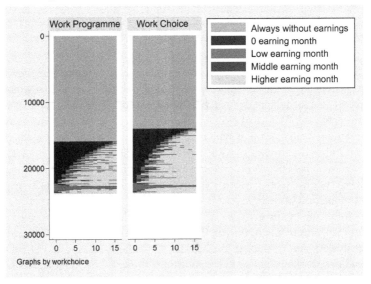

The majority of participants in both Work Programme and Work Choice are without any earnings record in the RTI (see the upper portion of Figure 7.7). Notably, a larger proportion of Work Programme participants are without earnings than their Work Choice counterparts (67 per cent of matched Work Programme participants have no earning record compared to 59 per cent of the Work Choice cohort). So in part the greater employment effects for the Work Choice programme can be understood as being driven by the greater number of participants on that scheme who do ultimately end up achieving paid employment. Work Choice participants do also enter employment more quickly following programme attachment, illustrated by the sharper gradient for colour changes. On average Work Choice participants enter employment after 4.4 months following programme attachment while matched Work Programme participants on average take 5.1 months.

The value of average monthly earnings among Work Choice participants is also higher. Across the months with non-zero earnings, the mean monthly earnings for Work Choice participants is slightly higher (at £772.84) compared to the average monthly earnings for Work Programme participants (£631.04). In more detailed analysis (not shown) that clusters similar earning trajectory types, Work Choice participants are also more likely to enter a stable earnings trajectory, that is, a sequence of month-to-month earnings that are not punctuated by spells of very low or no employment earnings.

Without a full process evaluation it is not possible to be explicit on the specific ways in which services and user experiences have varied across the schemes, but the variation in employment outcomes is in accordance with and *potentially* indicative of enhanced support experienced by Work Choice participants prior to employment entry. There is also a suggestion that *stability* of work (perhaps through enhanced in-work support) is heightened through Work Choice provision. It is important to be aware that the unit costs allocated through Work Choice, that is, the financial value of the per participant spending envelope available to invest in provision – is also understood to be larger than that for Work Programme participants (Learning and Work Institute, 2016). This may also interact with the variation in the quasi-marketised forms, such that Work Choice is *both* more generous in terms of resource and *softer* in terms of its orientation to provider priorities.

Discussion and conclusion

By extending from previous work investigating varieties of quasi-marketisation in public service delivery (Gingrich, 2011; Wiggan 2015a, b), this chapter introduces explicit *graduated dimensions* through which to understand variation in the way that quasi-markets may be constructed. The allocation dimension captures the form of financing for services (ranging from wholesale public funding to fully private provision) and the regulation of provider activity by the state (stretching from very light-touch or negligible regulation through to comprehensive scrutiny and service quality control). The production dimension captures three underlying axes:

- how 'open' and competitive the market is, spanning from an open, highly competitive and accessible market to a situation where access is constrained or limited;
- the specification of provider activity, ranging from a high degree of public sector control over provider activity to an increasingly outcomes-led approach, where the public sector takes a position of agnosticism on the means of securing specified outcomes; and
- the role of service user choice and voice, spanning from a situation where the preferences and concerns of participating citizens act as a powerful steering mechanism for provider behaviour to a state where service user choice and/or voice is constrained to such a degree that is has no traction for service provider actions.

Depending on the design of particular quasi-markets and their configurations with respect to these dimensions, providers and their service delivery activities will be differently responsive to the priorities and preferences of either the state, service users or providers themselves. This, in turn, is expected to have implications for the quantity, quality and distribution of services and consequently on any social outcomes achieved through such provision.

The benefit of setting out this framework as a series of graduated axes is first, to offer a clearer articulation of important underlying dimensions against which quasi-marketised arrangements vary. Second, by conceiving and visualising these axes as continua the framework is more alive to subtle variations in the variety of quasi-market under study. While quasi-markets *may* embody the 'pure' alternative types of either state-, user- or provider-directed forms, in practice *gradients* are likely to exist across these types. Quasi-market arrangements in practice are messy and the formulations on offer may straddle the clean-cut boundaries suggested in Gingrich's (2011) framework. This notion of softening or *hybrid quasi-market forms* has parallels with other work analysing employment support provision (Heins and Bennett, 2016, p 40), which has identified classification complexity when it comes to understanding 'the new welfare providers'. Although this work centres on service providers, the conclusions – that a process of hybridisation and boundary crossing is increasingly important in order to understand and address concerns around organisational change and service orientation – have clear echoes here.

The theoretical framework's ability to detect subtle variation in the formulation of quasi-markets is then utilised within the empirical study of the Work Programme and Work Choice. While on paper these programmes were commissioned according to the same commissioning strategy that sought to 'unleash' the innovation and entrepreneurialism of providers, the specific market formulation across the schemes varies in important ways. The positioning of the Work Programme against the dimensions described above suggests that it sits as a wholehearted exemplar of a provider-directed quasi-market configuration. Light-touch quality assurance on the allocation dimension is combined with a closed market with a questionable and seemingly limited (OECD, 2014) degree of ongoing competition between Prime providers. Within the Work Programme the state has rescinded control of which services are delivered to participants, the DWP has a weak regime for monitoring provider activity and service user preferences have no implication for providers. The promise of this provider-directed approach is that considerable freedom and discretion for providers will generate the dynamic entrepreneurialism and experimentation necessary to take employment outcome performance to a higher level (Wiggan, 2015a). By reifying provider interests, 'the state infers that the strength of the financial incentives built into the differential payment by result model is alone sufficient to drive providers to deliver appropriate [and effective] services for *all* users' (Wiggan, 2015a, p 126; emphasis added).

Critically, the enhanced outcome performance promised within the provider-led approach is *not* what we witness in practice. The empirical work shows that among matched programme participants with health conditions and disabilities, Work Programme performance is significantly *worse* than that achieved through Work Choice. Work Choice, in comparison to the Work Programme's wholehearted positioning as a provider-directed market, offers a more balanced or *hybridised* market position. The Work Choice arrangement counterpoises provider dominance through an enhanced role for the state in stipulating activity and regulating service quality and by furnishing service users with a (albeit limited) degree of choice. Although it leans towards the provider-led configuration Work Choice retains important elements of both a state-directed and user-responsive arrangement.

This balance or hybridity appears to be important when reading the empirical findings offered here alongside the now sizeable body of evidence on the Work Programme from within the DWP's official evaluation (Newton et al, 2012; Lane et al, 2013), from select committees (WPSC, 2011, 2013; PAC, 2012, 2013) and from academic research (Rees et al, 2014). This suggests that providers have not responded to the Work Programme's provider-led arrangement with innovative service offers tailored to the personalised support needs of programme participants. Instead, providers appear to have utilised their freedoms to maximise profits and reduce risk by cynically deprioritising services for those who – in providers' eyes – may be more difficult to move into work. This tallies with the findings here, which indicate that poor outcomes performance for those with health conditions and disabilities are *not inevitable* and that the employment and earnings outcomes for these groups are markedly better within the hybridised quasi-market configuration. Under the Work Programme the interests of providers are dominant, and in practice this arrangement appears to function in such a way that disadvantages unemployed programme participants with disabilities and health conditions, whose employment and earnings outcomes are significantly and sizeably lower than what they would have been had they participated in the alternative Work Choice scheme.

In sum, the variation in quasi-marketised form between the Work Programme and Work Choice emerges as an important mediator of programme participant experiences across the two schemes. In particular, the bolstered position for state and user preferences in the hybridised Work Choice example – which straddles across the state-, provider- and (to a lesser extent) user-directed forms outlined by Gingrich (2011) – serves as a defence against the worst perversities of a provider-dominated system. State stipulation of relatively intensive pre-employment engagement and guaranteed in-work support for Work Choice participants emerge in the evaluation material (Purvis et al, 2013) as facets that undergird the elevated employment outcomes for participants in this scheme.

The chapter, then, has implications for both research and practice. The theoretical framework offers the academic community a tool through which to systematically investigate variation in quasi-market formulations. The spur is to evaluate how alternative positions on allocation and production axes cascade incentives and ultimately influence service quality and the achievement of policy goals. The disappointing performance of the Work Programme for those with health conditions and disabilities, and the varying performance of Work Programme and Work Choice outlined for the first time in this analysis, should also have ramifications for current and future policy design.

UK employment schemes designed subsequent to Work Programme roll-out do appear to have made quasi-market design adjustments on some fronts. For example, in Northern Ireland the new Steps 2 Success employment support programme has explicitly rejected the black box approach and stipulates pan-programme minimum service standards in order to introduce greater public regulation than allowed for in the Work Programme (Wiggan, 2015a). What this chapter's framework offers policy-makers is a tool through which to consider how the full suite of levers at their disposal comes together to reify particular interests when structuring quasi-markets. With a fuller understanding of the variation in quasi-market types and further research on how this variation plays out in service experience, we will be able to make markets that better balance the competing priorities of government, service users and providers.

Note

1   In practice, one of the organisations classed as 'private sector' is a special purpose vehicle created by two voluntary sector organisations.

References

Armstrong, D., Byrne, Y., Cummings, C. and Gallen, B. (2010) *The commissioning strategy: Provider survey on early implementation*, DWP Research Report No 704, London: Department for Work and Pensions (www.gov.uk/government/uploads/system/uploads/attachment_data/file/214479/rr ep704.pdf).

Bonoli, G. (2010) 'The political economy of active labour market policy', *Politics & Society*, vol 38, no 4, pp 435-57.

Bonoli, G. (2013) *The origins of active social policy: Labour market and childcare policies in a comparative perspective*, Oxford: Oxford University Press.

Bryson, A., Dorsett, R. and Purdon, S. (2002) *The use of propensity score matching in the evaluation of active labour market policies*, Department for Work and Pensions Working Paper No. 4.

Brzinsky-Fay, C. (2007) 'Lost in transition? Labour market entry sequences of school leavers in Europe', *European Sociological Review*, vol 23, no 4, pp 409-22.

Carter, E. and Whitworth, A. (2015) 'Creaming and parking in quasi-marketised welfare-to-work schemes: Designed out of or designed in to the UK Work Programme', *Journal of Social Policy*, vol 44, no 2, pp277-96.

Conservative Party (2017) *Forward together: The Conservative manifesto, Our plan for a stronger Britain and a prosperous future* (www.conservatives. com/manifesto).

Considine, M., Lewis, J. and O'Sullivan, S. (2011) 'Quasi-markets and service delivery flexibility following a decade of employment assistance reform in Australia', *Journal of Social Policy*, vol 40, no 4, pp 811-33.

Disability Rights UK (2016) 'Statement on the DWP Green Paper: "Improving lives"' (www.disabilityrightsuk.org/statement-dwp-green-paper-%E2%80%9Cimproving-lives%E2%80%9D).

DWP (Department for Work and Pensions) (2008) *DWP commissioning strategy*, February, Cm7330 (http://webarchive.nationalarchives.gov. uk/20130128102031/http://www.dwp.gov.uk/docs/cs-rep-08.pdf).

DWP (2009) *Work Choice specification: Invitation to tender stage*, London: DWP.

DWP (2010) *Work Choice equality impact assessment* (www.gov.uk/ government/uploads/system/uploads/attachment_data/file/220225/ work-choice-equality-ia.pdf).

DWP (2012) *The Work Programme* (www.dwp.gov.uk/docs/the-work-programme.pdf).

Dorsett, R. and Lucchino, P. (2012) *Visualising the school to work transition: An analysis using optimal matching*, London: National Institute of Economic and Social Research (www.niesr.ac.uk/publications/ visualising-school-work-transition-analysis-using-optimal-matching).

Filges, T., Smedslund, G., Knudsen, A.S.D. and Jørgensen, A.M.K. (2015) *Active labour market programme participation for unemployment insurance recipients: A systematic review*, Oslo, Norway: Campbell Systematic Reviews.

Finn, D. (2012) *Subcontracting in public employment services: The design and delivery of outcome based and black box model contracts*, Brussels, Belgium: European Commission, DG Employment, Social Affairs and Inclusion (http://ec.europa.eu/social/main.jsp?catId=964).

Freud, D. (2007) *Reducing dependency, increasing opportunity: Options for the future of welfare to work*, London: Department for Work and Pensions.

Fuertes, V., Jantz, B., Klenk, T. and McQuaid, R. (2014) 'Between cooperation and competition: The organisation of employment service delivery in the UK and Germany', *International Journal of Social Welfare*, vol 23, pp 71-86.

Gash, T., Panchamia, N., Sims, S. and Hotson, L. (2013) *Making public service markets work: Professionalising government's approach to commissioning and market stewardship*, London: Institute for Government (www.instituteforgovernment.org.uk/sites/default/files/publications/Making_public_service_markets_work_final_0.pdf).

Gertler, P., Martinez, S., Premand, P., Rawlings, L. and Vermeersch, C. (2016) *Impact evaluation in practice*, Washington, DC: World Bank Group.

Gingrich, J. (2011) *Making markets in the welfare state: The politics of varying market reforms*, Cambridge: Cambridge University Press.

Greener, I. (2008) 'Markets in the public sector: when they work, and what do we do when they don't?', *Policy & Politics*, vol 36, no 1, pp 93-108.

Heinrich, C., Maffioli, A. and Gonzalo Vásquez, G. (2010) *A primer for applying propensity-score matching. Impact-evaluation guidelines*, Technical Note IDB-TN-161, Washington, DC: Inter-American Development Bank.

Heins, E. and Bennett, H. (2016) '"Best of both worlds"? A comparison of third sector providers in health care and welfare-to-work markets in Britain', *Social Policy & Administration*, vol 50, no 1, pp 39-58.

Jantz, B., Klenk, T., Larsen, F. and Wiggan, J. (2015) 'Marketization and varieties of accountability relationships in employment services: Comparing Denmark, Germany, and Great Britain', *Administration & Society*, vol 47, no 1, pp 1-25.

Lane, P., Foster, R., Gardiner, L., Lanceley, L. and Purvis, A. (2013) *Work Programme evaluation: Procurement, supply chains and implementation of the commissioning model*, London: Department for Work and Pensions.

Learning and Work Institute (2016) *Halving the gap: Making the Work and Health Programme work for disabled people*, Leicester (www.learningandwork.org.uk/sites/niace_en/files/files/Work%20and%20Health_Halving_the_Gap_FINAL_1.pdf).

Leuven, E. and Sianesi, B. (2003) psmatch2: Stata module to perform full Mahalanobis and propensity score matching, common support graphing, and covariate imbalance testing (http://ideas.repec.org/c/boc/bocode/s432001.html).

NAO (National Audit Office) (2012) *The introduction of the Work Programme*, London: The Stationery Office (www.nao.org.uk/wp-content/uploads/2012/01/10121701.pdf).

Newton, B., Meager, N., Bertram, C., Corden, A., George, A., Lalani, M., et al (2012) *Work Programme evaluation: Findings from the first phase of qualitative research on programme delivery*, London: Department for Work and Pensions.

Oakley, M. (2015) *Employment support for a high-wage economy*, York: Joseph Rowntree Foundation.

OECD (Organisation for Economic Co-operation and Development) (2014) *Connecting people with jobs: Activation policies in the United Kingdom*, Paris: OECD Publishing.

Mason, T. (2010) 'Shaw Trust relieved at DWP decision on Work Choice contracts', *Civil Society* (www.civilsociety.co.uk/news/shaw-trust-relieved-at-dwp-decision-on-work-choice-contracts.html).

PAC (Public Accounts Committee) (2012) *The Introduction of the Work Programme, Eighty-fifth report of session 2010-12*, London: The Stationery Office.

PAC (2013) *Work Programme outcome statistics, Thirty-third report of session 2012-13*, London: The Stationery Office.

Powell, M. (2015) 'Making markets in the English National Health Service', *Social Policy & Administration*, vol 49, no 1, pp 109-27.

Purvis, A., Foster, S., Lanceley, L. and Wilson, T. (2014) *Fit for purpose: Transforming employment support for disabled people and those with health conditions*, London: Centre for Economic and Social Inclusion.

Purvis, A., Foster, S., Lane, P., Aston, J. and Davies, M. (2013) *Evaluation of the Work Choice Specialist Disability Employment Programme: Findings from the 2011 Early Implementation and 2012 Steady State Waves of the research*, DWP Research Report No 846, London: Department for Work and Pensions.

Quintini, G. and Manfredi, T. (2009) *Going Separate Ways? School-to-Work Transitions in the United States and Europe*, OECD Social, Employment and Migration Working Papers, No. 90, OECD Publishing.

Rees, J., Whitworth, A. and Carter, E. (2014) 'Support for all in the UK Work Programme? Differential payments, same old problem', *Social Policy & Administration*, vol 48, no 2, pp 221-39.

Struyven, L. and Steurs, G. (2005) 'Design and redesign of a quasi-market for the reintegration of jobseekers: Empirical evidence from Australia and the Netherlands', *Journal of European Social Policy*, vol 15, no 3, pp 211-29.

Tarr, A. and Finn, D. (2012) *Implementing Universal Credit: Will the reforms improve the service for users?*, York: Joseph Rowntree Foundation.

Thompson, A., Trenell, P., Hope, M. and McPhillips, A. (2011) *Work Choice evaluation: Commissioning and transition of clients to the Programme*, DWP Research Report No 6, London: Department for Work and Pensions.

Whitworth, A. (2013) *Tailor made? Single parents' experiences of Employment Support from Jobcentre Plus and the Work Programme*, London: Gingerbread.

Wiggan, J. (2015a) 'Varieties of marketization in the UK: Examining divergence in activation markets between Great Britain and Northern Ireland 2008-2014', *Policy Studies*, pp 1-18.

Wiggan, J. (2015b) 'What variety of employment service quasi-market? Ireland's JobPath as a private power market', in Z. Irving, M. Fenger and J. Hudson (eds) *Social Policy Review 27*, Bristol: Policy Press.

WPSC (Work and Pensions Select Committee) (2011) *Work Programme: Providers and contracting arrangements*, Fourth Report of Session 2010–12, House of Commons, London: The Stationery Office.

WPSC (2013) *Can the Work Programme work for all user groups?* First Report of Session 2013-14, House of Commons, London: The Stationery Office.

Appendix

Supplementary table: covariates used in propensity score matching

Demographic	
	Self-reported disability
	Sex
	Age at programme attachment
	Ethnicity
	Cumulative effect of disability on day-to-day activities
	Presence of an International Classification of Diseases (ICD) code
	Disadvantaged through use of drugs, alcohol or ex-offender status
Employment history	
	Cumulative duration of out-of-work benefit claims (2- and 5- years prior to programme)
	Stability of out-of-work benefit claims (number of distinct spells in 2-years prior to programme)
	Duration of paid employment in 2-years prior to attachment (days)
	Stability of paid employment in 2-years prior to attachment (distinct spells)
Household	
	Has dependent children
	Lone parent status
Contextual	
	Resident local authority

Social policy and populism: welfare nationalism as the new narrative of social citizenship

Markus Ketola and Johan Nordensvard

Introduction

In recent years, ethnocentric nationalism has become a serious challenger to both social democratic and neoliberal welfare discourses. This chapter suggests that in the slipstream of the increasing popularity of the populist far-right across Europe we are also witnessing the emergence of a new social policy narrative. This new policy narrative is likely to have significant implications for the future development of social policy, as it is based on a heady mix of challenging expert knowledge as the basis of policy, prioritising the cultural claims of particular groups in society over others, and conflating the universal 'people' with the representatives of a particular cultural identity. Indeed, in this scenario the notion of 'universality' in terms of social rights becomes interpreted through a particular nationalist lens and the logic of access to welfare services rearticulated in narrower terms. What we are witnessing is a redefinition of social citizenship on the basis of welfare nationalism.

We make this claim with specific reference to the narratives employed by populist far-right politicians, and see these as a key instrument in the reframing of the welfare debate in more nationalist terms. In this chapter we investigate the narratives that influence the current reinterpretation of social policy priorities. While the argument put forward in this chapter is largely theoretical, we also draw on the case of Sweden in order to briefly exemplify the discursive strategies in play. Sweden is a particularly relevant case as in many ways it comes close to the ideal universal welfare state and multicultural society (Schierup et al, 2006), yet at the same time there has also been clear growth in welfare chauvinism from within the populist far-right (Norocel, 2016). By infusing facts with alternative meanings, the populist far-right contribute to the emergence of an alternative social policy narrative that aims at constraining social rights to native citizens.

Welfare chauvinist narratives are not new, so why are they gaining so much traction at this moment in time? One way to look at this is the merging into two crises that have generated the political opportunity structures for this to happen. First, the gradual but persistent erosion of the welfare state through its restructuring and retrenchment has resulted in the exclusion of substantial groups from long-established social rights in many European countries (Schierup et al, 2006). These are long-term patterns that have been exacerbated by the austerity policies of the last decade. In connection with this, the challenge of supranational integration within the European Union (EU) as well as broader concerns about immigration have contributed to what Delanty has termed 'anxieties about peoplehood', which significantly contributes to the argument as to how welfare and migration become interlinked as sources of instability' (Delanty, 2008, p 677).

In developing these narratives, European far-right populism can be understood to reflect the changing approach found among the electorate, who 'increasingly tend to privilege issue- and value-oriented forms of participation over ideology-oriented ones' (Betz, 1994, p 107). Betz makes an important distinction between two types of far-right populism: national and neoliberal. He suggests that ideologically driven libertarian and neoliberal far-right populism has been gradually sidelined by the value-driven politics of xenophobia and racism. In this chapter our focus is on the value-driven forms of far-right populism.

The chapter is structured as follows. The first section explains how we approach the concept of narratives and framing. The second looks at how populist narratives put forward particular understandings of social citizenship. Then the focus is cast on the case of Sweden, identifying the narratives of social policy employed by a far-right populist party. The final section concludes.

Framing, narratives and populism

The populist social policy narratives explored in this chapter should be understood as a particular approach to reframing the logic by which access to welfare is granted. As such, the narratives are often less focused on the actual content of welfare than they are on the eligibility criteria, particular for non-native claimants. Here we outline our approach to both framing and narratives, as well as their relationship to far-right populism.

Frames

Both framing and narratives should be seen as a natural part of interpretative studies (Alvesson and Sköldberg, 2003, p 90). Interpretative policy analysis diverges from mainstream positivist policy analysis by focusing on how policy actors interact, focusing on 'the social meaning of policies and the practices in which this meaning is embedded' (Durnova and Zittoun, 2011, p 103). Moreover, such a perspective seeks to 'develop a deeper, interpretative understanding of policy practices' by including 'perspectives on discourse, narration, governmentality and practice' (Durnova and Zittoun, 2011, p 103). Discourse analysis has an interest in how institutions and rules are spread through the usage of language as an approach commonly found in policy research (Hall, 1993; Cox, 2001; Hansen and King, 2001; Blyth, 2002; Béland, 2009; Béland and Cox, 2011). The focus is therefore less on explanation and more on meaningful understanding of social action (Heracleous, 2004). Frames and narratives are therefore discursive tools attached to particular meanings, which, in the party political context, enable the populist far-right to develop certain normative expectations about how social policy ought to be delivered, informed by welfare nationalism.

Frames are defined as 'schemata of interpretation' that guide individuals 'to locate, perceive, identify, and label' events and conditions around them (Goffman, 1974, p 21). Frame analysis focuses on policy controversies based on conflicting problem definitions, and its aim is to show how these controversies can be overcome (Daviter, 2007, p 657). In order to do so, Rein and Schön produce a normative theory of policy deliberation, that focuses on the social processes through which policy actors with conflicting frames and interests can reach consensus over policy issues (1996).

According to Snow and Benford, policy actors play an active role in shaping the policy process, yet their action is guided by values and meaning (1992, p 138). Their work conceptualises framing as 'a way of selecting, organizing, interpreting, and making sense of a complex reality so as to provide guideposts for knowing, analysing and acting' (Rein and Schön, 1991, p 236). In other words, policy frames enable actors to attach meaning to a policy problem, give it coherence and direct action (Rein and Schön, 1996). Although policy actors strategically engage with frames in order to dominate the policy process, their dominance depends on doubts, nature or habit (Peirce, 1992). Political actors use framing to convince the population or audience to support a specific policy alternative, yet the ideological frames are not the policy ideas per se, but are located in the discourse surrounding the policy alternatives under debate (Béland, 2005, pp 2-3).

Béland also points out that it is important to note how successful policy alternatives need to be framed in politically and culturally acceptable manners. He describes ideological frames as 'weapons of mass persuasion' where 'political actors must master the institutional "rules of the game" while manipulating the symbols available in existing ideological repertoires' (2005, p 12). Indeed, the need for policy-makers to frame issues using culturally accepted repertoires shows the continuing relevance of public opinion (Burstein, 1998).

Even when they use existing cultural symbols they can still use them in an original way. An important part of framing is to actually change and transform the frames of the stable ideological repertoires, and one way of doing this is through combining, manipulating, reconstructing or even outright changing the dominant frames. Frames and framing play an important role in creating consensus and creating consent for particular ideologies is about widening the popular appeal through extending frames.

Narratives

Narratives can be understood to function as tools of sense-making that imbue events with meaning and allow facts to be reinterpreted or embellished (Gee, 1999; Gabriel, 2004). In this way narratives have a close relationship with frames as they are both discursive tools used to make sense of our social world.

The key components of a narrative are the plotline, or a sense of a story (Jaworski and Coupland, 2000), together with a clear sense of a change from one set of circumstances to another. Often the sense of change is linked to a transition from a broken equilibrium to a new, stable one through a key event, or events, around which the narrative is constructed (Ochs, 1998). The narrative plot is further enriched by characters or forces that are pitched against each other (Todorov, 1977, p 111).

Narratives, in their core, are also a political activity. According to Ochs, we can see storytelling as 'crucial to the construction of a self, an "other", and a society', as it also 'allows members of communities to represent and reflect upon events, thoughts and emotions' (1998, pp 202-3). We can then see that the use of narratives by political parties in this way has the capacity to shape the narratives that members of communities associate with themselves as well as with other communities, and to generate harmony as well as discord through certain narrative interpretations.

We see narratives and framing as very much intertwined as narratives involves framing an issue or policy in a particular way depending on perspective. When someone analyses narratives, it is important to remember that narratives could be taken apart and rewritten with a new focus, a new plot and hereby a whole new narrative. There are no neutral stories, since we could always tell alternative stories that undermine the predominant way of looking at the world. Or, as Roe puts it:

> [T]he way to undermine a policy narrative is not by trying to subvert it empirically – a tactic that only increases uncertainty and, therefore, the pressure to retain the policy narrative being critiqued. A better way to undermine a policy narrative is by creating a counter narrative, finding ways to "rewrite" the dominant policy narratives, or engaging other dominant narratives that happen to run counter to the narrative being disputed. (1994, p 5)

We argue that welfare nationalism is rewriting the narrative around social policy to steer away from social democratic narratives and neoliberal narratives to focus more on ethnicity and culture as a foundation for both access to and content of social welfare.

Populist narratives: the core building blocks of the plotline

The populism at the core of the populist far-right in Europe warrants some unpacking and explanation. Like its associate, nationalism, populism is focused on 'the who of politics' (Stanley, 2008). Although not limited to right-wing politics, populism refers to a 'thin-centred ideology' (Mudde, 2004, p 544; 2007), a black-and-white separation between the economic and political elite on the one side and 'the people' on the other, making anti-elitism the one defining feature of the ideational narrative. The narrative refers to vague generalisations, where the elite are depicted as corrupt, selfish and colluding against the interest of the people, while the people are its counterpoint: an uncorrupt and unified entity legitimated to challenging elite rule by representing the majority interest (the general will) (Mudde, 2010). In fleshing out this 'thin ideology of populism', Stanley highlights four core concepts as being key: (1) the 'people' and the 'elite' as two homogenous units; (2) an antagonistic relationship between the people and the elite; (3) the idea of popular sovereignty; and (4) valorisation of the 'the people' and denigration of 'the elite' (Stanley, 2008, p 102; see also Rooduijn, 2014, p 573).

For Canovan (1999) and Laclau (2005), populism represents an avenue through which hitherto unheard voices are able to enter the democratic debate. Populism offers the means to rebalance the unequal structures of power within societies and generate counterhegemonic ideas and practices that are necessary elements of the democratic process.

While our focus in this chapter is strictly on the far-right variant of populism, a left-wing version of the same phenomenon exists. The populist far-left have shifted from a class-based references to the 'proletariat' to a more generic label of 'good people' to accommodate this, as Akkerman and Rooduijn argue (2015). However, the crucial difference between the two can be identified in the role of exclusion in the narrative. The far-left has not embraced the language of homogeneity and shies away from the exclusionary approach, particularly in relation to race and ethnicity (Schmidt, 2017).

However, as Müller argues, not all anti-elitists should be regarded as populists. He describes populism as a specific form of identity politics that combines anti-elitism and anti-pluralism while asserting a 'moral monopoly of representation' (2016, pp 2-3). In other words, the logic of popular sovereignty is taken to its extreme, suggesting that a support base of 51 per cent translates to fully legitimate majority to make policy decisions that favour the marginal majority at the expense of others. Populist parties of the right are therefore less concerned with developing alternative policy narratives and more focused on delegitimising their political opponents as unrepresentative of the people's concerns (Müller, 2016).

This, ultimately, serves as the central justification for the anti-pluralist argument in favour of the tyranny of the majority, and demonstrates a core problem of populist politics in relation to social policy: the black-and-white choice between rule by the 'people' or rule by the technocratic policy and political elite. This comes down to the concept of people and defining whether this an excluding or including conceptualisation. There has been strong argument that this far-right populism could fall into what some would call both an exclusive concept and an excluding process (Betz, 2001; Rydgren, 2005; Berezin, 2009). In linking welfare and social policy to the nationalist project in Finland and Sweden, Nordensvard and Ketola have argued that there is an deeper argument for linking welfare and social policy to the fundamental nature of far-right populism and the definition of people and social citizenship (2015).

Social citizenship

At its broadest one might consider two dominant approaches to acquiring citizenship rights and access to social policy – a blood-based (jus sanguinis) and a territorial-based (jus soli) system (Brubaker, 1992). However, such straightforward definitions of citizenship rarely reflect the complex reality of lived citizenship. There are different scales of being a citizen in practice, and we need to differentiate, for example, between the experiences of living at a place and being a full member of society with all the rights and duties that accompany it. These qualifications are important in the context of welfare chauvinism and right-wing populism, as these focus on both the rules of access to welfare and the nature of the welfare rights granted to citizens. The populist argument here is that citizenship rights ought to be differentiated on the bases of belonging; since migrants and minority ethnic groups belong 'less', we need to rethink both their overall access to welfare and the content of the welfare services they are entitled to. In this context, the relationship between the nation state and nationalism becomes an important variable to understand the access versus content debates.

The classic conceptualisation of social citizenship was formulated by T.H. Marshall (1950) who suggests a threefold model of citizenship rights that comprises civil, political and social rights. Civil citizenship refer to those rights that are necessary for us to enjoy individual freedom, such as freedom of speech, religion and fair treatment before the law, and emerged in the early 18th century as necessary preconditions for successful capitalist economic systems (Wagner, 2004, p 280). Political rights refer to the ability of individuals to participate in the political process, to hold office and to vote. Finally, social rights refer to access to a 'modicum of economic welfare and security' that is guaranteed through the provision of education, housing, healthcare and pensions as a matter of right (Marshall, 1950, p 11). This was in part an effort to guarantee the working classes a certain living standard independent of the market.

At least in the European context the dominant understanding of citizenship has become increasingly disconnected from the ethnic origins of the nation state. For example, the social democratic approach to welfare with its universal and egalitarian policies and principle of non-discrimination has been argued to create services that are decoupled from nationality or ethnic origin (Rothstein and Stolle, 2003, p 196; Rothstein and Uslaner, 2005). Residency tended to replace legal citizenship as the basis for access to welfare, underpinned by a gradual 'denationalization of solidarity practices' (Mau and Burkhardt, 2009, p 241). At the same time, the continuing integration of European nation states has eroded national sovereignty and led to a reaction against access to social policy on the bases of domicile, largely on the ground that this challenges a vision of welfare based on citizenship (Sainsbury, 2006). EU integration and subsequent loss of sovereignty on a range of social issues – both real and perceived – play a significant role in the rhetoric of the populist radical right.

Far-right populist narratives of social citizenship

Far-right populism has for a long time made the connection between the 'corrupt elites' who design and deliver social policy in a manner that fails to take into account the interests of the 'pure people' which, in this case, means the native common man and women. The far-right populist argument hinges on two basic narratives of welfare and social policy:

- First, the wrong people administrate welfare and social policy, so it is not in the interest of the native common man.
- Second, the corrupt elites, in their support for multiculturalism, have opened up access to undeserving migrants that undermines the nation state as well as diminishes the quality of welfare services.

With regards to the first narrative, the populist far-right takes a very particular citizenship perspective in how it criticises the way welfare is arranged and delivered in a manner that neglects the interests of the 'common man'. For example, the perception that the needs of asylum-seekers, refugees and migrants are prioritised over those of 'natives' is common across the globe (Spinney and Nethery, 2013). These parties claim that:

> … the welfare state is not adequately aimed at helping poor common people who are "really" in need and hence deserving of assistance … [and that the] welfare state, instead, provides well-paid and comfortable jobs for self-interested civil servants who cater to a class of "welfare scroungers" that freeload on the hard work of the "common man". (de Koster et al, 2013, p 6)

Nordensvard and Ketola (2015) discussed how far-right populism portrays economic globalisation, mass immigration and Europeanisation as an elite project that supports multiculturalism and undermines the nation and the nation state. It assumes that the political elite has used external forces (globalisation, immigration, the EU) to further its own interests and power. Far-right populists argue that the political elite has neglected the interests of the nation through EU polices, giving in to globalisation and opening up the borders to immigrants. This contributes to a critical attitude towards mainstream politics in general (Rydgren, 2007).

With regards to the second narrative, this gives momentum for an exclusive and exclusionist welfare state that favours ethnic nationals. Such ideas have been branded as welfare chauvinism, implying a strong support for economic redistribution with resistance toward distributing welfare services to immigrants (van der Waal et al, 2010). Chauvinism has often been portrayed by right-wing policy actors as a way to protect the welfare state through exclusion of migrants from welfare provision. This means that welfare and social policy is perceived as a proprietary right of the native ethnic majority (Mudde, 2007, p 47; de Koster et al, 2013, p 6). Andersen and Björklund summarise welfare chauvinism with the description that welfare services should be restricted on the basis of racial, national and/or cultural background (1990, p 212). Far-right populist parties in support of welfare chauvinistic positions claim they represent a more genuine form of economic egalitarianism, protecting the interests of the 'common man' (Betz, 1994; Meny and Surel, 2000) that challenges the mainstream rhetoric.

Recently, welfare chauvinism has received significant academic attention. One strand of this research has focused on the 'supply side' in the sense of interpreting welfare chauvinism at least in part as political opportunism by the far-right populist parties (as well as other parties) in Northern and Western Europe (Mudde, 2000, 2007; Jungar and Jupskås, 2014; Lefkofridi and Michel, 2014; Ennser-Jedenastik, 2016; Careja et al, 2016; Schumacher and van Kersbergen, 2016).

The 'demand side', looking at public attitudes to welfare and immigration, is the second core strand of research on welfare chauvinism. Such contributions reflect on survey data that highlight voter preference for differential access to welfare based on nationality or ethnicity (van Oorschot, 2006; van der Waal et al, 2010), and associate such trends with liberal and conservative welfare regimes (van der Waal et al, 2013). Alesina and Glaeser, in turn, have argued that 'racial heterogeneity' in the US explains why it has such a weak redistributive welfare state

(2004). Their position sees welfare chauvinism as a normal state of affairs as people are more likely to look favourably on their own group and subsequently prefer more limited redistribution of resources (2004). Ennser-Jedenastik (2017) also suggests there is some linkage between the nature of the welfare state and the prevalence of welfare chauvinism. He argues that policies that aim towards universal or means-tested benefits are more vulnerable to welfare chauvinism, whereas insurance-based systems are more resilient to welfare chauvinist interventions.

In the Nordic context, far-right populist parties are voicing their support for a vision where access to welfare is based on ethnic belonging and national borders. The Danish People's Party (Dansk Folkeparti) and the Norwegian Progress Party (Framstegspartiet) both support welfare discourses that aim to protect the welfare state from the drain of immigration (Rydgren, 2007, p 486; see also Kestilä and Söderlund, 2007). Using the examples of Sweden and Finland, Nordensvard and Ketola (2015) reveal a populist right-wing discourse that reframes the welfare state as being linked to a sovereign and exclusive political community with distinct national boundaries. Norocel (2016), in turn, shows how the Sweden Democrats merge welfare chauvinism and nostalgia for the old Swedish welfare model, popularly referred to as *folkhem* (the '[Swedish] people's home'). This interpretation stands in stark contrast to other mainstream parties that wish to transform the *folkhem* into a multicultural welfare state (Norocel, 2016). Keskinen (2016) also highlights the vulnerability of the Nordic model to far-right populist attacks on recent immigrants, evidencing in her research the tension between the universal welfare state ideology based on equality and equal treatment in terms of welfare access and the populist demands for differential treatment for those deemed not to belong to the nativist political community.

The case of Sweden

The Swedish welfare state has often been seen as a prime example of a universal and egalitarian approach to social policy found in the comparative welfare regime literature (Esping-Andersen, 1990). Nordic countries in general and Sweden in particular act as representatives of a distinctive approach to social policy, aligned with the ideal type of a social democratic regime. Esping-Andersen's criteria for a social democratic welfare state were closely modelled on what the Swedish welfare state was perceived to do: the state tries to de-commodify labour, it manages universal and solidaristic social programmes, it invests extensive resources into redistribution of income and it strives for full employment. Social transfers and welfare services are granted to everyone, and despite differences in wealth and resources, every citizen is of equal worth in access to social services (Eikemo and Bambra, 2008).

Although this institutional design is vulnerable to a welfare chauvinist narrative, compared to many other European countries Sweden remained an outlier, with only very limited electoral success for far-right parties until the 1990s (Andersen and Björklund, 1990, 2000). In the 1990s New Democracy (Ny Demokrati) received 6.7 per cent of votes in the 1991 parliamentary election based around two charismatic leaders: Bert Karlsson and Ian Wachtmeister (Taggart, 1996; Westlind, 1996). In many ways the party symbolised the traditional view of far-right populist parties that challenged mainstream political parties by claiming they fail to represent the 'people' and prioritised the reduction of immigration rates. Still the party retained a distinct neoliberal framing by, for example, promoting reduced levels of taxation as well as limited privatisation of the public sector (Rydgren, 2002; Taggart, 1996; Westlind, 1996). When the charismatic leaders Ian and Bert quit, followed by poor electoral results where the party received only 1.2 per cent of votes in the 1994 elections, the party soon disappeared.

The Sweden Democrats have been much more successful. They were founded in 1988 as a continuation of the Sweden Party (Sverigepartiet), which in turn was founded in 1986 as a merger of the Progress Party (Framstegspartiet) with the racist and far-right group Keep Sweden Swedish (Bevara Sverige Svenskt). The party spent much of the late 1990s cutting its links to extreme groups and becoming a more respectable mainstream party. When Jimmy Åkesson took over the party in 2005, he aimed to emulate the successes of the Danish People's Party and enter the national Parliament. In the 2014 election Sweden Democrats confirmed their place within mainstream politics by becoming the third biggest party in the Parliament. The party received 12.86 per cent of the vote – a doubling of their results from the 2010 election when they first entered the Swedish Parliament. In terms of social policy, Sweden Democrats prefer an ambiguous approach, straddling somewhere between nostalgia for the classical welfare state of the 1950s and 1960s and enthusiasm for neoliberal reforms premised on choice, decentralisation and new public management (see Table 8.1).

Sweden Democrats describe the state as essential for a society to function, and highlight that its core duties are the safety of the nation and its independence, the care of weak and vulnerable individuals, the upkeep of laws and the protection of the nation's historical heritage

Table 8.1: Framing the welfare narrative of Sweden Democrats

	Social policy access	Social policy content
Preferred policy	Welfare should be available first and foremost to citizens and there should be limitations on migrants/asylum-seekers' access to welfare services	Social policy should be designed to focus on Swedish citizens where there is a large focus on older people. There is quite an ambiguous view on neoliberal policies as choice is often seen as positive and for-profit providers of welfare services are seen as a complement to public services
Opposing	Migration from far away cultures that strain the welfare budget. Migrants having privileged access to the labour markets and Swedish citizens not having preferred access to national employment	Welfare services that are designed around migrants and promote their access to welfare, education in their own native language and cultures Unregulated labour markets that encourage immigrant workers, lead to higher costs and lower salaries for natives

together with its unique cultural characteristics. The party argues that education, heritage protection and welfare for the weak and sick should be financed by the public state through taxes. However, they further argue for pragmatism in relation to the size of the welfare state – certain services should be delivered by the state or municipalities while others by the private sector. Sweden Democrats describe their approach as result-oriented. For example, it is not important who fulfils a specific welfare task as long as it is performed in a way that gives the most utility for the citizens at the lowest possible cost (Sverigedemokraterna, 2011).

The party has highlighted on many occasions that the welfare state and the *folkhemmet* – a particular Swedish narrative of the welfare state as a family where everyone takes responsibility and is looked after – are based on a social conservative principle. The party argues for a revival of 'people's home', where community is not based around class, as was the case in the original conceptualisation of the *folkhemmet*, but around nationality. The party argues that all national citizens should be guaranteed a high welfare and social security. Their *Programme of principles* states that the party wants the welfare state to be based on solidarity and tax-financed welfare that supports equal opportunities. The party points to class inequalities and social injustice as threats to stability and a sense of community, tearing apart the nation. Welfare is portrayed as being based on identity and cultural belonging, which in turn pitches multiculturalism and the welfare state as being in conflict with each other (Sverigedemokraterna, 2011). This highlights an ambiguous and vague centre-right stand on welfare that aims to attract nationalist as well as conservative voters from both the conservative and social democratic corners of the electorate to vote for the party. It also clearly demonstrates the manner in which the Sweden Democrats take on existing frames by associating them with alternative narratives in an effort to reconceptualise and change the frames.

Sweden Democrats fulfils the basic requirement for far-right populist parties in arguing that elitist multiculturalism undermines Swedish society, and that the ruling elite has abandoned the interest of the common man and national interests for the sake of its own and external interests (Nordensvard and Ketola, 2015). The party suggests that it is in the national interest to limit the flow of immigrants to Sweden since this will protect Swedish culture, the welfare state, labour market and reduce crime. The interests of other cultures should be curtailed. The upshot is that Swedish people would be supported more through better welfare, better access to employment and increased safety. Elites neglect the interest of the 'common man', which would be more closely aligned with promoting a Swedish identity, promoting employment for Swedes, curtailing immigrants' alleged abuse of the welfare system, protecting Swedes from crime committed by immigrants and limiting the ability of foreign workers to compete with Swedish workers (Nordensvard and Ketola, 2015).

At the same time, the party has used an ambiguous neoliberal framing to portray immigrants as a cost to society and the welfare system. The party argues that immigrants tend to be unemployed and heavily reliant on the welfare state. This implies a dependence framework where immigrants are conveyed as free-riders and welfare tourists. Sweden Democrats has, therefore, included cutting spending on asylum and immigrants as an important part of its budget proposals. It argued in 2012 (with calculations that were widely disputed) that the net cost of new immigration is 119 billion Swedish Krona, while immigrants use social services 1.5 times more than ethnic Swedes. Additionally, here we encounter the argument that a reduction in the number of immigrants will lead to an overall improvement of the nation state and its citizens:

All political activity is about creating priorities and it is up to ourselves to decide where we want our common resources to go. Sweden Democrats have shown that one can, through immigration politics, free up resources that could be used to lower tax pressures and raise welfare. (Sverigedemokraterna, 2012)

Key policies for Sweden Democrats include not only restrictions on immigration but also initiatives to support people to leave Sweden, arguing that 'there should be an active and generous support to be given to immigrants who wish to return to their home countries' (Sverigedemokraterna, 2010).

However, one can also identify an important critique where the Sweden Democrats problematise the utility of a free labour market and elite corporations that behave irresponsibly. Sweden Democrats argue that free work immigration that was introduced in 2008 has placed a great strain on the labour market. It has meant that Swedes have been pushed out of jobs, and wages have been reduced: 'What happened in practice was that one transferred all responsibility to employers when it came to work immigration of people from outside the EU/EEA' (Sverigedemokraterna, 2011). This, in turn, has led to lower wages for people in the service industry in particular. In the absence of appropriate regulation of the labour market, therefore, it is assumed that immigrants lead to higher costs as well as lower salaries for Swedish workers and an overall decline in the labour market. The party concludes that Sweden should be a nation state and its welfare state ought to be first and foremost for Swedes: 'In our Sweden we help people in distress but the Swedish welfare and the well-being of the country will be the first priority. In our Sweden there will be responsible immigration politics' (Sverigedemokraterna, 2010, p 4). Temporary visas should be given to immigrants to fill gaps in the labour market, but the party insists that such workers should return home afterwards (Nordensvard and Ketola, 2015).

Conclusion

This chapter has attempted to demonstrate how framing and narratives can help us think about the way approaches to welfare, and to social citizenship in particular, are part of a discursive populist apparatus aimed at reframing the existing social democratic and neoliberal ideological frames.

For any political party, as Béland (2005) points out, it is important to frame welfare policies in a culturally acceptable manner. Moreover, for such framing to be convincing it needs to transform existing stable ideological frames used by other parties. In this chapter we have argued that frames are an important mechanism in creating consent for and widening the appeal of certain worldviews. By infusing experiences, policies and facts with alternative meanings, the far-right populists generate an alternative social policy narrative that draws on the typical populist, essentialist perception of homogeneous and culturally unified 'people'. This comes across clearly in the example of the *folkhemmeti* narrative, which blends together welfare chauvinist and conservative ideas in order to locate the *folkhemmet* within an alternative far-right populist frame.

The far-right populist narrative and storytelling, so crucial to the construction of a 'self' as well as an 'other' (Ochs, 1998), are appropriated in the telling of the story on the bases of certain experiences, granting the reflective rights only to those with particular, narrow, ethnic and cultural affiliation with the nation state. The far-right populist narrative draws on two fundamental critiques. First, that the political and policy elite in charge of welfare design and deliver it in ways that undermine the interests of the native common man. Second, these elites have, under the guises of multiculturalism, enabled immigration, which in turn dilutes the quality of the welfare available.

As the case of Sweden further demonstrates, by drawing on these two broad narratives, the welfare nationalism of Sweden Democrats is rewriting the narrative around social policy to steer away from social democratic narratives and neoliberal narratives to focus more on ethnicity and culture as a foundation for both access to and the nature of social welfare.

References

Akkerman, T. and Rooduijn, M. (2015) 'Pariahs or partners? Inclusion and exclusion of radical right parties and the effects on their policy positions', *Political Studies*, vol 63, no 5, pp 1140-57.

Alesina, A. and Glaeser, E. (2004) *Fighting poverty in the US and Europe: A world of difference*, Oxford: Oxford University Press.

Alvesson, M. and Sköldberg, K (2003) *Reflexive methodology: New vistas for qualitative research*, London: Sage.

Andersen, J.G. and Bjørklund, T. (1990) 'Structural changes and new cleavages: The Progress Parties in Denmark and Norway', *Acta Sociologica*, vol 33, no 3, pp 195-217.

Andersen, J.G. and Bjørklund, T. (2000) 'Radical right-wing populism in Scandinavia: from tax revolt to neo-liberalism and xenophobia', in P. Hainsworth (ed) *In the politics of the extreme right: From the margins to the mainstream*, London and New York: Pinter, pp 193-223.

Béland, D. (2005) 'The politics of social policy language', *Social Policy & Administration*, vol 45, no 1, pp 1-18.

Béland, D. (2009) 'Gender, ideational analysis, and social policy', *Social Politics*, vol 16, no 4, pp 558-81.

Béland, D. and Cox, R.H. (2011) *Ideas and politics in social science research*, New York: Oxford University Press.

Berezin, M. (2009) *Illiberal politics in neoliberal times: Culture, security and populism in the new Europe*, Cambridge: Cambridge University Press.

Betz, H.-G. (1994) *Radical right-wing populism in Western Europe*, New York: St Martin's Press.

Betz, H.-G. (2001) 'Exclusionary populism in Austria, Italy, and Switzerland', *International Journal*, vol 56, no 3, pp 393-420.

Blyth, M. (2002) *Great transformations: Economic ideas and institutional change in the twentieth century*, Cambridge: Cambridge University Press.

Brubaker, W.R. (1992) *Citizenship and nationhood in France and Germany*, Cambridge: Cambridge University Press.

Burstein, P. (1998) 'Bringing the public back in: should sociologists consider the impact of public opinion on public policy?', *Social Forces*, vol 77, pp 27-62.

Canovan, M. (1999) 'Trust the people! Populism and the two faces of democracy', *Political Studies*, vol 47, no 1, pp 2-16.

Careja, R., Elmelund-Praestekaer, C., Baggesen Klitgaard, M. and Gahner Larsen, E. (2016) 'Direct and indirect welfare chauvinism as party strategies: An analysis of the Danish People's Party', *Scandinavian Political Studies*, vol 39, no 4, pp 435-57.

Cox, R.H. (2001) 'The social construction of an imperative: Why welfare reform happened in Denmark and the Netherlands but not in Germany?', *World Politics*, vol 53, no 3, pp 463-98.

Daviter, F. (2007) 'Policy framing in the European Union', *Journal of European Public Policy*, vol 14, no 4, pp 654-66.

de Koster, W., Achterberg, P. and van der Waal, J. (2013) 'The new right and the welfare state: The electoral relevance of welfare chauvinism and welfare populism in the Netherlands', *International Political Science Review*, vol 34, no 1, pp 3-20.

Delanty, G. (2008) 'Fear of others: Social exclusion and the European crisis of solidarity', *Social Policy & Administration*, vol 42, no 6, pp 676-90.

Durnova, A. and Zittoun, P. (2010) 'Introduction: Interpretive policy analysis in a French setting. The Fifth Interpretive Policy Analysis Conference, Grenoble, June 2010', *Critical Policy Studies*, vol 5, no 2, pp 103-5.

Eikemo T. and Bambra C. (2008) 'The welfare state; A glossary for public health', *Journal of Epidemiology & Community Health*, vol 62, no 1, pp 2-6.

Ennser-Jedenastik, L. (2016) 'A welfare state for whom? A group-based account of the Austrian Freedom Party's policy profile', *Swiss Political Science Review*, vol 22, no 3, pp 409-27.

Ennser-Jedenastik, L. (2017) 'Welfare chauvinism in populist radical right platforms: The role of redistributive justice principles', *Social Policy & Administration*, vol 52, no 1, pp 293-314.

Esping-Andersen, G. (1990) *The three worlds of welfare capitalism*, Cambridge: Polity Press.

Gabriel, Y. (2004) 'Narratives, stories and texts', in D. Gran, C. Hardy, C. Oswick and L.L. Putnam (eds) *The Sage handbook of organizational discourse*, London: Sage, pp 61-79.

Gee, J.P. (1999) *An introduction to discourse analysis: Theory and method*, London: Routledge.

Goffman, E. (1974) *Frame analysis*, New York: Harper Books.

Hall, P.A. (1993) 'Policy paradigms, social learning and the state: The case of economic policymaking in Britain', *Comparative Politics*, vol 25, no 3, pp 275-96.

Hansen, R. and King, D. (2001) 'Eugenic ideas, political interests, and policy variance: Immigration and sterilization policy in Britain and the US', *World Politics*, vol 53, no 2, pp 237-63.

Heracleous, L.Th. (2004) 'Interpretivist approaches to organizational discourses', in D. Gran, C. Hardy, C. Oswick and L.L. Putnam (eds) *The Sage handbook of organizational discourse*, London: Sage, pp 175-92.

Jaworski, A. and Coupland, N. (2000) 'Introduction: Perspectives on discourse analysis', in A. Jaworskis and N. Couplands (eds) *The discourse reader*, London/New York: Routledge, pp 1-35.

Jungar, A.C. and Jupskås, A.R. (2014) 'Populist radical right parties in the Nordic region: A new and distinct party family?', *Scandinavian Political Studies*, vol 37, no 3, pp 215-38.

Keskinen, S. (2016) 'From welfare nationalism to welfare chauvinism: Economic rhetoric, the welfare state and changing asylum policies in Finland', *Critical Social Policy,* vol 36, no 3, pp 352-70.

Kestilä, E. and Söderlund, P. (2007) 'Local determinants of radical right-wing voting: The case of the Norwegian progress party', *West European Politics*, vol 30, no 3, pp 549-57.

Laclau, E. (2005) *On populist reason*, London: Verso.

Lefkofridi, Z. and Michel, E. (2014) *Exclusive solidarity? Radical right parties and the welfare state*, EUI Working Paper 2014/120, San Domenico di Fiesole, Italy: Robert Schuman Centre for Advanced Studies, European University Institute.

Marshall, T.H. (1950) *Citizenship and social class and other essays*, London: Cambridge University Press.

Mau, S. and Burkhardt, C. (2009) 'Migration and welfare state solidarity in Western Europe', *Journal of European Social Policy*, vol 19, no 3, pp 213-29.

Meny, Y. and Surel, Y. (eds) (2000) *Democracies and the populist challenge*, London: Palgrave.

Mudde, C. (2000) *The ideology of the extreme right*, Manchester: Manchester University Press.

Mudde, C. (2004) 'The populist Zeitgeist', *Government and Opposition*, vol 39, no 4, pp 542-63.

Mudde, C. (2007) *Populist radical right parties in Europe*, Cambridge/ New York: Cambridge University Press.

Mudde, C. (2010) 'The populist radical right: A pathological normalcy', *West European Politics*, vol 33, no 6, pp 1167-86.

Müller, J.W. (2016) 'Capitalism in one family', *London Review of Books*, vol 38, no 23, pp 10-14.

Nordensvard, J. and Ketola, M. (2015) 'Nationalist reframing of the Finnish and Swedish welfare states: the nexus of nationalism and social policy in far-right populist parties', *Social Policy & Administration*, vol 49, no 3, pp 356-75.

Norocel, O.C. (2016) 'Populist radical right protectors of the folkhem: Welfare chauvinism in Sweden', *Critical Social Policy*, vol 36, no 3, pp 371-90.

Ochs, E. (1998) 'Narrative', in T.A. van Dijks (ed) *Discourse as structure and process. Discourse studies: A multidisciplinary introduction. Volume 1*, London: Sage Publications, pp 185-207.

Peirce, C. (1992) *The essential Peirce: Selected philosophical writings, Volume 1 (1867–1893)*, Bloomington, IN: Indiana University Press.

Rein, M. and Schön, D.A. (1991) 'Frame-reflective policy discourse', in P. Wagner, C.H. Weiss, B. Wittrock and H. Wollman (eds) *Social sciences and the modern state: National experiences and theoretical crossroads*, Cambridge: Cambridge University Press.

Rein, M. and Schön, D.A. (1996) 'Frame-critical policy analysis and frame-reflective policy practice', *Knowledge and Policy*, vol 9, pp 85-104.

Roe, E. (1994) *Narrative policy analysis: Theory and practice*, London: Duke University Press.

Rooduijn, M. (2014) 'The nucleus of populism: in search of the lowest common denominator', *Government and Opposition*, vol 49, no 4, pp 573-99.

Rothstein, B. and Stolle, D. (2003) 'Social capital, impartiality and the welfare state: An institutional approach'. in M. Hooghe and D. Stolle (eds) *Generating social capital*, New York: Palgrave Macmillan, pp 191-210.

Rothstein, B. and Uslaner, E.M. (2005) 'All for one: equality, corruption, and social trust', *World Politics*, vol 58, no 1, pp 41-72.

Rydgren, J. (2002) 'Radical right populism in Sweden: Still a failure, but for how long?', *Scandinavian Political Studies*, vol 25, no 1, pp 27-56.

Rydgren, J. (2005) *Radical right-wing populism in Sweden and Denmark*, Beer Sheva: The Centre for the Study of European Politics and Society, Ben Gurion University.

Rydgren, J. (2007) 'Explaining the emergence of radical right-wing populist parties: case of Denmark', *West European Politics*, vol 27, no 3, pp 474-502.

Sainsbury, D. (2006) 'Immigrants' social rights in comparative perspective: welfare regimes, forms in immigration and immigration policy regimes', *Journal of European Social Policy*, vol 16, no 3, pp 229-44.

Schierup, C.-U., Hansen, P. and Castles, S. (2006) *Migration, citizenship, and the European welfare state: A European dilemma*, Oxford: Oxford University Press.

Schmidt, F. (2017) 'Drivers of populism: a four-country comparison of party communication in the run-up to the 2014 European Parliament elections', *Political Studies*, doi: 10.1177/0032321717723506.

Schumacher, G. and van Kersbergen, K. (2016) 'Do mainstream parties adapt to the welfare chauvinism of populist parties?', *Party Politics*, vol 22, no 3, pp 300-12.

Snow, D.A. and Benford, R.D. (1992) 'Master frames and cycles of protest', in A.D. Morris and C. McClurg Mueller (eds) *Frontiers in social movement theory*, New Haven, CT: Yale University Press, pp 133-55.

Spinney, A. and Nethery, A. (2013) '"Taking our houses": Perceptions of the impact of asylum seekers, refugees and new migrants on housing assistance in Melbourne', *Social Policy and Society*, vol 12, no 2, pp 179-89.

Stanley, B. (2008) 'The thin ideology of populism', *Journal of Political Ideologies*, vol 13, no 1, pp 95-110.

Sverigedemokraterna (2010) *99-förslag för ett bättre Sverige. Sverigedemokraternas kontrakt med väljarna 2010–2014 [99 suggestions for a better Sweden. Swedish Democrats' contract with voters 2010–2014]*, Stockholm: Sverigedemokraterna.

Sverigedemokraterna (2011) *Sverigedemokraternas principprogram 2011 [Programme of principles]*, Stockholm: Sverigedemokraterna.

Sverigedemokraterna (2012) 'Stora besparingar till följd av minskad invandring' (www.sverigedemokraterna.se).

Taggart, P. (1996) *The new populism and the new politics: New protest parties in Sweden in a comparative perspective*, Basingstoke: Palgrave Macmillan.

Todorov, T. (1977) *The poetics of prose*, Hoboken, NJ: Wiley-Blackwell.

van der Waal, J., Achterberg, P. and Houtman, D. (2010) '"Some are more equal than others": economic egalitarianism and welfare chauvinism in the Netherlands', *Journal of European Social Policy*, vol 20, no 4, pp 350-63.

van der Waal, J., de Koster, W. and van Oorschot, W. (2013) 'Three worlds of welfare chauvinism? How welfare regimes affect support for distributing welfare to immigrants in Europe', *Journal of Comparative Policy Analysis: Research and Practice*, vol 15, no 2, pp 164-81.

van Oorschot, W. (2006) 'Making the difference in social Europe: Deservingness perceptions among citizens of European welfare states', *Journal of European Social Policy*, vol 16, no 1, pp 23-42.

Wagner, A. (2004) 'Redefining citizenship for the 21st century: from the National Welfare State to the UN Global Compact', *International Journal of Social Welfare*, vol 13, no 4, pp 278-86.

Westlind, D. (1996) *The politics of popular identity: Understanding recent populist movements in Sweden and the United States*, Lund: Lund University Press.

NINE

What is 'impact'?
Learning from examples across the
professional life course

Tina Haux

Impact as a measure of academic work

The inclusion of research impact as the third element of the assessment of research excellence and research environment in the 2014 Research Excellence Framework in the UK (REF2014) has sparked debates around the definition, attribution and measurement of impact (see, among others, Holmwood, 2011; Brown, 2012; Borman, 2013; Penfield et al, 2014). In particular, the escalating costs of preparing a REF submission for departments (Sayer, 2015), the impact on individual careers when used as a managerialist tool (Docherty, quoted in Morrish 2015), the 'artificial, if not arbitrary' time limits on impact (Watermeyer, 2014), and incentivising a focus on current, safe, policy-relevant issues at the expense of more radical, and potentially uncertain, blue sky thinking (Smith and Stewart, 2016) have attracted critical commentary.

The initial announcement of the addition of 'impact' to the measurement of academic work was greeted with scepticism at best by the academic community (see, among others, Holmwood, 2011). Since then, the notion of measuring the influence of academics beyond academia has become more accepted. Nevertheless, there remains disquiet and discussion about what 'impact' is and how it can be measured. Martin (2011) argues that the current conceptualisation and proposed measurement of impact within the REF2014 suggested 'a linear model of how knowledge from an individual piece of research is subsequently taken up and used' (2011, p 250). Others have argued that impact can be 'conditional, even serendipitous' (Brewer, 2011), that it can be negative (the study on the supposed link between autism and the MMR vaccine being perhaps the most famous recent example), depends on the political leaning and agenda of respective governments (Brewer,

2011), does not sufficiently account for the time lag and cumulative nature of research and thus creates problems of attribution (Penfield et al, 2014) and does not capture excellence in teaching and curriculum development (Wade, 2013). Furthermore, Martin (2011) argues that any attempt to measure impact for REF purposes will become more cumbersome with each iteration, and that soon any 'impact' will be outweighed by the cost of the exercise.

Aims and objectives

The aim of this chapter is to examine the nature and scale of the impact of academic work on policy and practice outside academia. The objectives are to investigate how impact has been defined, how it has been achieved and by whom, and to develop a framework to compare the scale of impact achieved. The data sources for the analysis are highly ranked impact case studies from the Social Policy and Social Work REF2014 as well as the Economic and Social Research Council (ESRC) Early Career Impact Award prizewinners from the past four years, 2013–17.

What counts as impact?

Even though impact has been assessed in the REF2014, its interpretation and measurement remain elusive. For the purposes of the REF2014 impact has been defined as:

> … the "reach and significance" of impacts on the economy, society and/or culture that were underpinned by excellent research conducted in the submitted unit, as well as the submitted unit's approach to enabling impact from its research. (HEFCE, 2011, p 6)

The definition of impact in the REF2014 was deliberately broad, meaning that a whole range of activities and outcomes were captured. Tinkler (2012) argues that 'reach' stands for the extent and diversity of the beneficiaries of the impact while 'significance' represents the degree to which impact has been achieved through informing, enriching or changing public policy. Both are therefore viewed as components of demonstrating change.

Common features of guidance on impact are threefold: (1) that the researchers should be able to articulate the impact of their research beyond academia; (2) an assumption (sometimes explicit/ sometimes implicit) that this research will/should be uniformly positive (although 'for whom' remains unspecified); and (3) a belief that the distribution of research funding should (at least to some extent) reflect the researchers' ability to achieve 'impact' (Smith and Stewart, 2016, p 3).

The design of impact case studies in the REF2014 is based on a forward-looking approach using pieces of research as a starting point and then assessing its impact on subsequent policy-making and policy debates (Nutley et al, 2007). The main alternative is to take a policy change as a starting point and then to trace the influence on that policy change back to influential sources, academic and otherwise (Nutley et al, 2007). Capturing the use of research in the community is attempted by inviting policy users, for example, from the voluntary sector, to the academic panels. However, due to a 1:12 user-to-academics ratio and the general deference to research quality on both sides, their inclusion may have been mainly ceremonial, according to Watermeyer and Hedgecoe (2016). In their ethnographic study, they observed a university pilot exercise to evaluate potential impact case studies as well as interviews with (academic and user) REF panel members. The judgements on the quality of the underlying research strongly influenced the perception of the impact of said research. In other words, if the underlying research was perceived to be of high quality, for example, if it was published in a high-ranking journal, then the impact case study in that pilot exercise was much more likely to receive a high score. This was due, in part, to the difficulty of obtaining any/sufficient/convincing evidence (Watermeyer and Hedgecoe, 2016), but probably also due to the absence of a clear definition and agreed parameters for evaluating impact.

There have been a number of attempts to summarise and analyse the REF2014 impact case studies both as a whole as well as submissions by specific academic disciplines or professions. For example, previous analysis focused on an overview of all the case studies (Grant, 2015), the assessment process (Manville et al, 2015; Watermeyer and Hedgecoe, 2016), institutional contexts and strategies (Wilkinson, 2017) as well as more specifically on the REF impact of particular professions (Kelly et al, 2016, on nursing; Marcella et al, 2016, on information research; Ross and Morrow, 2016, on leadership in higher education; Syed and Davies, 2016, on business schools), research groups (Biri et al, 2014) or particular issues (Fordham and Noble, 2016, on end-of-life care). The number of studies focusing on research around health is striking, as is the absence of any analysis of the Social Policy REF impact case studies. Smith and Stewart (2016) identified the key concerns of social policy academics regarding the introduction of impact assessment into the REF2014, and cross checked those concerns against a selection of impact case studies submitted to the Social Policy and Social Work unit of assessment that received the best and worst ratings. Their brief analysis of the impact case studies confirms many of the points raised by the interviewees as well as other literature, for example, research critical of government being less likely to have an impact, an over-emphasis on instrumental and conceptual use of research, a link between the rating of the research and the impact case study, the absence of an ethics or contextual statement, an over-representation of national versus local impact, a lack of diversity in terms of the ethnic composition (although less so with regard to gender), and a reification of existing elites (Smith and Stewart, 2016). On the basis of the interviews, they have developed an impact ladder in which the degree and significance of impact move in the opposite direction to the ability to demonstrate said impact. For example, a policy report commissioned by a policy source is at the bottom of the ladder in terms of the degree and significance of the impact but at the top in terms of the ability to demonstrate impact, for example, through specific research reports. Conversely, changing the overall paradigm in which policy-makers think about an issue can only be demonstrated through the use of different language by policy-makers

Morton (2015a) has developed an alternative framework called the Research Contributions Framework (RCF). The key aims of this alternative framework are to better capture timing, attribution and context (Morton 2015a, b). Morton (2015a) distinguishes in her framework between research uptake, research use and impact. *Research uptake* is defined as: 'research users have engaged with the research: they have read a briefing, attended a conference … or engaged in some other activity which means they know the research exists' (Morton, 2015a, p 406). *Research use*, in contrast, is defined as 'research users *act* upon the research, discuss it, pass it on to others, adapt it to context, present findings, use it to inform policy, or practice developments' (Morton, 2015a, p 406; emphasis added). Finally, *research impact* 'changes awareness, knowledge and understanding, ideas, attitudes and perceptions, and policy and practice as a result of the research' (Morton, 2015a, p 406; emphasis added). The RCF was developed on the basis of an in-depth analysis of the impact of a small number of research programmes (Morton, 2015b).

Both the impact ladder by Smith and Stewart (2016) and the RCF by Morton (2015a, b) are useful starting points for the analysis of

Social Policy impact case studies. Both engage with the nature and demonstrability of impact perhaps more than how the impact has been achieved in terms of the nature of the underlying research, and both suggest a hierarchy of impact. The contribution of this chapter is an analysis and comparison of 'successful' Social Policy impact case studies with the aim of analysing and drawing links between the what, how and who of policy impact.

Methodology

The analysis in this chapter is based on two sources: first, on the rich and publicly available data of the REF2014 impact case studies. The REF2014 was set up as a 'process of expert review' (HEFCE, 2017b). Work was submitted to 34 subject-based units of assessment that were grouped into four main panels. Panel members consisted of senior academics, international members and research users (HEFCE, 2017b). The latter could be representatives from industry or the voluntary sector, for example, and their involvement focused on the assessment of the impact case studies. The ESRC Early Career Impact Award case studies have been included in the analysis to explore differences in impact achievement over the life course of an academic. These case studies have been assembled for a specific purpose and within a particular context (see also Smith and Stewart 2016), some of which is problematic. While the case studies themselves are publicly available, the supporting evidence is not, and this is a limitation of the analysis discussed later on.

Submissions to the Social Policy and Social Work panel were chosen for the following reasons: the impact case studies received higher scores than those submitted to the Sociology or Politics and International Relations sub-panels (THE, 2014). The higher scores may be a reflection of disciplinary orientation, that is, that for many social policy scholars, influencing the way policy is designed and implemented has always been one of their core aims (Page, 2010). Furthermore, social policy was one of the disciplines included in the REF impact pilot (HEFCE, 2014), and therefore as a discipline has had the advantage of learning from this exercise.

The focus in this chapter is on the top-ranked Social Policy impact case studies taken from REF2014. The five universities in REF2014 in the Social Policy and Social Work panel that performed most strongly were Oxford, the London School of Economics and Political Science (LSE), York, University of East Anglia (UEA) and Kent (see Table 9.1). Measuring impact as part of measuring research excellence was a new addition in 2014. The results of the impact case studies made up 20 per cent of the overall weighting. Each submission from a university to a sub-panel had to include a minimum of two case studies. If the submission included 15 academics or more, additional impact case studies needed to be submitted proportionally to the number of staff submitted (for further information, see REF2014, no date). Therefore, a better selection framework than the overall REF ranking for the purpose of this chapter is how well the universities did on impact specifically. When focusing on impact, four universities, which received a 100 per cent assessment for their impact activities, stand out: LSE, York, Oxford and University College London (UCL). Seven other universities achieved a 4★ rating for between 80 and 93 per cent of their impact case studies. Thereafter, Ulster came in at 67 per cent of 4★ research activity, that is, a noticeable drop-off. I have therefore chosen as the sample for this chapter the impact submissions from the 11 universities that scored 80 per cent or more on them. The sample includes 11 universities and a total of 38 case studies. As Table 9.1 demonstrates, the overall impact score is frequently but not always mirrored in a very good overall ranking,

Table 9.1: Impact and REF rankings based on the REF2014

University	% of impact case studies receiving 4* rating	Position in overall ranking
LSE	100	2
York	100	3
Oxford	100	1
UCL	100	11
Kent	93	5
Loughborough	90	19
Bath	84	=6
Dundee	80	37
UEA	80	4
Glasgow Caledonian	80	35
South Wales	80	=26
Ulster	67	=22
Strathclyde	63	=22
Nottingham	60	12

Notes: = refers to a joint position, for example, Ulster and Strathclyde were both ranked 22nd.

Source: Author, based on THE (2014)

for example, as in the case of LSE, Oxford, York and Kent. Obvious exceptions to this are South Wales and Glasgow Caledonian University, ranked joint 22nd in their overall REF score, and having had 80 per cent of their impact case studies rated as 4★ (see the Appendix at the end of this chapter for a full list).

The second source of impact case studies is drawn from the ESRC Impact Early Career Award prizewinners and runners-up. These have been included in order to be able to gauge impact across the different career stages of the academics. A full list of the winners and runners-up can be found in Table 9.4 later. The impact case studies from both sources have been analysed thematically using NVivo.

What counts as impact: measuring the scale of impact

When examining the *nature* of the impact achieved in the Social Policy and Social Work panel of REF2014 submissions, the following four groupings emerge: *policy creation*, *policy direction*, *policy discourse* and *policy practice* (see Table 9.3 later). The first group, *policy innovation*, is perhaps the most obvious but also the least frequent, and it is worth noting that the examples are spread all over the globe rather than being focused on the UK, as with the majority of the other examples. The claim made here is no less than that the research has directly led to a new policy being introduced. Examples that fall under this heading are the introduction of Universal Credit in the UK, trauma intervention in Palestine and anti-poverty interventions in sub-Saharan Africa. There are only two examples where a UK government has introduced a new policy or abolished an existing policy. The other examples refer to the European Union (EU) and other countries where at times external donors have financed the new policy. Therefore, achieving this kind of impact in terms of reach and significance can be particularly difficult, both in terms of the timing and policy openings, but also being able to attribute change on this scale to an individual or group of academics.

A number of studies claimed to have provided evidence on the different policy options to inform the decision-making and the *policy direction* (see Table 9.2). In other words, the claimed impact is to have shaped part of a policy rather than having provided the impetus through the research to introduce a whole new policy, thus smaller in scale. This category contains some of the most interesting examples, in my view, in that one case study claimed to have prevented a policy change that would have had detrimental effects, while another argued that it helped maintain the status quo. The latter argument is particularly reliant on supporting statements, as the claimed success is the absence of visible change. Influencing the direction can happen at different stages of the policy process. The target audience for this type of impact has tended to be the UK government.

The third group contains case studies that claim to have changed the *policy discourse* in terms of the framing of a group or an issue as well as through having contributed different policy options to existing discourse. In other words, the change is in how policies or social groups are being discussed rather than the nature of the policies themselves. Examples in this category vary in terms of the extent of the change in policy direction. At one end of the spectrum a new group is now regularly consulted about policy changes; at the other end the language of the reporting about a group has changed. The majority of the examples fall somewhere in the middle in terms of having either costed policy options, developed new/improved quantitative measurements for a phenomenon (usually commissioned) or provided an independent analysis of a contentious event/phenomenon. The inclusion of the development of new indicators for measuring existing concepts in this category is slightly problematic, but the argument is made that a new way of measurement, for example, of child wellbeing, first results in a new discourse itself and then enshrines it in future policy discourse through the regular publication of the figures. The audience for the change in policy discourse are key members of the policy-making community, that is, the government, MPs, civil servants, think tanks and the voluntary sector.

The final set of case studies is directed at the *policy practice* of professionals, mostly social workers and the police. The change that has supposedly been affected is to a particular group of professionals rather than (part of) a policy or policy discourse. It contains examples of (commissioned) reviews of practice, changes to practice guidance through new research as well as the development of different toolkits. The target audience for this last set of case studies have been the professional bodies.

Table 9.2 can be read as a hierarchy of impact, and this seems to be justified when focusing on policy discourse, policy direction and policy creation, with the latter most likely to be the most significant. Yet the impact on policy practice sits oddly at the bottom of the list. The categories relate to Nutley et al's (2007) model of conceptual versus instrumental impact in that the instrumental presentation and use of impact links to the policy direction and policy practice categories while the conceptual contribution of research in terms of awareness,

Table 9.2: Different types of policy impact, with examples

Type of impact	Examples
Policy creation	Universal Credit Justice deliberations in Afghanistan R&D in antibiotics Support for AIDS-affected children Microfinance Tackling extreme poverty War trauma treatment Abolition of the Child Support Agency
Policy direction	Modelling care needs Personal Independence Payment evaluation Microfinance: double bottom line Modelling options for financing long-term care Lone-parent policies Identifying high-risk children Disability Living Allowance/Attendance Allowance re-focusing 'Shortage occupation' migration policy Deprivation index Identifying successful parenting interventions Crime modelling Individual Budget evaluation Child wellbeing indicators Influence health policy on smoking Million-pound donors
Policy discourse	Children's experience of poverty Riots Poverty Child wellbeing Fuel poverty Decriminalisation of drugs Minimum Income Standard
Policy practice	Stop and search Justice deliberation Self-evaluation by older people Social workers' judgement Homicide investigations Intimate partner violence 'Designing' out crime Extension of treatment for mental health Child protection practice Adult Support and Protection Toolkit New interventions in instances of intimate partner violence Adult Social Care Outcomes Toolkit (ASCOT) Practice tools to improve safeguarding children Improving service delivery and guidance used by individuals with intellectual and development disabilities Training for social workers working in child protection

knowledge and understanding, ideas, attitudes and perceptions apply to the policy discourse category. One of the key differences to the hierarchical structure proposed by Smith and Stewart (2016) is that it places changing policy discourse below influencing policy direction. This is due to greater value being placed on change in policy elements over the discourse, given that the latter may or may not lead to policy change in the future.

Bringing the case studies together like this hides their *diversity*. Among those who claim to have instigated a new policy or a change in policy direction there are two clear sub-groups. The first treats the policy intervention as the impact and the case study therefore contains an evaluation of the policy against the stated goals. The change in behaviour and practice identified by Morton (2015a) is the policy implementation/ delivery, and the outcomes/contributions of the policy intervention are operationalised as the difference it has made to the lives of those targeted. The second group treats the policy change itself as the impact and therefore documents the influence on decision-makers through citations and letters of recommendation. The latter could be due to timing; for example, in some cases the policy has not been fully implemented and/ or the evaluations have not been carried out. However, it therefore leaves the question open as to whether the policy was a success compared to its original or subsequent intentions. This then re-opens the questions of impact: does only policy success count, and if so, who defines what counts as success and how, if at all, can the effect of the policy context on the subsequent design and implementation of a policy be accounted for? For research activities directed at professional bodies, impact is easier to demonstrate in terms of the proportion of professional groups that have taken up a new intervention or toolkit and the extent of changes or additions to the professional guidance. However, as with the second group, introducing the changes in guidance/toolkit, and so on is constructed as the policy change, while evidence of actual change in daily practice and any impact on the lives of users tends to be missing.

Regarding the demonstration of achievement and the geographical reach/audience of the work of academics analysed here, three observations stand out. The first is that the vast majority of the impact case studies have been directed at the UK government, as to be expected. The second is that there seems to be a clear language and perhaps cultural/institutional element that explains whether research found its way into other countries, with the next biggest group of countries being the Anglo-Saxon countries, predominantly the US but also Australia, New Zealand and Canada. The EU featured in only two case studies, as did the Scottish Parliament, while the Welsh Assembly did not appear at all in this selection. Finally, another substantial group of case studies claimed to have had impact in a substantial number of countries across the world. Therefore, overall it is fair to say that the case studies with the highest ratings have a particular focus on Westminster, but that a substantial proportion reached a truly international audience. The absence of the EU from most case studies examined here is somewhat surprising as it is otherwise comparable to the UK Parliament as a decision-making body that can be directly targeted by research dissemination and where impact can be evidenced through citations and supportive letters. It therefore raises the question as to whether the low number reflects an absence of engagement rather than an absence of demonstrable impact. Engagement with the EU was more prominent in the impact case studies submitted to other sub-panels, for example, Politics and International Relations.

How has impact been achieved, and by whom?

The focus on how impact has been achieved highlights the usefulness of different types of policy impact but also the importance of research capacity. Table 9.3 links different activities to the four types of impact identified in the discussion of the different types of impact above.

Perhaps more interesting, however, is a look at *who* achieved this kind of impact. Analysis as to whether case studies were attributed to individuals rather than teams suggests that the majority of submissions were based on the work of research teams, frequently based at different

Table 9.3: How impact is achieved

Type of impact	Methods
Policy creation	Communicating policy idea through think tanks Working with sponsors to introduce policy
Policy direction	Modelling options Assessing impact Evaluating pilots
Policy discourse	Developing new indicators Drawing attention to a particular issue or group Evaluating practice in other countries
Policy practice	Developing new toolkits Identifying new issues Reviewing current practice

universities. This did not seem to vary systematically across the different types of impact. However, it was noticeable that the examples for influencing the policy direction come disproportionately from research units within universities, such as the Social Policy Research Unit (SPRU) at York and the Centre for Health Service Studies (CHSS) at LSE and Kent. Research units represent a large infrastructure investment by universities and have the ability to carry out evaluations, which can, in turn, inform future policy, but have less of a focus on producing publications in high-quality journals. This is in contrast to research in the policy discourse category, which has predominantly been produced outside research units.

Another dimension worth considering is the 'commissioning of impact'. In a number of instances the government of the day commissioned (senior) academics to carry out reviews of policy issues, for example, the development of a new way of measuring a phenomenon or a review of practice. As long as there is no change of government in the interim, these recommendations tend to be implemented as the authors of such reviews tend to be carefully chosen and to be in close communication with civil servants and ministers about their thinking. Therefore, it is clear that the research has had impact in the sense that it has led to a change of policy or practice. Not only is the research likely to be delivered in a 'policy-ready' format (Brown, 2012), but policy-makers are also ready for it as they commissioned the research and thereby usually defined the question to be answered but have often also been supportive in other ways, for example, provided access to data that might not otherwise be easily obtainable. This is very different from an issue being highlighted by an academic/s that then has to be brought to the attention of policy-makers. While across the impact case studies examined in this chapter there has tended to be a range of seniority, the 'commissioned' impact tends to be limited to very senior academics.

To counterbalance the focus on senior academics whose work tends to be featured in the impact case studies, the following section moves beyond the REF2014 and investigates the ESRC Early Career Impact Award case studies. The inclusion of impact in the REF has influenced academic culture and allowed a new group of research stars to emerge, namely, younger scholars focusing on impact. In the following section the winners of the ESRC Early Career Impact Award Prize have been analysed to compare their 'impact' achievements to those in the REF2014 Social Policy case studies. As mentioned before, the definition of impact by the ESRC (2017) is slightly different than that of HEFCE's:

The impact of social science research can be categorised as:

- *Instrumental:* influencing the development of policy, practice or service provision, shaping legislation, altering behaviour
- *Conceptual:* contributing to the understanding of policy issues, reframing debates
- *Capacity building:* through technical and personal skill development.

The prizes were launched in 2013 and the prizewinners by year, institution and topics are listed in Table 9.4.

When analysing the ESRC Early Career Impact Award case studies, it seems the impact was achieved through either having highlighted:

- a new/under-researched phenomenon (foodbanks, rape of older people), or

Table 9.4: ESRC Early Career Impact Award prizewinners, 2013–17

Year	Name	Topic	Institution	Category
2017	Harriet Thomson	Fuel poverty in EU countries	University of Manchester	Winner
	Hannah Bows	Rape of older people	University of Durham	Runner-up
2016	Kath Murray	Stop and search by police in Glasgow	University of Edinburgh	Winner
	Martin Hearson	Tax treaties between developed and developing countries	LSE	Runner-up
2015	Jennifer Doyle	Linking social housing and social service provision	University of Manchester	Winner
	Oliver Owen	Nigerian police practice	University of Oxford	Runner-up
2014	Hannah Lambie-Mumford	Foodbanks	University of Sheffield	Winner
2013	John Jerrim	Links between educational background and attainment internationally	Institute of Education/UCL	Winner

- an incongruity (usually with the country in question doing worse, such as schools in England, stop and search in Scotland), or
- potential solutions (tax treaties, social housing and social service provision, fuel poverty in Europe and police practice) (see Table 9.5).

Table 9.5: Type of policy impact and examples by ESRC Early Career Impact Award prizewinners

Type of impact	Examples
Policy creation	No examples
Policy direction	No examples
Policy discourse	Rape of older people Foodbanks Link between education and background Fuel poverty in Europe
Policy practice	Stop and search Social housing and social service provision Nigerian police practices Tax treaties

When comparing the kind of impact the ESRC Early Career Impact Award prizewinners have achieved to that submitted to the REF2014, a number of differences stand out. First, impact seems to be focused on challenging the policy discourse and addressing professional practice. This may be a reflection of their status because early career researchers are unlikely to be commissioned to carry out reviews that later inform policy directions. At the same time, the scope of impact demonstrated by these early career academics is impressive and may be a reflection of the enhanced importance given to impact as a result of its inclusion in the REF2014, and thus more awareness about its general relevance. In addition, there is now funding and training for impact available at many universities.

Conclusion: looking ahead to REF2021

Impact will form part of the next research assessment exercise, that is, REF2021 (HEFCE, 2017a). The definition of impact will be aligned with that of the research councils and also pay greater attention to public engagement and impact on teaching (HEFCE, 2017a). However, the ratio of case studies to research submissions as well as the timescales for when the research can have been carried out and when the impact can have taken place are likely to be similar to REF2014 (HEFCE, 2017a).

This therefore seems an appropriate moment to pause and reflect on the nature or 'significance' of impact and the effects of impact as an additional measurement of academic work.

Starting with the meaning of impact in social policy, the question is whether impact is the introduction of a new policy or the impact said policy has had. Morton's framework (2015a) considers not only the research uptake and research use, but also the research impact, and in her example refers to the impact of a policy change rather than the policy change itself (Morton, 2015b). In the context of the REF2014 it has been left ambiguous as to whether impact refers to the change of policy/direction/discourse/practice or the impact the change has had, and examples of case studies receiving high scores include both. The disparity is most visible among the examples of the first group, that is, the policy creation (see Table 9.1). In one group of examples the introduction of a policy is argued to be impact in itself. For example, the introduction of Universal Credit is claimed to be the impact of the academic work. The case study does not include any assessment of the impact of the policy itself, for example, the number of people affected, whether it improved their lives as intended and if so, by how much. This compares to other examples where impact is defined as the impact of the policy, that is, the impact case study for the measures introduced to support children affected by HIV contains evidence for the impact the policy itself has had on children's lives such as the number of children who have received treatment and the changes this has made to their wellbeing. It is worth noting that in the three instances where the impact case studies included the effect of the policies introduced (support for HIV-affected children, extreme poverty and war trauma-affected children), the research teams seem to have had considerable control over the design and implementation of the policy in a country. The same cannot be said for Universal Credit, making the headlines in the autumn of 2017 due to considerable delays in payments and emerging evidence of increasing hardship even where it is received. What might have seemed liked a good but challenging policy idea between 2012 and 2014, that is, the assessment period of the REF, would be viewed less favourably now.

Yet how significant in terms of the contribution of the research is change, if the government has requested research? This relates back to Smith and Stewart's (2016) emphasis on challenging and changing existing ideas as much as policy. Without having access to the testimonials and carrying out interviews with the officials involved at the time concerned, it is difficult to establish the extent to which the impact of research has been 'symbolic' (Watermeyer, 2014) or truly additional (Nutley et al, 2007). This demonstrates the limit of analysing the publicly available material of the REF2014, but also of the forward-looking approach chosen in the REF.

Moving on to the effects of the introduction of impact on academic work and life, the introduction of impact and possibly a Knowledge Exchange Framework (THE, 2017) takes place within the context of what some have called 'oppressive acceleration', 'quantitative control', marketisation and de-professionalisation (see Burrows, 2014; Vostal 2015). Measuring academic output has become a central feature of contemporary, neoliberal universities. Burrows (2014) argues that any single academic in the UK can potentially be measured against more than 100 different measures. The proliferation and flaws as well as the negative impact on academic life of the measures have been documented elsewhere (see Collini, 2013; Burrows, 2014; Vostal, 2015). At the same time, for many social policy scholars having an impact is the key reason for choosing the discipline in the first place, and the examples of the ESRC Early Career Impact Award prizewinners demonstrates that real excellence in impact can be found across the professional life course. Therefore, the increased recognition in terms of time, funding and promotion criteria arguably plays to the strengths and orientation of many social policy academics.

In summary, this chapter contains an attempt to analyse the nature and significance of impact, and sits alongside other work on impact of social policy and other disciplines. The story of the REF impact case studies analysed in this chapter includes elements of status and funding bringing advantages. However, the ESRC Early Career Impact Award case studies demonstrate that achieving impact is not limited to the later stages of the academic life course. The establishment and validation of impact as a measure of academic work as part of the REF and most research funders as well as universities' own measurement and validation of academic outputs means that all sides, from academics to universities and users, from new to old impact stars, will be better prepared for demonstrating impact in the REF2021. Demonstrating impact has become a far more resource-intensive exercise. Ironically it comes at a time when the possible impact on policy-making by the current government is likely to be limited given the spending constraints and ideological differences. And yet, there are opportunities and challenges in shaping social policies in post-Brexit Britain. Thus, is the golden era of impact only about to start?

References

Biri, D., Oliver, K.A. and Cooper, A. (2014) *What is the impact of BEAMS research? An evaluation of REF impact case studies from UCL BEAMS*, STEaPP Working Paper, London: Department of Science, Technology, Engineering and Public Policy, University College London.

Bormann, L. (2013) 'What is societal impact of research and how can it be assessed? A literature review', *Journal of the American Society for Information Science and Technology*, vol 64, no 2, pp 217-33.

Brewer, J.D. (2011) 'The impact of impact', *Research Evaluation*, vol 20, no 3, pp 255-6.

Brown, C. (2012) 'Exploring the concepts of knowledge adoption and conceptual impact: Impact for educational research submissions to the Research Excellence Framework 2014', *Education, Knowledge and Economy*, vol 5, no 3, pp 137-54.

Burrows, R. (2012) 'Living with the h-index? Metric assemblages in the contemporary academy', *The Sociological Review*, vol 60, no 2, pp 355-72.

Collini, S. (2013) 'Sold out', *London Review of Books*, vol 35, no 20 (www.lrb.co.uk/v35/n20/stefan-collini/sold-out).

ESRC (Economic and Social Research Council) (2017) 'What is impact?' (www.esrc.ac.uk/research/celebrating-impact-prize/what-is-impact/).

Fordham, F.T. and Noble, B. (2016) 'What is in a name? Evidence of impact in palliative and end-of-life care in the 2014 REF is difficult to find', *BMJ Supportive and Palliative Care*, vol 6, issue 3, pp 248-50.

Grant, J. (2015) *The nature, scale and beneficiaries of research impact: An initial analysis of Research Excellence Framework (REF) 2014 impact case studies*, London: King's College London and Digital Science (www.kcl.ac.uk/sspp/policy-institute/publications/Analysis-of-REF-impact.pdf).

HEFCE (Health Education Funding Council for England) (2011, updated 2012) *Assessment framework and guidance on submissions*, Bristol: HEFCE.

HEFCE (2014) 'Impact pilot exercise' (www.ref.ac.uk/2014/background/pilot/).

HEFCE (2017a) *Initial decisions on the Research Excellence Framework 2021*, Bristol: HEFCE (www.ref.ac.uk/media/ref,2021/downloads/REF2017_01.pdf).

HEFCE (2017b) 'What is the REF?' (www.ref.ac.uk/about/whatref/).

Holmwood, J. (2011) The impact of "impact" on UK social science', *Methodological Innovations Online*, vol 6, no 1, pp 13-17.

Kelly, D., Kent, B., McMahon, A., Taylor, J. and Traynor, M. (2016) 'Impact case studies submitted to REF 2014: The hidden impact of nursing research', *Journal of Research in Nursing*, vol 21, no 4, pp 256-68.

Manville, C., Guthrie, S., Henham, M.L., Garrod, B., Sousa, S., Kirtley, A., et al (2015) *Assessing impact submissions for REF 2014: An evaluation*, Cambridge: RAND Europe.

Marcella, R., Lockerbie, H. and Bloice, L. (2016) 'Beyond REF 2014: The impact of impact assessment on the future of information research', *Journal of Information Science*, vol 42, no 3, pp 369-85.

Martin, B.R. (2011) 'The Research Excellence Framework and the "impact agenda": Are we creating a Frankenstein monster?', *Research Evaluation*, vol 20, no 3, pp 247-54.

Morrish, L. (2014) 'Against REFonomics: Quantification cannot satisfy the demands of rationality, equity and tolerability', LSE Impact Blog, 22 December (http://blogs.lse.ac.uk/impactofsocialsciences/2014/12/22/refonomics-and-reformations/).

Morton, S. (2015a) 'Progressing research impact assessment: A "contributions" approach', *Research Evaluation*, vol 24, no 4, pp 405-19.

Morton, S. (2015b) 'Creating research impact: The roles of research users in interactive research mobilisation', *Evidence & Policy: A Journal of Research, Debate and Practice*, vol 11, no 1, pp 35-55.

Nutley, S., Walter, I. and Davies, H.T.O. (2007) *Using evidence: How research can inform public services*, Bristol: Policy Press.

Page, R.M. (2010) 'The changing face of social administration', *Social Policy & Administration*, vol 44, no 3, pp 326-42.

Penfield, T., Baker, M., Scobie, R. and Wykes, M. (2014) 'Assessment, evaluations, and definitions of research impact: A review', *Research Evaluation*, vol 23, pp 21-32.

REF2014 (no date) 'REF2014 impact case studies' (http://impact.ref.ac.uk/CaseStudies/FAQ.aspx).

Ross, F. and Morrow, E. (2016) 'Mining the REF impact case studies for lessons on leadership, governance and management in higher education', LSE Impact Blog, 8 June (http://eprints.lse.ac.uk/67282/).

Sayer, D. (2015) 'Why did REF2014 cost three times as much as the RAE? Hint: It's not just because of the added impact element', LSE Impact Blog, 3 August (http://blogs.lse.ac.uk/impactofsocialsciences/2015/08/03/why-did-the-2014-ref-cost-three-times-as-much-as-the-2008-rae-hint-its-not-just-because-of-impact/).

Smith, K.E. and Stewart, E. (2017) 'We need to talk about impact: Why social policy academics need to engage with the UK's Research Impact Agenda', *Journal of Social Policy*, vol 46, no 1, pp 109-27.

Syed, J. and Davies, J. (2016) 'Diversity in the authorship of journal articles and REF impact case studies: How are UK business schools shaping up?', in BAM (British Academy of Management) 2016 Conference Proceedings.

Tinkler, J. (2012) 'The REF doesn't capture what government wants from academics or how academic impact on policymaking takes place', British Politics and Policy at LSE (http://blogs.lse.ac.uk/politicsandpolicy/ref-academic-impact-policy-making-tinkler/).

THE (Times Higher Education) (2014) 'Research Excellence Framework 2014: Institutions ranked by subject', 17 December (www.timeshighereducation.com/sites/default/files/Attachments/2014/12/17/x/o/z/sub-14-01.pdf).

THE (2017) 'Jo Johnson plans for KEF to measure knowledge exchange', 12 October (www.timeshighereducation.com/jo-johnson-plans-kef-measure-knowledge-exchange).

Vostal, F. (2015) 'Academic life in the fast lane: the experience of time and speed in British academia', *Time & Society*, vol 24, no 1, pp 71-95.

Wade, P. (2013) 'The REF's narrow definition of impact ignores historical role of teaching in relation to the social impact of the university', LSE Impact Blog, 12 August (http://eprints.lse.ac.uk/72036/1/blogs.lse.ac.uk-The%20REFs%20narrow%20definition%20of%20impact%20ignores%20historical%20role%20of%20teaching%20in%20relation%20to%20the%20social%20im.pdf/).

Watermeyer, R. (2014) 'Issues in the articulation of "impact": the responses of UK academics to "impact" as a new measure of research assessment', *Studies in Higher Education*, vol 39, no 2, pp 359-77.

Watermeyer, R. and Hedgecoe, A. (2016) 'Selling "impact": peer reviewer projections of what is needed and what counts in REF impact case studies. A retrospective analysis', *Journal of Education Policy*, vol 31, no 5, pp 651-65.

Wilkinson, C. (2017) 'Evidencing impact: a case study of UK academic perspectives on evidencing research impact', *Studies in Higher Education*, pp 1-14.

Appendix: REF impact case studies from selected universities

University	Number	Topics
LSE	6	Better measures for fuel poverty
		Reading the riots
		Improving policy and practice to promote better mental health
		Shaping the financing of long-term care
		Child protection: improving practice
		Re-igniting R&D for antibiotics
York	4	Child support research and policy impacts
		The impact of research on child wellbeing
		Personalisation in health and social care: the Individual Budget evaluation
		Development of a 'single working-age benefit' and impact on welfare reform
Oxford	4	Regulating labour immigration: labour markets, welfare states and public policy
		Targeting resources and interventions in deprived areas using small area level indices of deprivation in the UK and South Africa
		Improving evidence-based policy and programming for AIDS-affected children in sub-Saharan Africa
		Reducing child anti-social behaviour through effective parenting interventions: internal impact on policy, practitioners and families
UCL	2	Situational crime prevention policy and practice
		Improving police practice and reducing the incidence of crime through mapping and analysis
Kent	6	Paying for social care
		Improving outcomes of social care services: the impact of ASCOT
		Million-pound donors: shaping policy and professional practices in philanthropy and fundraising from high net worth individuals
		Improving illicit drug policy
		Behaving badly? Managing challenging behaviour among people with intellectual and developmental disabilities (IDD)
		Empowering people with intellectual and developmental disabilities: the importance of community living and active support6

L'borough	2	Improving outcomes of services for children in need through research and changes in national and international practice
		Measuring poverty: A Minimum Income Standard for the UK
Bath	5	Improving the social performance of microfinance globally
		Encouraging policy-makers to listen to children when developing policies to address childhood poverty
		Reducing the tobacco industry's ability to influence public health policies
		Sustainable livelihoods and wellbeing
		Lone-parent families: work, welfare and wellbeing
Dundee	2	Protecting and supporting vulnerable adults in Scotland: impacting public policies, services, health and welfare
		Evidence-based model for child trauma in war-torn contexts
UEA	2	Influencing reform of disability benefits for older people
		Preventing child death from maltreatment
Glasgow Caledonian	2	Poverty: challenging perceptions and informing practice
		Transforming families: improving safety, minimising risk: how research has changed practice in interventions and assessment for intimate partner violence
South Wales	2	Contributions to new methods of homicide investigations
		A new hybrid model of the justice system in Afghanistan 2
Total	37	

Source: HEFCE (2015)

Part Three
Excavating social policy lessons from the New Labour era

James Rees

As L.P. Hartley famously wrote, 'The past is a foreign country', and indeed, surveying the current social policy landscape – rocked by populist insurgency and riven by social inequality and a variety of social tensions that were exposed by the fallout from the Brexit vote in June 2016 – it is often hard to believe that between 1997 and 2010 a 'New' Labour government seemed to have shifted the centre ground of British politics to a Third Way consensus that married economic growth, healthy tax receipts, re-investment in public services and expansion of a variety of novel social programmes. Today we frequently hear complaints about cronyism, failure to assess the impact of policy changes, and more broadly, a seemingly implacable austerity and deep cuts to even mainstream public services – these were all mirrored in the New Labour period by, at the very least, strong rhetoric about evidence-based policy, 'what works' evaluation, equality impact assessments, policy experimentation and consultation, and representativeness of public institutions.

Adding to the sense of distance between the contemporary period and that of pre-2010 is the almost complete repudiation of the legacy of New Labourism by the Corbyn-led Labour Party: centrism is much mocked for its milquetoast failure to challenge vested interests, and cautious incremental improvement is out of fashion among those sympathetic to the Momentum movement that favours radical and sweeping changes such as nationalisation, expansion of public spending on public services and enhanced redistribution. Clearly, on a broader canvas the New Labour experiment was ultimately undone by the unparalleled impact of the 2008 financial crisis, which, it is now clear, caused a significant rupture in the public's willingness to support the compromises inherent in the New Labour project: relative freedom for the market, selective marketisation within public services, and acceptance of relatively high immigration. Nevertheless, the typical social policy challenges remain starkly apparent in the UK, and the aim of this themed section was to ask what can still be learned from the approaches developed by New Labour: what is worth salvaging and indeed resurrecting wherever possible in the contemporary terrain with its ever-present constraints of austerity and Brexit.

Area regeneration was a major priority of the incoming Labour administration in 1997, and in their chapter, Ruth Lupton and Richard Crisp ask what, if anything, can be learned from the approach that developed, especially in an era following the Brexit vote that re-focused attention on 'left behind' areas and people. They begin by noting that we are now in a 'post-regeneration' era: as in many policy fields the Coalition ended funding for area-based initiatives and dismantled the policy architecture that had focused on less prosperous areas. Instead, from 2010, urban regeneration was recalibrated as a policy field dominated by a growth-based rather than a needs-based approach. In approaching the New Labour approach to regeneration they argue that regeneration policy should be seen as an ongoing tension between competing logics of 'transformation' and 'amelioration' – indeed, the balance between these logics shifted over time in the New Labour era, and partly contributed to undermining the support for its regeneration policies. They draw out four big lessons from the New Labour period: first, that regeneration as a policy domain is always weakly embedded in the architecture of government, and this is an important lesson for social policy scholars interested in the 'durability' of policy support for a particular issue. They argue that Labour's devaluation of its own *ameliorative* achievements was misguided, and this has implications for the argument between those keen to denigrate the Labour years and those often vilified as 'Blairites' who want to defend key approaches that brought social progress. Next they argue that genuine and significant improvements were made through Labour's emphasis on national regeneration frameworks with a longer-term view. Relatedly, it is clear that area regeneration alone cannot do all the heavy lifting of tackling entrenched spatial inequalities whose roots lie in wider structural trends. They finish by attempting to apply these lessons with a call for a blueprint based on a national framework for regeneration with coordination across government, enhanced devolution and a commitment to inclusive growth as a fundamental guiding approach.

There were clear similarities and linkages between New Labour's regeneration policy and its adherence to the notion of 'community cohesion', as well as a set of related concepts like social inclusion, community empowerment and integration. Community cohesion as a policy originated in 2001 in response to the so-called race riots in the northern English towns of Bradford, Oldham and Burnley, but as Matthew Donoghue makes clear, it was a politically and ideologically specific response to that unrest, which makes it difficult to simply transpose the policy response of New Labour on to recent frameworks. Nevertheless, the social fractures highlighted by Brexit – along the lines of race, class and age – are clearly similar, so there is an opportunity to examine New Labour's approach to community cohesion in order to learn what a reinvigorated approach to cohesion *should* and *shouldn't* do. Crucially, Donoghue points out that community cohesion policy was targeted at 'problem' groups, and that this legacy endures today in Conservative approaches to such issues as extremism and 'parallel lives'. Thus, in its response to the 2011 riots, the government failed to learn the lesson of community cohesion policy that communities were promised empowerment, but instead created more responsibility without being given the means to follow it through. In its approach to extremism, illustrated in the government's Prevent Strategy that has been widely perceived as unfairly focusing on Muslims, 'instead of engendering mutual respect between social and ethnic groups and the state, communities have been divided. Thus, "cohesion" becomes an empty promise, associated more with political rhetoric than with meaningful integration.' Donoghue argues convincingly that something like community cohesion is still needed following Brexit, although the lessons from New Labour are primarily of the 'what not to do' variety. A rejuvenated response would ditch the assimilationist approach that tackles problem groups, and abandon the securitised approach that has disproportionately targeted Muslims, and instead promote a more mutual form of integration as well as progress on tackling socioeconomic divisions.

Ian Greener's chapter considers in some detail the reforms implemented by New Labour in the hugely significant policy field of the NHS. The chapter approaches Labour's reforms to the NHS between 1997 and 2010 as representing a series of 'programme theories' to consider what we can learn from them about healthcare and public reorganisation more generally. It suggests Labour's programme theory of 'delivery' had, through the Quality and Outcomes Framework (QOF), potential for learning how better to handle performance management, but that 'choice and competition' has not achieved the goals asked of it. The theory represented by the Private Finance Initiative (PFI) presents a significant legacy and challenge to policy-makers and NHS organisations today because of the financial commitments it requires of organisations that put in place poorly negotiated deals. The first positive point that Greener makes about Labour's reforms is that they managed to implement a remarkable degree of reorganisation without the opposition that was generated by the reforms of the 1990s and the Lansley reforms post-2010. Greener attributes this to an approach that avoided 'big-bang' reforms, and involved consultation especially with senior clinicians, the key message being 'health reorganisation by stealth' can achieve very significant change. Meanwhile, focusing more on delivery than headline reforms, the experience of the QOF and the comparison of approaches in hospitals and GP surgeries suggests that such initiatives work better when pay-for-performance mechanisms work with the grain of clinicians' desire to do a good job and make evidence-based interventions: it is crucial to consider 'the exact means by which such systems are meant to work, and their potential effects on staff motivation using more sophisticated ideas than simple "carrot and stick" models.' More generally, in the case of reforms based on choice and competition, there needs to be continued emphasis on nuanced analyses of the exact institutional arrangements being created rather than broad-brush ideological debates. That said, Greener also suggests that the strongest driver for the very clear improvements in health and public satisfaction with the NHS was increased funding – both of which now risk being undermined.

Rikki Dean and Moira Wallace's chapter reminds us that in the field of child and adolescent wellbeing, New Labour invested significant public expenditure and policy effort in trying to remedy multi-dimensional problems of adolescent social exclusion. The Labour government made remarkable progress in reducing youth disadvantage, and the effects were intended to be long-term and multifaceted. A considerable legacy of data also allows the authors to evaluate progress across individual programmes, and as the generation of children whose life course coincided with most of these policy and expenditure changes is now making the transition to adulthood, it is a good time to ask what happened to them when they reached adolescence. The chapter outlines the distinctive policy approach taken by the New Labour government, documenting the policy experimentation that was intended to reduce teenage pregnancies, keep young people in school, improve their educational attainment, smooth their transition to post-16 education and work, reduce youth crime, and reduce drug and alcohol misuse. It then analyses the outcomes data on these dimensions of adolescent social exclusion. In particular, the remarkable decline in teenage pregnancy is well documented, but more generally their analysis shows a similar or greater magnitude in reductions across the other indicators of youth exclusion for the cohort who experienced these policies. In the final section, like the other authors in this themed section, they draw out the implications from this period for current and future policy – what can be learned from the successes on adolescent social exclusion, are they durable, and what remains to be done?

There is a consistent message that emerges from these four chapters, focusing as they do on quite disparate policy fields – notwithstanding that New Labour was always at pains to highlight the interlinked nature of social issues, and to establish 'joined-up government' responses, as demonstrated by the early work done by the Policy Action Teams set up soon after the election victory in 1997. The message is that they put in sustained investment into these policy fields (although Greener draws attention to important phasing of investment in health), with long-term commitments, underpinned by clear national frameworks that established priorities and set the tone for sub-national and local action (particularly clear Chapter Ten). Finally, the evidence is clear that very substantial (although variable, and certainly not perfect) progress was made as a result of this committed and largely well-principled political and policy direction – as Dean and Wallace make clear in Chapter Thirteen on tackling youth disadvantage. There is therefore clearly a case for social policy scholars to continue to excavate the key implications and wider messages from the 'policy soup' of the New Labour period, and to consider how these might be applied in our austere and fragmented policy landscape.

TEN

Regeneration redux? What (if anything) can we learn from New Labour?

Ruth Lupton and Richard Crisp

Introduction

England,[1] it is commonly accepted, is currently in a 'post-regeneration' policy era (O'Brien and Matthews, 2015). The election of the Coalition government marked both the end of funding for large-scale area-based initiatives (ABIs) and the dismantling of much of the policy architecture that had enabled a broader focus on less prosperous areas: Regional Development Agencies (RDAs), some regional data series and requirements on Local Strategic Partnerships (LSPs) to develop neighbourhood renewal strategies (Lupton and Fitzgerald, 2015; Pugalis, 2016). From 2010, urban regeneration was recalibrated as a policy field dominated by a growth-based rather than a needs-based approach (Deas, 2013; Pugalis and McGuinness, 2013; Crisp et al, 2014). This 'Local Growth' agenda (BIS, 2011; DCLG, 2011, 2012) included the establishment of new city regional institutions (Local Enterprise Partnerships [LEPs] and combined authorities); new funding streams to support a range of interventions around housing and planning, skills, transport and economic development; and the emergence of locally negotiated City Deals, Growth Deals and Devolution Deals as mechanisms for funding allocation. This set of initiatives is widely regarded as the abolition of central government regeneration policy. Unlike the other nations in the UK, England now has no national strategy for regeneration, which is seen as a policy function for local or city regional institutions (DCLG, 2011, 2012).

However, the shock of the European Union (EU) referendum result, and perhaps also the 'austerity fatigue' that became evident in the 2017 General Election campaign, has led to a refocus in public policy debate on the plight of older industrial areas that voted predominantly to leave the EU (RSA, 2017). To some extent this echoes Tony Blair's pledge, in his inaugural speech as Prime Minister (Blair, 1997), to focus on the people and places that had been 'forgotten' by government and left out of growing prosperity. A new department has been established with responsibility for industrial strategy, with an early Green Paper (HM Government, 2017, p 107) signalling that 'recognition of the importance of place will be at its heart'. It also points to the need to reduce spatial economic imbalances through infrastructure and R&D (research and development) investment, targeted programmes to raise skills, and the strengthening of place-based institutions. At the same time as the political parties battle for the votes of 'left behind' people and places, and in the wake of the Grenfell Tower disaster, Labour has also begun to rediscover 'regeneration', with a critique of public–private partnership schemes as state-led gentrification and social cleansing (Corbyn, 2017), an argument that has repeatedly been made in the academic literature (see, for example, Bridge et al, 2012; Lees and Ferreri, 2016; Hochstenbach, 2017).

This constellation of circumstances creates space for thinking anew about reviving and reconfiguring regeneration policies to address enduring forms of place-based disadvantage. If place-based policy is set to make a comeback, what form could or should 'regeneration redux' take? To address this, this chapter takes a close look at the 'New' Labour approach to urban regeneration from 1997 to 2010 and what can be learned from it. With the benefit of elapsed time since the 2010 election, we are able to present a new synthesis of the academic and 'grey' (policy evaluation) literature covering this period too, including our own previous contributions. We also offer a new conceptual analysis of how the New Labour years were characterised by a tension between 'ameliorative' and 'transformative' policy logics, with valuable ameliorative outcomes around improving neighbourhood conditions eventually reassessed as failure through the lens of transformative objectives around wholesale economic regeneration. Drawing on this analysis, we suggest that the most important lessons from this period are not so much about 'what works' (although there are plenty of these), but about what regeneration is and can be, and about how it is contested. In order to achieve a period of greater policy stability in which the interests of the 'forgotten' people and places of England are meaningfully addressed, these tensions and contestations need to be acknowledged and resolved in less binary and divisive ways than in recent policy history. We suggest some of the possibilities for doing so in the current policy context.

New Labour's approach(es) to urban regeneration

Seen through the lens of critical urban policy, the New Labour era is often conceived as a period of 'rollout neoliberalism', a corrective phase where 'experimental governance, promarket reregulation, and all manner of short-term fixes, bandaids and bromides – complete with their own limits and contradictions' succeeded the 'rollback' phase of 'deregulation, dismantling, deconstruction, and downsizing' of earlier rounds of predominantly property-led regeneration (Peck, 2012, pp 629-30). While recognising this broad critique, we offer a more nuanced account that captures more fully the heterogeneity and dynamic tensions of New Labour policies, and pulls out in more detail the contradictions within and across policies, in order to draw some detailed lessons for current and future policy-making.

Developing a conceptualisation first presented in earlier papers (see Lupton and Tunstall, 2008; Lupton and Fuller, 2009; Lupton et al, 2013) and influenced by urban scholars including Fainstein and Fainstein (1982) and Cochrane (2007), we argue that regeneration policy can be seen as an ongoing tension between competing logics of 'transformation' and 'amelioration' (see Table 10.1) that gain or lose dominance at different times under different political and institutional contexts.

By an 'ameliorative' logic we mean that the purpose of intervention is primarily to improve a particular place and the circumstances of the people who already live there – as Pugalis (2016) puts it, a 'use' philosophy. It centres on a dominant analysis of neighbourhood-level disadvantage (or 'social exclusion') as a consequence of long-term economic restructuring that public service providers have thus far failed to address. Through ameliorative approaches, state-led interventions seek to provide additional funding or 'bend' mainstream spending to support incremental improvements to tackle the multiple and mutually reinforcing causes of poverty. This ameliorative logic can be read as a form of place-based social policy, with interventions seeking to improve services and amenities to address the social impacts of economic transition.

The alternative 'transformative' logic describes approaches whose purpose is to change the functional role of an area within its wider labour or housing markets, often through physical property-led forms of regeneration. This logic centres on an understanding of neighbourhood-level disadvantage as driven by the failure of land and property markets, thereby locking in concentrations of poverty that become self-perpetuating through compounding 'area effects' (see Manley et al,

2012, for a fuller discussion of area effects). The aim of transformative interventions, therefore, is to change the function of areas to serve purposes beyond the interests of current residents such as stimulating new industries and economic growth; incentivising investment and raising land values; and creating new residential opportunities for people in professional occupations to live near work and enhance 'social mix'. They are primarily about the 'exchange' value of a place, not its 'use' value (Pugalis, 2016). In practice, of course, many regeneration schemes involve some element of both (for example, transformational schemes may also involve some renewal of social housing and community facilities), but one or the other logic can be identified as dominant.

In early New Labour policy, an ameliorative logic was highly prominent. Following a report by the Social Exclusion Unit, *Bringing Britain together* (SEU, 1998), detailing the multiple problems of the poorest areas, the policies of the first Blair government placed a strong emphasis on tackling these forms of social exclusion by improving housing, amenities and public services. This approach came to be described as 'neighbourhood renewal'. Pursuing the goal that 'no one should be seriously disadvantaged by where they live' (SEU, 2001), the government established a National Strategy for Neighbourhood Renewal (NSNR), aiming to impact across six main domains: employment, education, health, housing, liveability and crime. Reflecting its implict focus on the use value of neighbourhoods, a particularly strong emphasis was placed on living conditions, such that 'all neighbourhoods in the country should be free of fear', and 'we should not have neighbourhoods where so many people's number one priority is to move out' (SEU, 2001, p 24). A desire for greater equity in the distribution of services, opportunities and economic and social goods was given expression in a set of 'floor targets' described as 'the social equivalent of the Minimum Wage'. To this end, new ABIs were set up, most significantly the New Deal for Communities (NDC) programme that targeted 39 small areas for substantial investments (£50 million per area) in place and service infrastructure as well as people-based programmes. In all of these policies, the scale of action was the neighbourhood, and there was a strong emphasis on community engagement (Batty et al, 2010).

New Labour's early regeneration policy was not just limited to ameliorative forms of neighbourhood renewal. Larger-scale physical and economic regeneration with a stronger transformative logic, including remediation of large brownfield sites, was handled through its new RDAs, English Partnerships[2] as well as through establishing Urban Regeneration Companies (URCs) in 1999. A Housing

Table 10.1: A conceptual framework of transformative and ameliorative approaches

	Transformation	Amelioration
Dominant analysis of problem	Market failure State-induced dependency	Economic restructuring Public service failure Social exclusion
Relationship between place and poverty	Poor neighbourhoods as cause of poverty Residents as contributing factor to poverty (eg cultures of poverty)	Poor neighbourhoods as consequence of poverty Residents as victims of wider economic and social change
Dominant logics for intervention	Exchange value Restoring housing and labour market functionality Attracting investment Reducing public spending Deconcentrating poverty Stimulating economic change to improve social outcomes	Use value Improving conditions for existing residents Investing in existing housing, facilities and services More effective public spending Tackling multiple and overlapping causes of poverty Addressing social consequences of economic change
Mode of intervention	Physical and economic development	Social welfare Some physical and economic development
Primary policy domains	Economic development Housing Employment and skills	Employment and skills Education Health Crime Housing and physical environment Community development
Spatial scale for intervention	Cities (often city centres) and city-regions May have neighbourhood element as part of strategic focus on role of places in wider housing and labour markets	Focused on neighbourhoods
Spatial imaginary	Urban renaissance Reshaping areas to make them more attractive places to live and work	Neighbourhood renewal Improving living conditions to narrow gap with more affluent areas
Target population	Attracting new and aspirational residents to create more mixed communities	Supporting existing residents and stemming outflow of households to more affluent areas
Role of the state	Entrepreneurial Promoting competitiveness Reducing risk for private investors	Welfarist Providing and coordinating services
Nature of the partnership	Strong emphasis on private sector involvement	Cross-sectoral, with some private sector involvement

Market Renewal (HMR) scheme introduced in 2003 also had large-scale physical regeneration at its heart, aiming to restructure housing markets that were deemed to be failing. Perhaps most significantly in terms of policy logics, the idea of 'urban renaissance' – a commitment to breathing new life into Britain's large urban areas after decades of industrial decline and depopulation – was evident as early as 1998 when architect Richard Rogers was commissioned to lead an Urban Task Force. The Task Force's recommendations included densification, improving neighbourhood connectivity, brownfield redevelopment, social mixing and high-quality urban design (Urban Task Force, 1999; Rogers and Power, 2000) – transformative ideas that were no doubt in tension with the ameliorative approaches of neighbourhood renewal (Lees, 2003; Colomb, 2007).

This brief synopsis shows how an ameliorative 'neighbourhood renewal' approach existed *alongside* a more transformative 'urban renaissance' agenda into the second term of New Labour. By 2004/05, however, the tensions between these two approaches, and resolution in favour of a transformative logic, became evident in a growing focus on low levels of economic activity (Cabinet Office, 2004, p 12) and on the problems of 'concentrated poverty' that were seen as holding back economic growth and urban potential. In 2007, a Treasury review of sub-national economic development and regeneration (HM Treasury et al, 2007), later incorporated in the Brown government's *Transforming places, changing lives* Regeneration Framework (DCLG, 2008), signalled the end of the neighbourhood renewal agenda. This was replaced with a regeneration approach more clearly rooted in transformative, exchange value logics of restoring housing and labour market functionality by means of sub-regional economic development. The purposes of regeneration were re-defined as: improving economic performance, improving rates of work and enterprise and creating sustainable places where people want to live and work and businesses want to invest (DCLG, 2008, p 5).

In contrast to earlier policy documents that had advocated a greater alignment of spending and services to need, the Regeneration Framework set out a specific ambition to reduce the cost to the taxpayer of 'subsidising rather than transforming lives'. At the same time, the Neighbourhood Renewal Unit (NRU) and its floor targets were disbanded, and the HMR programme become increasingly focused on supporting economic growth (Ferrari, 2007; Audit Commission, 2009). Barely a decade since Blair's Aylesbury Estate speech, the neighbourhood renewal approach to regeneration policy had effectively been abolished.

Lessons from the New Labour years

New Labour's strong commitment to evaluation leaves today's policy-makers with much practical guidance about aspects of policy and practice that do and do not 'work'. Key lessons around community engagement, partnership working, the sequencing of design and delivery, the mix of 'quick wins' and longer-term investment, and the appropriate size of target areas are well summarised in our previous work (see, for example, Lupton et al, 2013; Crisp et al, 2014, 2015) as well as programme evaluation reports in which ourselves and others have been involved (see, for example, Amion Consulting, 2010; Batty et al, 2010). In this chapter, however, we do not wish to rehearse these practical points again but rather, to highlight four bigger lessons that we draw from the academic and 'grey' literature and relate to our understanding of the broader policy objectives and tensions at play.

The first lesson is that even within governments (never mind between them), *regeneration policy lacks a single clear purpose and identity, and for that reason, tends to be weakly embedded institutionally and vulnerable to political caprice.* Its form reflects the ways in which the competing logics of amerioloration and transformation are articulated, contested and made manifest in policy and spending decisions at different times. We do not have room here to explore all the reasons for the policy shifts described above. Durose and Rees (2012) argue that at least part of what happened can be accounted for by changing perceptions of the electoral capital that could be gained through pledges to 'neighbourhoods'. The key point here is that different political and economic contexts see these tensions resolved in different ways. Labour's internal debates about what and who renegeration was for need to be revisited as we reflect on the form that policy could take in the changed context of 2018.

Second, Labour's own *devaluation of its ameliorative achievements was misguided.* Although part of the policy narrative from the mid-2000s onwards was that ameliorative strategies had failed (measured against a different set of objectives) and therefore did not represent value for money, much of the evidence does not support this. New Labour's ameliorative strategies were often successful in improving neighbourhoods and reducing the chance that people would be seriously disadvantaged by the areas in which they lived. For example, the NSNR evaluation reports showed that many residents agreed that the streets were cleaner, that the quality of parks and open spaces had improved, and that environmental conditions were better (Amion Consulting, 2010). The NDC evaluation also reported statistically significant evidence of greater improvement than in comparable areas on indicators of place – such as perceptions of the environment, being a victim of crime and satisfaction with the area (Batty et al, 2010). In addition, residents credited the much-maligned time-limited, area-based, neighbourhood-scale NDC partnerships for having been effective agents of change (DCLG, 2010a). Qualitative studies also consistently reported residents welcoming new services and environmental improvements (Bashir and Flint, 2010; Eisenstadt, 2011; Power et al, 2011).

At the same time, the broader targeting of (increased) mainstream government funding towards disadvantaged areas also resulted in significant changes: a reduction in the number of vacant or poor quality homes as a result of the HMR and Decent Homes programme; the expansion of childcare services and facilities as a result of Sure Start and Neighbourhood Nurseries and, towards the end of the latter part of the period, investment in new school buildings through Building Schools for the Future; and an increase in frontline police officers and Police Community Support Officers (Lupton et al, 2013). Ameliorative gains were played down but they were significant. Moreover, amid austerity narratives of profligate and ineffective public spending, the evidence on spending is also important to recall. Compared with mainstream policy areas, Labour's spending on neighbourhood renewal was very small in scale. Looking at the tail end of the New Labour period, average annual spend on regeneration was £9.1 billion in the period 2009-11 compared with £182.8 billion in 2010–11 on tax credits and benefits (see Crisp et al, 2014, for a full account). The comparatively small-scale of spend makes the outcomes documented above all the more significant.

Our third lesson is that *systematic improvements were achieved through central government adopting responsibility for spatial inequalities and developing national regeneration frameworks with a longer-term view.* Perhaps the most striking point that emerges from a detailed review of the New Labour years is just how quickly the principles underpinning policy were redefined, arguably paving the way for the much more fundamental abandonment of central government responsibility for regeneration witnessed under subsequent Coalition and Conservative governments. Yet the early New Labour model is in many respects a classic example of how changes in outcomes at a very local level could be driven by central government. Elements included:

- the establishment of targets for individual neighbourhoods, types of neighbourhoods or for a general closing of the gap between disadvantaged neighbourhoods and others;

- a commitment to collecting and analysing neighbourhood-scale data;
- guidance from central government on the responsibility and accountability of local partnerships for area-based regeneration;
- mechanisms to coordinate policy across government departments in the form of the NRU and floor targets, which also led to effective and spatially progressive 'bending' of mainstream spending and programmes (see DCLG, 2010b).

This is not to say New Labour had the balance between central direction and local control exactly right. Attempts in the latter half of the 2000s to persist with a targets regime from central government while allowing nascent combined authorities (in the form of Multi-Area Agreements) to determine their own priorities were generally regarded as too locally insensitive, while some centralised uses of data ran roughshod over local issues and priorities. However, a lesson can be learned that when central government takes responsibility for spatial inequalities and tackling the problems of the 'worst' neighbourhoods, significant and coordinated local and national action can be engineered.

Fourth, we learn that, despite New Labour's successes, *spatial inequalities cannot be solved in the short term or by regeneration policies alone.* This should perhaps go without saying. The differences in opportunities and life chances encountered in richer and poorer neighbourhoods have been decades, if not centuries, in the making. They are the product of a complex series of factors cutting across wider spatial scales including global financial flows and regulatory regimes; the hollowing out of labour markets and wage suppression in low-paid sectors; the impact of welfare reforms; growing income inequalities leading to social segregation through residential sorting; and the failure of weak regional policies to spatially rebalance the economy (Lupton and Tunstall, 2008; Dorling, 2011; Donald et al, 2014; Beatty and Fothergill, 2016; Martin et al, 2017). These disparities will take generations to tackle.

Indeed, the regional disparities that had been emerging during the late 1980s and 1990s continued to grow (Martin et al, 2017). London's resurgence as a global financial and business centre fuelled rapid growth in the capital and the South East. Some of England's smaller and larger cities benefited from the growth of technological, knowledge-based and service industries, enabling an 'urban renaissance' in parts as young professionals discovered the benefits of city living (Rae, 2013). But few non-metropolitan or peripheral areas were able to reinvent themselves in the post-industrial era. A substantial body of evidence now shows that even before the financial crisis and the ensuing austerity policies with their uneven geographical effects, different types of poor neighbourhoods were on very different trajectories as the local economies of which they were part flourished or struggled (see, for example, Lupton et al, 2013).

And overall, despite New Labour's substantial commitments and effort, very large gaps remained between poorer neighbourhoods on a whole range of indicators. The National Equality Panel, which reported in 2010 on a range of economic indicators including educational outcomes, earnings, incomes and wealth, drew attention to 'profound gaps' on all these measures between more and less advantaged neighbourhoods, and concluded that the 'neighbourhood renewal agenda is itself in need of renewal' (Hills et al, 2010, p 6). While 'forgotten people' and places had benefited from the investments made, England was not a substantially more equal society in spatial terms.

Regeneration redux? Applying these lessons in the current context

As indicated at the start of this chapter, the context in which we might now think about applying these lessons is somewhat different to the one that most 'post-regeneration' commentators have been writing about. The period from 2010 to 2017 has been, and still is, dominated by a growth-based rather than needs-based approach, with an implicit transformational logic (Deas, 2013; Pugalis and McGuinness, 2013; Crisp et al, 2014; Mayer, 2017). Funding allocations through local growth initiatives are now largely determined by the ability of local stakeholders to convince central government of their capacity to promote growth and establish good governance, as embodied in the opaque and highly uneven distribution of funding through devolution deals to date (NAO, 2016; Tomaney, 2016).

However, Theresa May's pledge to create a 'country that works for everyone' (May, 2016) and the resurgence of interest in spatial imbalances, 'left behind' places and industrial strategies for places that have missed out on prosperity all seem to invoke the concerns of the incoming Labour government in 1997 – concerns that led to the regeneration policies described above. However, the very different economic climate, the ongoing English devolution process (NAO, 2016), developments outside government including the recent RSA commission on inclusive growth (RSA, 2017) and the experience of 20 years of varying policy all make this a very different environment to the one facing the new Blair administration, or indeed the Cameron government that effectively abolished central government regeneration policy in 2010. So how might the learning from the New Labour period play into policy developments now? We make three proposals around: a new national framework for regeneration; integrated place-based working; and alignment of social and economic policy.

A new national framework and coordination mechanisms

One possibility is that there may be an opportunity, given widespread concerns about 'left behind' places, to gain cross-party consensus for a new national approach that might garner non-partisan and long-term support – bringing England back into line with the other devolved nations of the UK and providing greater policy stability than in the 1997–2017 period.

This framework could play a valuable role in articulating a vision for regeneration, while explicitly recognising the tensions that surfaced in the New Labour years between ameliorative and transformative approaches. This means acknowledging efficiency versus equity trade-offs and defining an appropriate balance, as the recent Industrial Strategy Commission (2017) advocates. In other words, central government needs to recognise that investment in ameliorative approaches may bring important place-based improvements to existing residents without generating transformative change, while transformative investments in areas best placed to grow may not have immediate benefits to residents in the least prosperous areas. The point is to strike an appropriate balance, not privilege one over the other as the current growth-based approach does.

A regeneration framework could also identify connections across national strategies through, for example, outlining how the UK's nascent Industrial Strategy could contribute to regeneration objectives. A cross-departmental policy unit could also help to ensure coordination across policy domains and secure departmental support for ensuring their respective strategies, policies and programmes consider impacts in less prosperous areas. A commitment to providing data to understand change in low-income neighbourhoods may help to cement this.

Supporting integrated place-based working through devolution

The current devolution agenda also provides opportunities to develop coordinated forms of place-based working to improve outcomes in low-income neighbourhoods, learning from Labour's successes and limitations in that regard. Specifically, it provides a mechanism for developing locally sensitive solutions that address concerns that past forms of neighbourhood renewal were spatially selective, overly prescriptive and insensitive to local need (Rae et al, 2016). Clearly, there is a risk of simply devolving national agendas, especially in a deal-making process where funding may be allocated on the basis of willingness to support central government priorities as recent research shows in the case of housing and planning policy (Crisp et al, 2017). However, there are nascent signs that local and combined authorities are increasingly asserting public sector muscle in securing funding and flexibilities, and pursuing projects that at least begin to run counter to neoliberal models of dispossession and accumulation. The Leeds City Region, for example, has made 'inclusive growth' a defining principle of its recently refreshed Strategic Economic Plan (LCR LEP and WYCA, 2017), and other areas are looking to follow suit.

These tentative steps suggest that devolution may refocus attention on the most disadvantaged groups and areas. This could be embedded more systematically within the devolution process by making any further allocations of funding to LEPs or combined authorities conditional on outlining impacts on, say, areas in the bottom quintile of the English Index of Multiple Deprivation. Enshrining a '20 per cent principle' within the currently opaque deal-making processes of devolution would at least ensure a new and consistent focus on tackling area-based deprivation. It would also help to reinstate the neighbourhood as a legitimate spatial scale for investment alongside cities and city regions and reintroduce a degree of spatial literacy lost in the current era of local growth initiatives.

A new integration of social and economic policy: towards inclusive growth?

Finally, the emerging inclusive growth agenda may provide both an opportunity and an imperative to resolve the ameliorative/transformative tension in new ways. Many different versions of the meaning of inclusive growth are in play, and it may yet turn out to be the case that the dominant form may turn out to be one that effectively subordinates ameliorative *social* goals to transformative *economic* objectives (RSA, 2017) by positioning a renewed assault on poverty as a means of unlocking latent talent to drive productivity and growth. But this could be complemented by a focus on reconfiguring economic policies to deliver valuable social outcomes. For example, a more inclusive approach could mean influencing the nature of labour market demand through, for example, ensuring that procurement practices of anchor institutions create jobs accessible to local people or opportunities for businesses in local supply chains, while also working to improve pay through Living Wage charters, as currently being pursued in the Leeds City Region (LCR LEP and WYCA, 2016; While et al, 2016; Devins et al, 2017). More radically, it could include developing mechanisms for areas to capture and redistribute wealth in a way that is not conditional on individuals securing positions in the labour market. Examples might include land value capture mechanisms to benefit from the uplift in land values that result from granting planning permission or remunicipalisation of services such as energy provision for collective benefit. Any financial gains could be reinvested in services or amenities to benefit the wider community, perhaps through some kind of 'community wealth' fund.

Such developments would offer a new integration of economic and social policy at the local level that would provide a more stable and productive basis for neighbourhood policies: avoiding repeating the mistake of measuring ameliorative approaches against transformative yardsticks and vice versa. However, they do require an explicit recognition of the tensions and trade-offs involved, something that we hope has emerged more clearly from our analysis of the New Labour period.

Conclusion

The three broad proposals outlined above highlight ways in which a new generation of regeneration policy could draw on the lessons of the New Labour years and begin to address the issues facing 'left behind' communities. Undeniably, however, there is a long way to go. These proposals rely on a fundamental willingness of central government to explicitly recognise the trade-offs between transformative and ameliorative interventions, and to reinstate the principle of need in urban regeneration policy. Without this there is a danger that a devolution process already 'fraught with confusion, complexity and competing spaces of governance' (Pugalis, 2015, p 128) will further lock in spatially regressive outcomes. Growth potential and good governance cannot be the sole basis for allocations of discretionary funding, as the recent collapse of numerous devolution deals in less prosperous areas highlights (see Ayres et al, 2017).

There is also the fundamental question of resources. It perhaps seems naive to call for extra funding under current conditions of 'super-austerity' (Lowndes and Gardner, 2016), but it is equally naive to expect change without a significant increase in investment. New analysis shows that total central government spending on the 'local growth' agenda is actually considerably less than on urban regeneration policy prior to 2010 (Crisp et al, 2018: forthcoming).

We must also be realistic about what even well-funded regeneration strategies, policies and programmes can achieve. As is already well understood, the roots of poverty and area deprivation lie largely outside the area affected themselves and cannot be tackled by area-based policy alone. Many of the policy levers likely to impact on localised concentrations of poverty such as those relating to tax, benefits, wages, the terms and conditions of employment, and access to health and education are determined at a national level and therefore largely outside the scope of regeneration (Powell et al, 2001; Lupton, 2003; Lawless et al, 2011). Effective regeneration policy also has to be part of a wider set of economic and political strategies to generate more equitable place-based outcomes, not least in terms of spatially rebalancing the UK economy away from London and the South East (Martin et al, 2017).

Despite these caveats, we contend that regeneration is a project worth pursuing to address spatial forms of disadvantage. The ameliorative-transformative conceptualisation developed in this chapter contributes to understandings of how this might happen by highlighting the need to recognise the tensions inherent in this policy area. This moves us beyond a narrow, reductive emphasis on 'what works', which, on its own, only generates 'fragmented understandings' (Cochrane, 2007, p 4) of the effectiveness of particular interventions. Our aim is to show that regeneration is vulnerable to downscaling if these tensions go unrecognised as ameliorative interventions are assessed – and find wanting – through a transformative lens. Better understanding of these tensions could lead to a more balanced approach where trade-offs are made explicit and expectations framed accordingly. Interventions to improve living conditions for existing residents may not dramatically reconfigure the role of neighbourhoods, for example, but may still increase its 'use value' in meaningful ways for those who live there.

This analysis also adds nuance to periodisations of urban policy through a critical urban policy frame that see the New Labour years very much as an example of 'rollout' neoliberalism. It may be true that many of the ameliorative interventions of the neighbourhood renewal era were mere 'sticking plasters' relative to the scale of negative externalities of large-scale economic and political processes. But it remains important to excavate – and sometimes legitimate – the features of this particular form of urban policy under New Labour, not least because its unresolved contradictions arguably paved the way for the post-2010 recalibration of urban policy. The failure of New Labour to create a 'defensible space' around the regeneration policy paradigm and to distinguish between different and sometimes competing objectives rendered it vulnerable in the unforgiving fiscal and ideological terrain of the political landscape that followed. Perhaps now there is scope to draw on some of the bigger lessons of the past to develop a form of regeneration redux capable of addressing left behind places and forgotten people.

Notes

[1] Area regeneration is a devolved policy area in the UK, so New Labour's policies applied only to England. Different paths were followed in Scotland, Wales and Northern Ireland, and are not the subject of this chapter.

[2] English Partnerships was a national regeneration agency constituted as a non-departmental public body sponsored by the Department for Communities and Local Government. It was replaced by the Homes and Communities Agency in 2008.

References

Amion Consulting (2010) *Evaluation of the National Strategy for Neighbourhood Renewal. Final report: Summary*, London: Communities and Local Government.

Audit Commission (2009) *Housing Market Renewal: Programme review*, London: Audit Commission.

Ayres, S., Flinders, M. and Sandford, M. (2017) 'Territory, power and statecraft: Understanding English devolution', *Regional Studies* [Online first].

Bashir, N. and Flint, J. (2010) *Residents' perceptions of neighbourhood change and its impacts*, Sheffield: Centre for Regional Economic and Social Research, Sheffield Hallam University.

Batty, E., Beatty, C., Foden, M., Lawless, P., Pearson, S. and Wilson, I. (2010) *The New Deal for Communities experience: A final assessment. Volume 7. New Deal for Communities evaluation final report*, London: Communities and Local Government.

Beatty, C. and Fothergill, S. (2016) *Jobs, welfare and austerity: How the destruction of industrial Britain casts a shadow over present-day public finances*, Sheffield: Centre for Regional Economic and Social Research, Sheffield Hallam University.

BIS (Department for Business Innovation and Skills) (2011) *Local growth: Realising every place's potential*, London: The Stationery Office.

Blair, T. (1997) Speech at the Aylesbury Estate, Southwark, 2 June (www.youtube.com/watch?v=q_HGgT--AGs).

Bridge, G., Butler, T. and Lees, L. (eds) (2012) *Mixed communities: Gentrification by stealth?*, Bristol: Policy Press.

Cabinet Office (2004) *Improving the prospects of people living in areas of multiple deprivation in England*, London: Cabinet Office.

Cochrane, A. (2007) *Understanding urban policy: A critical approach*, Oxford: Blackwell.

Colomb, C. (2007) 'Unpacking New Labour's "Urban Renaissance" agenda: towards a socially sustainable reurbanisation of British cities?', *Planning Practice and Research*, vol 22, no 1, pp 1-24.

Corbyn, J. (2017) Speech to the Labour Party Conference, full speech available at: https://www.totalpolitics.com/articles/news/jeremy-corbyn%E2%80%99s-2017-labour-conference-speech-full-transcript

Crisp, R., Gore, T. and Pearson, S. (2015) 'Rethinking the impact of regeneration on poverty: a (partial) defence of a "failed" policy', *Journal of Poverty and Social Justice*, vol 23, no 3, pp 167-87.

Crisp, R., Gore, T. and Wells, P. (2018: forthcoming) *Unbalancing the economy? Why devolution policies will not help less prosperous areas.*

Crisp, R., Cole, I., Eadson, W., Ferrari, F., Powell, R. and While, A. (2017) *Tackling poverty through housing and planning policy in city regions*, York: Joseph Rowntree Foundation.

Crisp, R., Gore, T., Pearson, S. and Tyler, P. with Clapham, D., Muir, J. and Robertson, D. (2014) *Regeneration and poverty: Evidence and policy review*, Sheffield: CRESR, Sheffield Hallam University.

DCLG (Department for Communities and Local Government) (2008) *Transforming places, changing lives: A framework for regeneration*, London: HMSO.

DCLG (2010a) *Making deprived areas better places to live: Evidence from the New Deal for Communities Programme: The New Deal for Communities national evaluation final report, Volume 3*, London: DCLG.

DCLG (2010b) *Improving outcomes for people in deprived neighbourhoods: Evidence from the New Deal for Communities Programme: The New Deal for Communities national evaluation: Final report, Volume 4*, London: DCLG.

DCLG (2011) *Regeneration to enable growth: What government is doing in support of community-led regeneration*, London: DCLG.

DCLG (2012) *Regeneration to enable growth: A toolkit supporting community-led regeneration*, London: DCLG.

Deas, I. (2013) 'Towards post-political consensus in urban policy? Localism and the emerging agenda for regeneration under the Cameron government', *Planning Practice and Research*, vol 28, no 1, pp 65-82.

Devins, D., Gold, J., Boak, G., Garvey, R. and Willis, P. (2017) *Maximising the local impact of anchor institutions: A case study of Leeds City Region*, York: Joseph Rowntree Foundation.

Donald, B., Glasmeier, A., Gray, M. and Labao, L. (2014) 'Austerity in the city: Economic crisis and urban service decline?', *Cambridge Journal of Regions, Economy and Society*, vol 7, no 1, pp 3-15.

Dorling, D. (2011) *Injustice: Why social inequality persists*, Bristol: Policy Press.

Durose, C. and Rees, J. (2012) 'The rise and fall of neighbourhood in the New Labour era', *Policy & Politics*, vol 40, no 1, pp 39-55.

Eisenstadt, N. (2011) *Providing a Sure Start: How government discovered early childhood*, Bristol: Policy Press.

Fainstein, N. and Fainstein, S. (1982) 'Restoration and struggle: urban policy and social forces', in N. Fainstein and S. Fainstein (eds) *Urban policy under capitalism, Urban Affairs Annual Review 22*, Beverley Hills, CA: Sage.

Ferrari, E., (2007) 'Housing Market Renewal in an era of new housing supply', *People, Place and Policy Online*, vol 1, no 3, pp 124-35.

Hills, J., Brewer, M., Jenkins, S., Lister, R., Lupton, R., Machin, S., et al (2010) *An anatomy of economic inequality in the UK – Report of the National Equality Panel executive summary*, London: London School of Economics and Political Science.

HM Government (2017) *Building our industrial strategy, Green Paper*, London: HM Government.

HM Treasury, BERR (Department for Business, Enterprise and Regulatory Reform) and DCLG (Department for Communities and Local Government) (2007) *Review of sub-national economic development and regeneration*, London: HM Treasury.

Hochstenbach, C. (2017) 'State-led gentrification and the changing geography of market-oriented housing policies', *Housing, Theory and Society*, vol 34, no 4, pp 399-419.

Industrial Strategy Commission (2017) *The final report of the Industrial Strategy Commission*, Manchester/Sheffield: University of Manchester and University of Sheffield.

Lawless, P., Overman, H.G. and Tyler, P. (2011) *Strategies for underperforming places*, SERC Policy Paper 6, London: Spatial Economics Research Centre (SERC), London School of Economics and Political Science (LSE).

LCR LEP (Leeds City Region Local Enterprise Partnership) and WYCA (West Yorkshire Combined Authority) (2016) *Leeds City Region strategic economic plan 2016-2036*, Leeds: LCR/WYCA.

Lees, L. (2003) 'Visions of "urban renaissance": The Urban Task Force report and the Urban White Paper', in R. Imrie and M. Raco (eds) *Urban renaissance? New Labour, community and urban policy*, Bristol: Policy Press, pp 61-82.

Lees, L. and Ferreri, M. (2016) 'Resisting gentrification on its final frontiers: learning from the Heygate Estate in London (1974-2013)', *Cities: The international Journal of Urban Policy and Planning*, vol 57, pp 14-24.

Lowndes, V. and Gardner, A. (2016) 'Local government under the Conservatives: super-austerity, devolution and the "smarter state"', *Local Government Studies*, vol 42, no 3, pp 357-75.

Lupton, R. (2003) *Poverty Street: The dynamics of neighbourhood decline and renewal*, Bristol: Policy Press.

Lupton, R. and Fitzgerald, A. (2015) *The Coalition's record on area regeneration and neighbourhood renewal 2010-2015*, Social Policy in a Cold Climate Working Paper 19, London: Centre for Analysis of Social Exclusion.

Lupton, R. and Fuller, C. (2009) 'Mixed communities: a new approach to spatially concentrated poverty in England', *International Journal of Urban and Regional Research*, vol 33, no 4, pp 1014-28.

Lupton, R, and Tunstall, R. (2008) 'Neighbourhood regeneration through mixed communities: A "social justice dilemma"?', *Journal of Education Policy*, vol 23, no 2, pp 105-17.

Lupton, R., Fenton, A. and Fitzgerald, A. (2013) *Labour's record on neighbourhood renewal in England: Policy, spending and outcomes 1997-2010*, London: Centre for Analysis of Social Exclusion.

Manley, D., van Haam, M. and Doherty, J. (2012) 'Social mix as a cure for negative neighbourhood effects: Evidence-based policy or urban myth?', in G. Bridge, T. Butler and L. Lees (eds) *Mixed communities: Gentrification by stealth?*, Bristol: Policy Press, pp 35-41.

Martin, R., Pike, A., Tyler, P. and Gardiner, B. (2017) 'Spatially rebalancing the UK economy: towards a new policy model?', *Regional Studies*, vol 50, no 2, pp 342-57.

May, T. (2016) First statement as Prime Minister in Downing Street, 13 July (www.gov.uk/government/speeches/statement-from-the-new-prime-minister-theresa-may).

Mayer, M. (2017) 'Whose city? From Ray Pahl's critique of the Keynesian city to the contestations around neoliberal urbanism', *The Sociological Review*, vol 65, no 2, pp 168-83.

NAO (National Audit Office) (2016) *English devolution deals*, London: NAO.

O'Brien, D. and Matthews, P. (eds) (2015) *After urban regeneration: Communities, policy and place*, Bristol: Policy Press.

Peck, J. (2012) 'Austerity urbanism', *City*, vol 16, no 6, pp 626-55.

Powell, M., Boyne, G. and Ashworth, R. (2001) 'Towards a geography of people poverty and place poverty', *Policy & Politics*, vol 29, no 3, pp 243-58.

Power, A., Willmott, H. and Davidson, R. (2011) *Family futures: Children and poverty in urban neighbourhoods*, Bristol: Policy Press.

Pugalis, L. (2015) 'English urban policy debate: an urban policy for all', *Town Planning Review*, vol 86, no 2, pp 125-31.

Pugalis, L. (2016) 'Austere state strategies: Regenerating for recovery and the resignification of regeneration', *Local Government Studies*, vol 42, no 1, pp 52-74.

Pugalis, L. and McGuinness, D. (2013) 'From a framework to a toolkit: Urban regeneration in an age of austerity', *Journal of Urban Regeneration and Renewal*, vol 6, no 4, pp 339-53.

Rae, A. (2013) 'English urban policy and the return to the city: a decade of growth, 2001–2011', *Cities*, vol 32, pp 94-101.

Rae, A., Hamilton, R., Crisp, R. and Powell, R. (2016) *Overcoming deprivation and disconnection in UK cities*, York: Joseph Rowntree Foundation.

Rogers, R. and Power, A. (2000) *Cities for a small country*, London: Faber & Faber.

RSA (Royal Society for the encouragement of Arts, Manufactures and Commerce) (2017) *Inclusive Growth Commission: Making our economy work for everyone*, London: RSA.

SEU (Social Exclusion Unit) (1998) *Bringing Britain together: A national strategy for neighbourhood renewal*, Cm 4045, London: SEU.

SEU (2001) *A new commitment to neighbourhood renewal: National strategy action plan*, London: SEU.

Tomaney, J. (2016) 'Limits of devolution: Localism, economics and post-democracy', *The Political Quarterly*, vol 87, no 4, pp 546-52.

Urban Task Force (1999) *Towards an urban renaissance*, London: Spon.

While, A., Crisp, R., Eadson, W. and Gore, T. (2016) *Major development projects: Connecting people in poverty to jobs*, York: Joseph Rowntree Foundation.

ELEVEN

Back to the future of community cohesion? Learning from New Labour

Matthew Donoghue

Introduction

New Labour embarked on an ambitious social project that sought to unite disparate social groups through mechanisms such as integration, social inclusion and the empowerment of different groups and 'communities'. A specific element of this was community cohesion policy. Designed in response to so-called race riots in northern England in 2001, community cohesion aimed to improve relations and contact between, primarily, ethnic communities that had been charged with leading parallel lives (Home Office, 2001a, b). Although its main focus was race relations (McGhee, 2003; Worley, 2005; Cheong et al, 2007), it emphasised among other things the virtues of paid work, not only as the best route out of poverty but also as a method of integrating into one's community-at-large (Lister, 2003, p 428; DWP, 2006, p 2; DCLG, 2007; Hulse and Stone, 2007, p 114). Thus its aim was to smooth tensions between multiple different social groups.

The current period has exhibited multiple instabilities that suggest community cohesion may be able to provide some lessons on dealing with such tensions – both in terms of what to do and what *not* to do – in times of relative uncertainty. Social cohesion, for example, has been linked to Theresa May's shared society, but also as a potential solution to preventing radicalisation and acts of terror. Yet running parallel to this are social divisions emphasised and exacerbated by the European Union (EU) referendum vote, discussions on the meaning and role of Britishness, and a heightened sense of inequality both in terms of income and power that has on more than one occasion manifested itself in anger on the streets. Community cohesion was designed to address these issues. What does the continued presence of these issues say about the success of community cohesion? Importantly, can we draw lessons about what to do, and what *not* to do, when it comes to building cohesion?

This chapter reappraises community cohesion in light of the current political, social and economic landscape. It draws on published work (see Donoghue, 2013, 2014, 2016) based on critical discourse analysis (CDA) of UK welfare reform and community cohesion policy documents from 2001–10, and a series of focus groups conducted in Bradford and Birmingham in 2012 that investigated everyday perceptions and understandings of community, cohesion and welfare. A number of implications of these findings are contrasted with recent events. This provides an opportunity to contextualise some of the failures and successes of community cohesion, and provide some tentative suggestions as to how this can be adapted for use by current and future governments. In particular, the chapter argues that any new formal policy response designed to increase cohesion should not reduce social division to ethnic difference, and should especially avoid securitising the subject. Crucially, those who are subject to such policies should be given a genuine voice in its development, rather than the promise of empowerment coupled with too great an increase in responsibility.

A brief history of community cohesion

Community cohesion as a discrete policy response originated in 2001 in response to unrest in the northern English towns of Bradford, Oldham and Burnley (Clarke, 2001; Richie, 2001; Kalra, 2003; Hussain and Bagguley, 2005). The government's approach to implementing cohesion strategies was split between national legislation and local initiatives, with the aim of making a national framework responsive to differing local contexts. The Community Cohesion Unit was established in 2002 to begin the process of mainstreaming community cohesion across various policy areas, including housing, youth and community work, policing, education and employment (Robinson, 2005, pp 1411-12). The promotion of community cohesion became a requirement within legislation, such as, for example, the Education and Inspections Act 2006 and the Equality Act 2006. This mainstreaming ensured that community cohesion remained on the policy agenda for some time, unlike more recent related initiatives such as the Big Society.

How the unrest in northern England was characterised set the tone for community cohesion. The media described the events in Bradford, Oldham and Burnley as 'race riots', as well as being some of the worst in the UK's history (see, for example, BBC News, 2001; Harris, 2001). The government concluded that ethnic groups were divided in education, employment, religion and language. This prevented 'meaningful interchanges' from taking place between different 'communities' (Home Office, 2001a, p 9). The Cantle Report remarked on 'the depth of polarisation in our towns and cities' (Home Office, 2001a, p 9), while the Denham Report asserted that '[w]e cannot claim to be a truly multi-cultural society if the various communities within it live, as Cantle puts it, a series of parallel lives which do not touch at any point' (Home Office, 2001b, p 13).

This represented a depoliticised account of the unrest, which has been countered by many. Amin (2003, p 461) argues that tensions were fuelled not by a lack of cross-cultural or ethnic understanding, but rather by 'deprivation and desperation'. Kalra (2003) highlights anger and frustration levelled at the police coinciding with media reports of racially motivated crime by south Asians against whites, which enabled the British National Party (BNP) to mobilise in the area (Kundnani, 2001; Bagguley and Hussain, 2003). Thus, the riots were a culmination of more than just 'parallel lives'; they were symptomatic of 'communities fragmented by colour lines, class lines, and police lines. It was the violence of hopelessness. It was the violence of the violated' (Kundnani, 2001, p 105). It should not be forgotten that the riots took place in areas of sharp industrial decline, exacerbated by the fact that 'the jobs to which South Asian migrants had once been drawn had disappeared and there were few alternative opportunities either for them or for working class whites' (Ratcliffe, 2012, p 264). Regardless of the socioeconomic situation on the ground, ethnicity became the overriding factor in community cohesion, with significant focus placed on the 'mores of minorities' (Cheong et al, 2007, p 26) over more intractable structural problems (see, for example, Blackledge, 2006; Letki, 2008, p 121; Ratcliffe, 2012, p 263). This is despite the fact that throughout New Labour's time in office, it retained a strong commitment to tackling social exclusion (Lister, 1998, 2003; Powell, 2000; Worley, 2005). Of course, it is important to remember that New Labour was famously 'nonchalant about rising inequality', and meekly invoked community as a counterbalance (Levitas, 2012, p 330). In addition, the original reports on the riots and community cohesion came under the Home Office's remit, making a focus on social order (for a discussion on social cohesion as social order, see Misztal, 2013) more likely than giving marginalised groups agency.

Responses to social exclusion and the development of community cohesion were implemented with different ends in mind, although there was some overlap. Important for this chapter is the framework that underwrote New Labour's adoption of both: Robert Putnam's development of social capital. In the words of Arneil (2007, p 42, cited in Husband and Alam, 2011, p 43), social capital provided 'the language of civic renewal to buttress New Labour's critique of the welfare state while justifying its reform in softer packaging.' Putnam (2000, p 19) described social capital as 'the associations among individuals – social networks and the norms of reciprocity and trustworthiness that arise from them.' This description clearly resonates with the notion of tackling groups living parallel lives. The state's role in this context is to facilitate the construction of institutions that will contribute to the accumulation of social capital, thus lessening the risk of social exclusion (Navarro, 2002, p 425) and increasing connections, interactions and mutual benefit between groups (Putnam, 1995, p 67). Indeed, Ferragina and Arrigoni argue that:

> In this context, the objective of creating social capital, through the empowerment of families and communities and the decentralisation of social services, became one of the main driving forces of New Labour's political action. (2017, p 360)

UK policy-makers were enthusiastic adopters of Putnam's distinction between bonding and bridging social capital. Bonding capital refers to the networks *within* relatively homogeneous groups while bridging capital refers to the networks *between* groups. Unsurprisingly, considering the Cantle and Denham Reports' focus on parallel lives and ethnic segregation (see, for example, Husband and Alam, 2011, pp 45-57), community cohesion focused on building bridging capital over bonding capital. Bonding capital was 'routinely seen as the lamentable characteristics of the dispossessed working classes and the minority communities still mired in "identity politics"', couched within a wider context of 'a consensual assertion of the failure of multiculturalism' (Husband and Alam, 2011, p 42; see also, McGhee, 2003). This runs against the findings of Zetter et al (2006, pp 23-5) that Putnamesque social capital requires *both* the bridging and bonding elements to be successful (indeed, following Putnam himself in this example).

Discourses around mistrust, parallel lives and ethnic segregation, especially in the post-9/11 and 7/7 context, made the ground fertile for a securitisation of community and cohesion. This securitisation has involved a process of 'othering' groups, especially Muslims, as not in step with British values. In fact, Muslims have been increasingly constructed as the 'new enemy within' (Husband and Alam, 2011, p 33). This has led, Worley argues, to a 'discourse of blame directed towards new migrants and especially British Muslim communities, who are expected to show "which side they are on", though an allegiance to a "phoney" construction of Britishness. This choice is not demanded of those who are white and not Muslim' (Worley, 2005, p 491; see also Kundnani, 2005).

Recent examples of responses to unrest

I have argued elsewhere that community cohesion represents a politically and ideologically specific response to social unrest (Donoghue, 2014, pp 87-8). In this sense, it is not possible to simply transpose the policy response of New Labour on to recent frameworks. However, the principles and assumptions underlying New Labour's approach to community cohesion remain alive and well in, for example, the Prevent Strategy, although the relationship between the two is certainly problematic (Jarvis and Lister, 2013). One can find more solid connections between community cohesion as a discrete policy area and responses to unrest in the current period via the underpinning assumptions of and approaches to British identity and values, citizenship and participation, as well as how the Coalition and Conservative governments have responded to destabilising and 'crisis' events, such as the refugee crisis and the ongoing political, economic and social fallout from the EU referendum result.

The event that perhaps invites the clearest comparison with 2001 specifically is the riots of 2011, which took place in London, Birmingham and Manchester. The Riots, Communities and Victims Panel (2012) concluded that the riots could not be traced to one single cause, but rather a combination of material deprivation, inequality, poor parenting and suspicion of the police. Thus, comparisons were more easily drawn to the Brixton riots of 1981 than the northern riots of 2001 (see, for example, Samad, 2013, p 270). Yet this characterisation of the 2011 riots chimes strongly with Kundnani, Kalra and Ratcliffe's explanations of the 2001 riots highlighted earlier. This suggests that there is a need to acknowledge that community cohesion is concerned with, and the result of, addressing multiple and interlinking social problems. Although it may be possible to identify a single trigger, arguing that any unrest is the result of a single underlying cause should be met with scepticism.

In the wake of the riots, David Cameron proclaimed that the unrest was a symptom of '[c]rime without punishment. Rights without responsibilities. Communities without control'. His solution was 'Stronger families. Stronger communities. A stronger society' (Kirkup et al, 2011). Notwithstanding Cameron's appeal to traditional conservative values, he echoed community cohesion's preoccupation with rights and responsibilities (Donoghue, 2013) and with building stronger, resilient communities (Craig, 2007). Cameron also continued the Labour government's focus on British (that is, Liberal) values and national identity as a major driver of cohesion. Identifying 'passive tolerance' as central to the segregation of communities, Cameron explicitly targeted Muslims as a problem group in which 'backward attitudes' of a minority of Muslim men encouraged gender segregation, radicalisation and extremism. The solution that was proposed, beyond rejecting 'passive tolerance' and 'being more assertive about liberal values', was to provide free English lessons specifically to Muslim women. This draws parallels with David Blunkett's conception of British 'home' as the 'English language – specifically, the ability of ethnic minorities to speak English and thereby take full part in wider society' (Alexander et al, 2007, p 784).

A particularly stark crisis event that had the potential to threaten social cohesion across Europe was the refugee crisis of 2015. In the UK (as elsewhere) tensions were increased as a result of aggressive government rhetoric against those fleeing countries such as Syria. Nils Muižnieks, the Council of Europe's human rights commissioner at the time of the crisis, remarked that Theresa May, the then Home Secretary, was determined to create a 'really hostile' environment for illegal immigrants, while 'criminalising irregular migrants' and 'failing to highlight the positive impact of immigration in Britain' (quoted in Travis, 2016). This was a crisis that would have benefited from an overt and explicit policy of community cohesion. However, the UK has no formal integration policy for refugees and asylum-seekers (Bakker et al, 2016). Rather, refugees find themselves excluded and in locations away from where 'social network formation might be possible' (Bakker et al, 2016, p 122). Bakker et al (2016, p 122) go as far as to argue that the UK's asylum and refugee support system 'can be regarded as a mechanism of social exclusion.' There have also been several acts of extremism in recent years – events that community cohesion policy, alongside initiatives such as Prevent, were designed to combat and prevent. Perhaps the two starkest events were the murders of Lee Rigby and Jo Cox, respectively. Lee Rigby, a soldier stationed at the Royal

Artillery Barracks in London, was attacked and killed by two men with knives and a cleaver as an act of retaliation against the killing of Muslims by the British armed forces. One of the attackers, Michael Adebolajo, was, according to *The Guardian*, under surveillance by MI5, and 'was detained by Kenyans for suspected extremist activity in 2010 and later deported to Britain' (Dodd and Halliday, 2013). Jo Cox, the MP for Batley and Spen in West Yorkshire, was shot and stabbed multiple times by Thomas Mair. Mair, who had links to the National Front and an interest in white supremacy, attacked and killed Cox because of her support for migration and the EU, describing her as a traitor to her 'race' (that is, white people) (Cobain, 2016).

Putting to one side the specific nature of these two events, seen within a broader timeline that includes other acts of terror and extremism, there is a growing popular feeling of increased social division rather than social cohesion. The British Social Attitudes survey characterises the UK as 'a country divided', particularly regarding the EU referendum and immigration. Rather than the referendum vote reflecting a lack of trust in politicians and government, it reflected 'the concerns of older, more "authoritarian" or social conservative voters who were particularly worried about immigration' (NatCen, 2017). This period also saw a significant increase in racial tension: *The Independent* reported that in the months following the referendum, the number of hate crimes recorded by police forces across the country rose by 100 per cent (Sharman and Jones, 2017). Ashcroft and Bevir (2016, p 355) argue that tensions between cultural pluralism, national identity and citizenship have been 'exacerbated by the prominence of immigration in the referendum campaign, the democratic deficit in the EU and the longer-term erosion of the welfare state.'

Although the social fractures discussed above are not new, they have been emphasised and exacerbated by recent events, alongside more long-term developments such as the erosion of potentially solidaristic institutions like the welfare state. Does this mean that community cohesion has failed? Rather than writing it off, the UK could benefit from a renewed prioritisation and development of social cohesion as a distinct policy area. For this to be successful it is crucial to examine New Labour's approach to community cohesion in order to learn what a reinvigorated approach to cohesion *should* and *shouldn't* do.

Assessing community cohesion

This chapter draws on research conducted during the New Labour and Coalition governments concerned with understanding the discursive presentation and legitimisation of government strategies towards cohesion, and the responses of citizens directly affected by the policies. This section summarises the findings and arguments developed from the research, which will then be revisited in the current context. In-depth and dedicated analysis and discussion can be found in Donoghue (2013, 2014, 2016). This work consists of a CDA of 12 Green Papers, White Papers and consultation documents on Community Cohesion and welfare reform, alongside focus groups conducted in Bradford and Birmingham in 2012. The focus groups allowed for an assessment of community cohesion and its legacy not long after a change of government. This also enabled participants to begin to place the legacy and impact of community cohesion within the context of David Cameron's Coalition government.

CDA was used to critically engage with the specifically constructed understanding and presentation of (community) cohesion within New Labour's policy on the subject, including how competing approaches to community cohesion were emphasised and/or de-emphasised, thus legitimising as 'common sense' and ubiquitous a politically and socially subjective approach to social cohesion (for more on the use of CDA in general, see van Dijk, 2004; for more on my specific approach to CDA, see Donoghue, 2014, pp 83-6, 92-106; 2017). The research identified three central political logics that contribute to the discursive presentation and legitimisation of community cohesion: the logic of conditionality, the logic of rights and responsibilities, and the logic of assimilation and integration. These logics operate within the broader social logics of welfare and cohesion. Where the social logics contain the rules on how a citizen should act, what is acceptable behaviour and so on, the political logics provide the mechanisms through which the rules are developed and transmitted. It is the political logics, then, that can provide most insight into the influence of discourses of cohesion found in policy documents on citizens (for details on social and political logics, see Howarth, 2005, p 323).

The focus groups were conducted in diverse and relatively deprived neighbourhoods, and both have had attention placed on them regarding levels of community cohesion. Participants were recruited through gatekeepers (Barbour and Schostak, 2005, p 44), such as community organisations. These proved especially important regarding access to the field in Bradford, as the population was particularly wary of an increased focus on the town by academics and policy-makers since 2001. Participants were asked questions regarding opinions and experiences of their community, how different groups interact, and how much say they have over local decision-making. They were also asked about experiences with the welfare system and overall perceptions of it. The focus groups were originally analysed using CDA to enable a greater analysis of and comparison between them and the analysis of policy documents. This enables the research to contrast discursive constructions of cohesion with everyday experiences of the policy.

CDA of New Labour policy (Donoghue, 2013) highlighted that although on the surface there was a commitment to the empowerment of communities, the policy was constructed in a way that in fact significantly increased the responsibilisation of communities and individuals for their own community cohesion, as well as community and individual welfare. For example, within the logic of rights and responsibilities, a notional idea of rights was used to legitimise a notable increase in responsibilities; the discursive construction of these utilised the ideal of 'rights' to soften the blow of this increase in responsibility (Donoghue, 2013, pp 91-3). This accompanied the construction of a logic of assimilation and integration in which assimilation – here understood as a process of the 'outside' group becoming subsumed into the 'host' group, representing a diminished position of power – was legitimised via an emphasis on the language of integration, which promises a more mutual process of coming together. The 'outside' group are able to articulate the need for different elements of culture and values to remain distinct from the 'host' group.

These logics were perhaps best represented by a participant from one of the Bradford focus groups. In the following extract he discusses his experiences of racism as a British-Asian. He has lived in Bradford all his life, and thus qualifies as a member of the 'host' community. However, the focus of community cohesion policy on Muslim groups makes this participant's connection to the host group problematic, particularly as 'host' is often taken as being synonymous with 'white British' (see, for example, Worley, 2005):

> As a community or as south Asian or Muslim etcetera, we use the word discrimination, racism as an excuse sometimes.... I think we're more racist sometimes than the host community, about wanting to integrate, about wanting to get together – we would

rather stay out of it. (Fieldwork participant, cited in Donoghue, 2016, p 8)

This participant belongs to a number of interconnected communities: his neighbourhood, his ethnic and religious heritage and his national identity (British). These identities enable him to discuss racism from an authoritative position, and from multiple perspectives. Yet he deliberately separates Muslim and Asian from 'host' in the above extract, while also responsibilising himself to 'do more' to integrate into *his own* host community. He effectively polices himself, invoking elements of conditionality (in that he should integrate more in order to deserve fair treatment), thus emphasising responsibility and de-emphasising rights.

This also demonstrates that discourses emphasised and developed through policy do have an effect on those that are the focus of such policies, as they are drawn on in order to make sense of social problems as well as to situate individuals and groups within the social and policy world (see Donoghue, 2016). This is especially true for New Labour's community cohesion policy. Its strong discursive framing restricted *how* people were able to understand and approach social division and integration, legitimising heavily constrained notions of community and cohesion. The policy, in framing and constructing these understandings, constrained ways of 'thinking about, doing and being communities' (McGhee, 2003, p 391). It is therefore important to understand the general direction in which community cohesion policy travelled up until the end of the New Labour years, and continues today, especially within the language of 'resilient communities' (see, for example, Macdonald and Hunter, 2010; Spalek and Davies, 2012; Havering, 2013).

Community cohesion has become increasingly more closely entwined with the anti-radicalisation and anti-extremism strategy of the UK government. This is most clearly associated with the Prevent and Counter-terrorism (Contest) Strategies that seek to identify individuals vulnerable to radicalisation and prevent this from happening (Jarvis and Lister, 2013). It is locally focused, and emphasises 'hearts and minds' tactics. It also focuses on increasing the resilience of communities, addressing grievances and 'challenging and disrupting ideologies sympathetic to extremism' (Thomas, 2010, p 444). The cohesion of communities is central to this conception, because strong and confident communities with well-developed networks and bridging social capital are more resilient to threats of extremism and radicalisation. The major tension between cohesion and counter-extremism is in the overwhelming focus on Muslims that, as Thomas (2009) highlights, stands in contradiction to community cohesion's focus on inter-ethnic contact. This focus should be seen as superficial, especially in more recent years, as notions of cohesion become more securitised. This produces both an implicit and explicit target; the 'enemy within' and the 'home-grown terrorist' both invoke feelings of disbelief that 'one of us' could commit such an act, and are thus not 'one of us' at all (see Havering, 2013, pp 349-53). Within this context, community cohesion is no longer about bringing groups together, but rather weeding out threats to the established – white British – 'community'. This takes place in a problematic framework in which the location, role and utility of conflict is unclear; the securitisation of community cohesion necessitates a sharp focus on conflict, yet there is an 'implicit rhetorical conflation of community cohesion with the removal of conflict' (Husband and Alam, 2011, p 222) throughout the policy framework. This pervades current understandings and deployments of community cohesion, which may lead to more problems than it solves.

Placing findings in the current context

The previous sections have established that community cohesion policy during the New Labour years was overly targeted at what the government saw as 'problem' groups, and that this legacy continued with the Coalition and Conservative governments. Although the Conservative government is unlikely to revive wholesale a Labour initiative, there are still lessons that can be applied to recent events.

Riots and unrest

On the surface there is perhaps little for community cohesion to speak to regarding the English riots in 2011 considering that they were quickly characterised as having nothing to do with race and ethnicity. Yet, like in 2001, the English riots were an outburst of frustration against unfavourable conditions and a perceived controlling and/or uncaring state. One focus group participant in Birmingham, when asked what 'community' meant to him, replied that:

> ... to me a community is a group of people who are ... battling against the decision makers ... it's like if you've got a family member that is in charge of the house, and doesn't really listen to anybody and does their own thing ... everyone ... is going to get frustrated. (cited in Donoghue, 2014, p 249)

Community for this participant was understood as its own entity in charge of its own wellbeing. Yet it is inherently linked to the state through implicit claims on rights, and in this sense community becomes understood as a defensive resource, battling 'against the decision-makers'. Contrary to Cameron's position during the 2011 riots, the participant sees communities within his area as particularly strong. Yet rather than having all rights and no responsibilities, the community is understood as a vehicle to realise rights. This is an important distinction that should be taken into account when considering current approaches to cohesion. A particular issue with community cohesion was that it promised empowerment but instead created more responsibility without necessarily providing communities the wherewithal to discharge it (see, for example, Donoghue, 2014, p 300). This will inevitably lead to frustration, apathy and anger.

Attitudes towards refugees, immigration and integration

Community cohesion was concerned with the idea that ethnic groups were living 'parallel lives' and not interacting; this caused fear and mistrust that led to the unrest of 2001. However, the form of integration pursued through community cohesion was heavily assimilationist. The example taken from Donoghue (2016) in the previous section illustrates how pervasive the assimilationist approach taken in the policy could be, moving beyond the integration of immigrants into settled communities; it extended assimilation to include conforming to accepted norms and values – something that can be seen in Cameron's response to the English riots in 2011. This can quickly diminish the legitimacy of various groups that do not, for example, live up to a dominant understanding of 'British values'.

The lack of focus on integration during the recent migration crisis also points to the need for a change of focus regarding social cohesion. The focus on security alongside the need to accept dominant norms can erect barriers to integration for all categories of migrants. Those who are most able to negotiate these barriers are wealthier, voluntary migrants who are likely more able to integrate via employment or even through already established networks. This is not the case for forced migrants, such as refugees and asylum-seekers who have felt compelled or have been forcibly removed from their home countries. In such situations, new arrivals, as the outsider group, cannot be expected to shoulder entirely the responsibility to integrate, as is the case in current UK cohesion policy that deploys a 'discourse of blame directed towards new migrants' that compels them to declare 'which side they are on' (Worley, 2005, p 491).

Extremism

It has been well documented that community cohesion's focus was overwhelmingly on Muslims, with the same applying for counter-extremism strategies. The Prevent Strategy, in its early years, was closely linked to community cohesion with the latter aiming to win over hearts and minds while the former introduced strategies to identify and police threats. Both can be seen as operating within the notion of 'problem communities'. Husband and Alam (2011, p 74) highlight that many saw Prevent as a vehicle to spy on and target Muslim communities. They point to the Communities and Local Government Committee of the House of Commons 2010 report, entitled *Preventing violent extremism*, which characterised 'the single focus on Muslims in *Prevent*' as 'unhelpful', 'stigmatising', 'potentially alienating' and containing 'a pre-occupation with the theological basis of radicalisation, when the evidence seems to indicate that politics, policy and socio-economics may be more important factors in the process' (CLGC, 2010, p 3, cited in Husband and Alam, 2011, p 74). Considering this, the Bradford participant's policing of his own membership of different 'communities' discussed earlier can be understood as the outcome of a sustained policy initiative that unfairly targeted a religious and ethnic group based on largely unfounded assumptions around religion and values.

This is perhaps the area in which most can be learned. On the surface, the most prominent problem is that instead of engendering mutual respect between social and ethnic groups and the state, communities have been divided. Thus, 'cohesion' becomes an empty promise, associated more with political rhetoric than with meaningful integration. It can be argued that this was an inevitable outcome of the securitisation of social cohesion through the interrelation of community cohesion and Prevent, considering the positionality towards Muslims in much of the community cohesion canon as well as an assimilationist approach that weighted power significantly away from those groups deemed as 'in need' of cohesion. As such, it becomes more important to lessen the overt, and more implicit discursive, focus on Muslims as 'problem' groups, and focus more on socioeconomic and structural barriers to effective *socioeconomic* as well as ethno-cultural integration.

'Brexit'

Well publicised in the popular media after the referendum vote for the UK to withdraw from the EU was the increase in racially motivated violence and hate speech. According to Morgan (2017, p 123),

> ... the core concerns of post-Brexit policy in the UK seem likely to be tightly focused on the economy because of the disruption created by Brexit. They are unlikely to be concerned directly with inequality, social mobility, democratic accountability and social cohesion as the problems that helped to trigger Brexit.

Richards and Heath (2017) argue that both the vote to leave the EU and the actual process of leaving may act as a weathervane for social cohesion in the post-EU era in terms of values: attitudes towards immigration, or Brexit as an anti-establishment act, for example. Yet they frame this strongly in terms of class differences rather than adherence to or deviation from supposed shared *national* values.

This re-emphasises a major problem with community cohesion, in that it was too preoccupied with ethnicity and culture, rather than addressing the socioeconomic divisions that may cause ostensible differences in attitudes and values. Proclaiming a shared set of universal values, as community cohesion did and present politicians continue to do, elides many of the core drivers of unrest and division. Yet it is politically expedient because it enables governments to make social division a problem of 'them' not thinking like 'us', generating a set of moral implications based on supposed 'universal' values. As unpopular as it currently may be politically, any reimagination of community cohesion for the current period must prioritise tackling inequality and structural barriers such as social exclusion and low-paid work – especially considering the emphasis on integration via paid work within much of the social exclusion and cohesion debates in Europe and North America (see, for example, Levitas, 2005; Hulse and Stone, 2007).

Conclusion

A rejuvenated strategy for community or social cohesion would be of benefit to UK society, although certainly not without its problems. It is essential that any new development of cohesion policy does not also continue to pursue a primarily assimilationist strategy that targets arbitrarily defined 'problem' groups. A new cohesion policy provides the opportunity to break from assimilationist rhetoric, still preferred by government, that places undue emphasis on a set of 'universal values' that, although politically convenient, shifts focus from the more pressing socioeconomic divisions in British society. It also opens space for a re-imagination of cohesion aimed at developing a more mutual form of integration that involves the 'host' community playing a larger supporting role rather than placing the burden almost entirely on the shoulders of the 'out' groups that are unlikely to have the necessary resources or capitals to fully integrate without the appropriate support. Such changes must begin at the level of policy-makers and politicians. Discursive moves toward empowerment and mutual support must be reflected in concrete policy initiatives that, first and foremost, directly involve those the policies will affect the most.

A significant problem facing the transformation of the arguments in this chapter into policy recommendations is the current lack of political will to either focus more on socioeconomic inequality or to 'de-securitise' cohesion discourse and thinking in the UK. Programmes that aim to tackle inequality are not particularly compatible with the UK's ongoing austerity programme and the government's political preoccupations, as indicated by the recent resignations of every member of the government's Social Mobility Commission. Alan Milburn MP, the committee chair, argued that the government's focus on UK/EU negotiations eclipsed other concerns, despite the commission itself publishing a report highlighting the social divisions 'laid bare by the Brexit vote' (Pickard, 2017).

A Corbyn-led Labour government would present more potential for a rejuvenated Social Cohesion strategy, although this would likely look very different from New Labour's community cohesion strategy. Recommendations here should focus on the relationship between socioeconomic inequality and feelings of difference, not only between ethnic groups but also between a range of social groups based on income, employment status and even geographical location. In this sense, the concept of social cohesion, when removed from its current social and political frame, provides the opportunity to acknowledge that cohesion – like social exclusion, for example – is highly multifaceted, and as such, any programmes to encourage and engender cohesion must take this into account.

Thinking more modestly, there is also clear potential for renewing social cohesion broadly within the existing framework, retaining the primary concern of the integration of different ethnic groups. Such an approach should focus strongly on decoupling social cohesion with security, which will, in turn, help address the implicit and explicit problematisation of 'outsider' communities, especially Muslim groups that have been disproportionately affected by community cohesion since 2001. As part of this process, social cohesion should be reimagined so that it prioritises in reality mutual processes of communication and deliberation that are led from the bottom up, rather than simply promising such processes through empowering rhetoric.

This chapter asked whether present-day scholars and policy-makers can learn anything from New Labour's community cohesion policy. The ensuing discussion has led to the argument that although there are a number of positive take-aways, much of the community cohesion framework provides us with an example of what *not* to do. This does not mean that, for example, the strategies employed within the framework have not been successful in building communities resilient to extremism or helping to combat terrorism (and indeed, this is not the focus of this chapter). Rather, the argument is that this is not what community (or social) cohesion should be about. The securitisation of cohesion coupled with the disproportionate focus on Muslims within the UK severely limited the policy's ability to bring communities together. The conspicuous lack of concern for socioeconomic inequalities compounded division, focusing instead on a nebulous set of British values that made cohesion in the UK more about assimilating and conforming to dominant norms than about bringing different groups together in a process of navigating barriers between them. As such, even as a concern now mainstreamed throughout much social and public policy, it has not been able to deal with the divisions that have resurfaced in recent years.

References

Alexander, C., Edwards, R. and Temple, B. (2007) 'Contesting cultural communities: Language, ethnicity and citizenship in Britain', *Journal of Ethnic and Migration Studies*, vol 33, no 5, pp 783-800.

Amin, A. (2003) 'Unruly strangers? The 2001 urban riots in Britain', *International Journal of Urban and Regional Research*, vol 27, no 2, pp 460-3.

Arneil, B. (2007) 'The meaning and utility of social capital', in R. Edwards, J. Franklin and J. Holland (eds), *Assessing social capital: Concept, policy and practice*, Newcastle: Cambridge Scholars Publishing, pp 29-52.

Ashcroft, R. and Bevir, M. (2016) 'Pluralism, national identity and citizenship: Britain after Brexit', *Political Quarterly*, vol 87, no 3, pp 355-9.

Bagguley, P. and Hussain, Y. (2003) 'The Bradford "Riot" of 2001: A Preliminary Analysis', in C. Barker and M. Tyldesley (eds) *Ninth International Conference on Alternative Futures and Popular Protest*, pp 1-17. Manchester: Manchester Metropolitan University.

Bakker, L., Cheung, S.Y. and Phillimore, J. (2016) 'The asylum-integration paradox: Comparing asylum support systems and refugee integration in The Netherlands and the UK', *International Migration*, vol 54, no 4, pp 118-32.

Barbour, R.S. and Schostak, J. (2004) 'Interviewing and focus groups', in B. Somekh and C. Lewin (eds) *Research methods in the social sciences*, London: Sage.

BBC News (2001) 'Race "segregation" caused riots', 11 December (http://news.bbc.co.uk/1/hi/england/1702799.stm).

Blackledge, A. (2006) 'The racialisation of language in British political discourse', *Critical Discourse Studies*, vol 3, no 1, pp 61-79.

Cheong, P.H., Edwards, R., Goulbourne, H. and Solomos, J. (2007) 'Immigration, social cohesion and social capital: A critical review', *Critical Social Policy*, vol 17, no 1, pp 24-49.

Clarke, T. (2001) *Burnley speaks, who listens? A report of the Burnley Task Force*, Burnley: Burnley Council.

Cobain, I. (2016) 'Jo Cox killed in "brutal, cowardly" and politically motivated murder, trial hears', *The Guardian*, 14 November.

CLGC (Communities and Local Government Committee) of the House of Commons (2010) *Sixth report of session 2009-10, Preventing violent extremism*, HC 65. London: The Stationery Office.

Craig, G. (2007) 'Community capacity-building: something old, something new …?', *Critical Social Policy*, vol 27, no 3, pp 335-59.

DCLG (Department for Communities and Local Government) (2007) *What works in Community Cohesion*, London: The Stationery Office.

Dodd, V. and Halliday, J. (2013) 'Lee Rigby murder: Michael Adebolajo and Michael Adebowale found guilty', *The Guardian*, 19 October.

Donoghue, M. (2013) 'Welfare and cohesion contested: a critical discourse analysis of New Labour's reform programme', *British Politics*, vol 8, no 1, pp 79-100.

Donoghue, M. (2014) '"Cohesion" in the context of welfare and citizenship: discourse, policy and "common sense"', PhD thesis, Oxford Brookes University.

Donoghue, M. (2016) 'Cohesion as "common sense": everyday narratives of community and cohesion in New Labour's Britain', *Politics*, vol 36, no 3, pp 262-76.

Donoghue, M. (2017) 'Beyond hegemony: elaborating on the use of Gramscian concepts in critical discourse analysis in political studies', *Political Studies*, doi: 10.1177/0032321717722362

DWP (Department for Work and Pensions) (2006) *A New Deal for Welfare: Empowering people to work*, London: The Stationery Office.

Ferragina, E. and Arrigoni, A. (2017) 'The rise and fall of social capital: requiem for a theory?', *Political Studies Review*, vol 15, no 3, pp 355-67.

Harris, P. (2001) 'Race riots ignite Bradford', *The Observer*, 8 July.

Havering, A. (2013) 'Managing integration: German and British policy responses to the "threat from within" post-2001', *Journal of International Migration and Integration*, vol 14, no 2, pp 345-62.

Home Office (2001a) *Community Cohesion: A report of the Independent Review Team*, London: The Stationery Office.

Home Office (2001b) *Building cohesive communities: A report of the ministerial group on public order and Community Cohesion*, London: The Stationery Office.

Howarth, D. (2005) *Discourse theory in European Politics: Identity, policy and governance*, Houndmills: Palgrave Macmillan.

Hulse, K. and Stone, W. (2007) 'Social cohesion, social capital and social exclusion', *Policy Studies*, vol 28, no 2, pp 109-28.

Husband, C. and Alam, Y. (2011) *Social cohesion and counter-terrorism: A policy contradiction?*, Bristol: Policy Press.

Hussain, Y. and Bagguley, P. (2005) 'Citizenship, ethnicity and identity: British Pakistanis after the 2001 "riots"', *Sociology*, vol 39, no 3, pp 407-25.

Jarvis, L. and Lister, M. (2013) 'Disconnected citizenship? the impacts of anti-terrorism policy on citizenship in the UK', *Political Studies*, vol 61, no 3, pp 656-75.

Kalra, V, (2003) 'Police lore and community disorder: diversity in the criminal justice system', in D. Mason (ed) *Explaining ethnic differences: Changing patterns of disadvantage in Britain*, Bristol: Policy Press, pp 139-52.

Kirkup, J., Whitehead, T., Gilligan, A. (2011) 'UK riots: David Cameron confronts "Britain's social collapse"', *The Daily Telegraph*, 14th August, https://www.telegraph.co.uk/news/uknews/crime/8701371/UK-riots-David-Cameron-confronts-Britains-moral-collapse.html

Kundnani, A. (2001) 'From Oldham to Bradford: the violence of the violated', Institute of Race Relations, Comment, 1 October (www. irr.org.uk/news/from-oldham-to-bradford-the-violence-of-the-violated/).

Letki, N. (2008) 'Does diversity erode social cohesion? Social capital and race in British neighbourhoods', *Political Studies*, vol 56, no 1, pp 99-126.

Levitas, R. (2005) *The inclusive society? Social exclusion and New Labour*, Basingstoke: Palgrave Macmillan.

Macdonald, M. and Hunter, D. (2010) 'Security, population and governmentality: UK counter-terrorism discourse (2007-2011)', *Critical Approaches to Discourse Analysis across Disciplines*, vol 6, no 2.

McGhee, D. (2003) 'Moving to "our" common ground – A critical examination of Community Cohesion discourse in twenty-first century Britain', *The Sociological Review*, vol 51, no 3, pp 376-404.

Morgan, J. (2017) 'Brexit: Be careful what you wish for?', *Globalisations*, vol 14, no 1, pp 118-26.

NatCen (2017) 'Brexit' (www.bsa.natcen.ac.uk/latest-report/british-social-attitudes-34/brexit.aspx).

Navarro, V. (2002) 'A critique of social capital', *International Journal of Health Services*, vol 32, no 3, pp 423-32.

Levitas, R. (2012) 'The just's umbrella: Austerity and the Big Society in coalition policy and beyond', *Critical Social Policy*, vol 32, no 3, pp 320-42.

Lister, R. (1998) 'From equality to social inclusion: New Labour and the welfare state', *Critical Social Policy*, vol 18, no 55, pp 215-25.

Lister, R. (2003) 'Investing in the citizen-workers of the future: Transformations of citizenship and the state under New Labour', *Social Policy & Administration*, vol 37, no 5, pp 427-43.

Misztal, B.A. (2013) *Trust in modern societies: The search for the bases of social order*, Oxford: Blackwell.

Pickard, J. (2017) 'Theresa May's Social Mobility Commission walks out', *Financial Times*, 3 December (www.ft.com/content/e4426dce-d808-11e7-a039-c64b1c09b482).

Powell, M. (2000) 'New Labour and the third way in the British welfare state: a new and distinctive approach?', *Critical Social Policy*, vol 20, no 1, pp 39-60.

Putnam, R. (1995) 'Bowling alone: America's declining social capital', *Journal of Democracy*, vol 6, no 1, pp 65-78.

Putnam, R. (2000) *Bowling alone: The collapse and revival of American community* (2nd edn), New York: Simon & Schuster.

Ratcliffe, P. (2012) '"Community Cohesion": Reflections on a flawed paradigm', *Critical Social Policy*, vol 32, no 2, pp 262-81.

Richie, D. (2001) *Oldham Independent Review: One Oldham, one future*, Oldham: Oldham Council.

Richards, L. and Heath, A. (2017) '"Two nations"? Brexit, inequality and social cohesion', British Academy blog (www.britac.ac.uk/blog/%E2%80%9Ctwo-nations%E2%80%9D-brexit-inequality-and-social-cohesion).

Riots, Communities and Victims Panel (2011) *After the riots: The final report of the Riots Communities and Victims Panel*, London: The Stationery Office.

Robinson, D. (2005) 'The search for Community Cohesion: Key themes and dominant concepts of the public policy agenda', *Urban Studies*, vol 42, no 8, pp 1411-27.

Samad, Y. (2013) 'Community cohesion without parallel lives in Bradford', *Patterns of Prejudice*, vol 47, no 3, pp 269-87.

Sharman, J. and Jones, I. (2017) 'Hate crimes rise by up to 100 per cent across England and Wales, figures reveal', *The Independent*, 15 February.

Spalek, B. and Davies, L. (2012) 'Mentoring in relation to violent extremism: A study of role, purpose and outcomes', *Studies in Conflict and Terrorism*, vol 35, no 5, pp 354-68.

Thomas, P. (2009) 'Between two stools? The government's "Preventing Violent Extremism" agenda', *Political Quarterly*, vol 80, no 2, pp 282-91.

Thomas, P. (2010) 'Failed and friendless: The UK's "Preventing Violent Extremism" programme', *British Journal of Politics and International Relations*, vol 12, no 3, pp 442-58.

Travis, A. (2016) 'Refugee crisis: human rights chief hits out at Cameron and May', *The Guardian*, 23 March.

van Dijk, T.A. (2004) 'Critical discourse analysis', in D. Schriffen, D. Tannen and H.E. Hamilton (eds) *The handbook of discourse analysis*, Oxford: Blackwell.

Worley, C. (2005) '"It's not about race. It's about the community": New Labour and "Community Cohesion"', *Critical Social Policy*, vol 25, no 4, pp 483-96.

Zetter, R., Griffiths, D., Sigona, N., Flynn, D., Pasha, T. and Beynon, R. (2006) *Immigration, social cohesion and social capital: What are the links?*, York: Joseph Rowntree Foundation.

TWELVE

Learning from New Labour's approach to the NHS

Ian Greener

Introduction

Policy-makers seem to find the urge to reorganise healthcare almost irresistible. Doing so, however, as governments across the world have repeatedly found out, is expensive and time-consuming. In the UK, the National Health Service (NHS), after experiencing relative stability between its founding in 1948 and its first substantial reorganisation in 1974, has been subject to substantial changes with increasing frequency. In the 1980s the NHS Management Inquiry (DHSS, 1983) led to changes attempting to make the service better run. In the 1990s, an 'internal market' was introduced (HM Government, 1989) that attempted to create a dynamic where a split between purchasers and providers would generate improvements to services. After their election to power in 1997, Labour engaged in an almost hyperactive series of changes to the organisation of the NHS in England (with devolution taking other UK countries down a different path). Such a period of intense policy-making offers us significant opportunities for learning, both in terms of the NHS, and for health policy more generally.

While it is relatively straightforward to try and draw lessons from individual, specific policy changes, trying to disentangle the effects of one change from another, especially because they came with such frequency under Labour, is a more significant challenge. Finding a method of achieving this is a difficult but important task. To try and address these challenges, this chapter adopts an approach based on Pawson's realism, especially in the context of realist review (Pawson et al, 2005; Pawson, 2006, 2013), in trying to extract contextually sensitive programme theories from Labour's reorganisation to learn lessons from the changes between 1997 and 2010 for policy today.

In contrast to more conventional approaches to evaluation and review, Pawson suggests that we need to consider not only evidence about what appears to have worked in specific instances, but also the context within which those changes occurred, the theory that they appear to draw from and the outcomes that resulted as a consequence. The patterns between context, mechanism and outcome can be used to compare evidence of what happened in each case with both policy-makers' expectations and existing theories to generate learning that we might be able to use to inform future policy.

Perhaps Pawson's most celebrated example is around 'naming and shaming', which he shows applies to a range of different approaches to public service change. Here interventions as diverse as ASBOs (Anti-social Behaviour Orders), sex offender regulations and the use of league tables of performance measures all share an underlying theory in which the use of public censure of one kind or another is meant to influence behaviour to drive it in the direction policy-makers sought, but with very different outcomes. By seeking patterns of outcomes and how they related to specific contexts and the mechanisms introduced, we can generate a 'programme theory' of how and when naming and shaming interventions might work, and when they do not. Generating programme theories in this way allows us to link findings from a particular public service to attempts to reorganise services in another area, as well as with theories of change more generally.

The context of health policy under Labour

A first step in exploring what lessons we can draw from Labour therefore has to take account of the wider context of the 1990s and 2000s. This in itself represents a formidable challenge as it is difficult to find a boundary to differentiate which elements of context to include as relevant and which to exclude. We can, however, find some key factors in the existing literature that set a context which Labour inherited in coming to power, and shaped their health policy while in office.

A central part of understanding the 'New Labour' project comes in the positioning of the party as economically credible and business-friendly (Mandelson, 2011). To achieve this, the first Blair government initially promised to remain within the spending limits set by the Conservatives before them. This set an initial economic context where increases in public service expenditure were very limited. This was apparent in Labour initially suggesting that any problems faced by the NHS were not due to its relative low level of funding compared to other health systems

(Secretary of State for Health, 1997). At the same time, however, it was increasingly becoming clear that building infrastructure was in need of significant capital investment that had not been achieved by previous attempts to address that challenge (Mohan, 2002).

A second key contextual factor was that Labour inherited an NHS in 1997 where an 'internal market' for healthcare put in place in the early 1990s was lying mostly dormant except for some experimentation around GP purchasing (Wainwright, 1998). Instead, there was an increased stress on partnership working (Secretary of State for Health, 1996).

Into this financial and organisational context we can see three phases in Labour's health policy in their early years in power (Greener, 2004). In 1997, there was an election promise to reduce waiting times, and a White Paper claiming Labour was abolishing the internal market on the grounds that it was bureaucratic and wasteful (Secretary of State for Health, 1997), and with a pragmatic, partnership-based approach being advocated instead. However, the 'Old Labour' Health Secretary Frank Dobson made way in 1999 for his ambitious junior minister Alan Milburn, giving a new direction to health policy that was more distinctly 'New Labour'.

Milburn's appointment takes us to the second phase of Labour policy. In 2000, Tony Blair appeared to spontaneously promise on television that his government would increase NHS funding to that of the European average (which may have happened without him consulting his Chancellor first; see Klein, 2006), and which paved the way for the NHS Plan (Secretary of State for Health, 2000), with its focus on improving performance while promising increased investment. Budget constraints began to be relieved as the government and its Chancellor Gordon Brown established economic credibility (Keegan, 2003), and the government faced concerns about the lack of reform progress (Giddens, 2002).

This led to Labour beginning to seek an alternative model where welfare expenditure could be increased. The answer was the founding of an economic model based on an implicit agreement with the City of London in which Labour avoided regulating the activities of new financial areas such as derivatives, and reduced corporate taxation for those engaged in trading activities in the City on the grounds that this was entrepreneurial. In return, the growth of the City of London would help fund an expansion in welfare services (Richards, 2010).

The clearest signal of the change in direction for the NHS came from Milburn's publication of the NHS Plan (Secretary of State for

Health, 2000), which combined a promise of new investment with a requirement that the NHS changed, and which put in place a new performance management system to measure the improvements that government was demanding.

The third phase of new Labour's health policy is specific to England, with devolution leading Scotland especially down a different path. After 2002, and driven by demands from Blair to be more radical in public service change more generally (Blair, 2010), there was an emphasis on the use of choice and competition combined with a funding system that sought to reward providers of care that could attract contracts for their services (DH, 2001, 2002). The period after 2003, in many respects, was about Labour working through these different threads, with the gradual extension of the market for healthcare to encourage greater non-public competition proving perhaps the most contentious (Crisp, 2011).

Mechanisms of health policy change under New Labour

Labour's period in government, especially between 1997 and 2003, represented a hyper-active period of health policy-making. Any attempt to cover every aspect of what they attempted in their whole period of government would require more space that is available here. What I can do, in line with the method outlined above, is attempt to capture the most significant elements of health policy change in a series of four programme theories, justified and explained below, of delivery, choice and competition, the Private Finance Initiative (PFI), and funding.

Delivery

The first programme theory is that of 'delivery' and is based on Labour's use of performance management, not only in the NHS, but also across the public sector. A government 'delivery unit' was established to attempt to ensure that the Prime Minister's expressed frustrations about the ability of the public sector to achieve change were confronted and dealt with (Barber, 2007). Alongside the delivery unit, a range of changes was made to healthcare regulation, but here we focus on the performance management aspects of 'delivery' because of their importance in understanding New Labour's health policy, and the extensive research exploring performance management that allows us to assess its effects.

The 'delivery' programme theory was based on the iterative setting of targets against which performance was measured to ensure that central policy was being carried out by those responsible for it. The government's concern to be seen to be meeting the promises they had made the electorate meant that they would attempt to more proactively measure and monitor the targets they were setting for public services than had been the case before.

In the NHS we can see two main variations of the 'delivery' programme theory – one in hospitals in England, and one in GP practices in both England and Scotland. In English hospitals, targets were set, often at a high level, for a range of outcomes with waiting times a special concern because of their public visibility, but also because of Labour's promises to reduce them as one of their 1997 election pledges. From these targets, composite measures were constructed to grade the overall performance of a hospital, initially based on traffic lights (red, amber, green) (Secretary of State for Health, 2000), but later using scales with measures such as 'good' and 'poor', but with both measures and scales changing from year to year. Labour claimed to offer 'earned autonomy', new funding, freedoms from inspection and even new organisational statuses to those that were able to show they could consistently meet these targets.

In GP surgeries, 'delivery' was handled in a different way. In the Quality and Outcomes Framework (QOF), targets were put in place after extensive consultation with leaders from the profession as part of the introduction of a new GP contract. Targets were at a less abstract level, were grounded in everyday clinical practices such as smoking cessation, and were presented as being based on clinical evidence rather than on politically motivated goals such as waiting times. The way GPs practices were funded was changed to try and link successful measured performance in the QOF to them hitting or exceeding their targets.

We therefore have two different forms of 'delivery', and a comparison between the two forms a central part of the analysis of the programme theory below.

Choice and competition

Labour's second programme theory of 'choice and competition' captures perhaps the most contentious of Labour's changes – their use of market mechanisms, and their extension from the quasi-market approach of the 1990s to include private providers as a means of increasing competition (Mays et al, 2011). This approach of making use of 'choice and competition' went across the whole NHS in England, spanning GP, hospital and even public health provision.

Choice and competition was designed to increase NHS responsiveness (Greener and Powell, 2009) by increasing competition for care contracts between both public and non-public providers, and asking patients to choose between different providers of care for secondary care referrals especially. This 'competition and choice' approach was intended to work, much like the Conservative internal market of the 1990s, by making sure financial flows rewarded the providers of care that were successful in attracting care contracts (DH, 2002), but was extended over the decade to give a more significant role for private sector providers of care. Labour's approach had an important advocate in Le Grand (see his justification in Le Grand, 2007), who worked in a role with the government as an adviser during this period.

Private Finance Initiative (PFI)

Labour's third programme theory represented their attempt to deal with the infrastructure challenges facing the NHS through the Private Finance Initiative (PFI). PFI deals were negotiated locally between the NHS and private contractors, with the latter providing financing and expertise for the building of new facilities, with an undertaking also to maintain the buildings, and the former then paying fees over an extended period of typically 25–30 years. The PFI programme theory here was that public infrastructure need and funding would be matched with private sector enterprise and delivery to address infrastructural gaps and bypass the delays in public infrastructural funding that had beset previous attempts at increasing capital expenditure.

PFI was inherited from the Conservative government, but was Labour's preferred model of funding public infrastructure as PFI deals appeared in government accounts in such a way that they appeared 'off balance sheet' and so did not technically breach the government's expenditure rules on paper, while at the same time allowing significant investment to take place.

Funding

Finally, 'funding', as the name implies, represents Labour's increase in the NHS budget, especially after 2002 and the review of NHS financing (Wanless, 2002). Labour moved from their initial position that NHS funding was not a barrier to service improvement to one accepting that a significant financial investment was needed. This shift appeared to be based on the Prime Minister personally intervening in the face of negative NHS publicity from the media after a difficult winter, combined with an acceptance from the government that funding was lagging significantly the levels given to healthcare in other countries (Watt, 2000).

The programme theory here was that increased funding would lead to improved services – and was made explicit from the government in speeches at the time (see, for example, Reid, 2004), in which a clear deal was presented to NHS staff (following from the NHS Plan) – that significant investment would be made, but only if significant reform followed.

Having outlined the four main mechanisms by which Labour attempted to improve the NHS, we now explore their outcomes.

Outcomes

There are a range of measurable improvements in health indicators between 1997 and 2010. There was a rise in GPs and hospital doctors per 1,000 population that was above trend. Both male and female life expectancy figures rose throughout the period, and there was a rise in treatments such as hip replacements and cataract operations that was above trend as well. Waiting times for treatments such as cataract surgery fell significantly (especially in Scotland), as they did for hip and knee replacements. Trends in amenable mortality for both men and women fell across the decade. Public satisfaction with the NHS at the end of the decade was at an all-time high (Bevan et al, 2014).

Accepting some national variations, the overall picture, then, is one that appears to suggest that the NHS in the 2000s did achieve a range of notable successes. However, there were also problems, including perhaps most notably the emergence of the care failings at Stafford Hospital at the end of the decade. We attempt to explore the extent to which the programme theories outlined above seem to have contributed to both these positive and negative results.

Delivery

The result of use of the 'delivery' programme theory can be usefully compared in the different contexts of hospitals and GP surgeries. In English hospitals, targets were effectively imposed on hospitals rather than being negotiated with clinical representatives or being linked through evidence to system-wide goals for health improvement. As such, the targets were often seen by those in hospitals as being political in nature, and so imposed on staff working in those settings. The targets were also seen by managers as being career-ending if they were not achieved, or if their hospital was indicated to be poorly performing in relation to others – they were called 'P45' targets[1] (Bevan and Hood, 2006).

The result of hospital targets being seen as externally imposed, political and potentially career-ending for managers resulted in them being extensively 'gamed'. A variety of different means of such gaming appeared, from waiting times being manipulated through patients being offered appointments they were unlikely to accept (around holiday times), and then being moved to the back of the waiting list if they refused, through to simple fraud and patients being removed from lists returned to the Department of Health. It was characterised as a time of 'targets and terror' (Hood, 2006).

At Stafford Hospital a series of care failing took place that the independent inquiry that followed (Francis, 2013) linked directly to the use of targets. The inquiry found that staff had lost sight of providing actual care itself, so focused were they on achieving financial improvements and hitting targets (Dixon-Woods et al, 2014). The inquiry's findings cast a deep shadow over New Labour's use of targets in hospitals.

In GP surgeries, the QOF worked in a different way. Doctors were consulted on how it was set up, and the targets were presented as being based on clinical evidence and measures of quality to an extent that GPs regarded them as legitimate (Checkland et al, 2007). GPs then went about organising their practices to achieve the maximum scores they could under the system, and boosting activities that the QOF system measured to a point where they secured significant funding increases. There is much less evidence of the systematic gaming of QOF systems compared to hospitals (Roland and Guthrie, 2016), and it seems that GPs engaged in practice reorganisation to make best use of the full range of health professionals, so that patients could be seen in more efficient ways (McDonald et al, 2007). From the perspective of achieving behavioural change, the QOF represents a remarkable success.

There were also concerns, however, with the QOF. GPs expressed concerns about their lives becoming dominated by form-filling and screen-driven prompts that interfered with them providing the best possible care (McCartney, 2016). There were also questions about whether target thresholds were initially set too low to achieve significant improvements in health outcomes, or that the targets were not adapted over time to drive sustained improvements (Doran et al,

2014). These concerns, among others, led to the QOF being removed in Scotland. However, QOF is remarkable in that it at least initially led to improvements in measured performance (and so behavioural change) that few public performance management systems have ever achieved.

Because of devolution, the NHS in Scotland offers us a means of comparing the results of seeing an increase in funding of the same scale as appeared in England in the 2000s, but without the use of 'delivery' in respect of hospitals (Scotland did use the QOF during Labour's terms in office), and in an era in Scotland of remarkable continuity in terms of formal organisational structures (Steel and Cyclus, 2012). Such a comparison will always be imperfect, but is nonetheless worth attempting, even in the face of differences in respect of health need and in the way that data is collected.

Research comparing the four nations of the UK in terms of health service performance in the 2000s (Bevan et al, 2014) presents the remarkable finding that, at the end of the first decade of the new millennium, there was almost nothing to choose between the health service performance of England and Scotland that can be measured. This means we can see similar measured improvements in both English and Scottish health and healthcare during Labour's governments, but with Scotland not having engaged in the use of 'delivery' in hospitals (or 'choice and competition'). This would suggest that we need to look elsewhere for the reasons why the NHS improved under New Labour.

Choice and competition

There are two main interpretations of the result of Labour's 'choice and competition' approach to health reorganisation. The first is that the use of the purchaser–provider split between 1989 and 2010 (including a brief interlude between 1997 and 2001 when Labour claimed to have abolished it) has been a significant error. The argument here is that the separation of purchaser and provider services did not lead to sufficient improvements for the costs of these reorganisations to exceed any benefits they have generated. This was the view of the House of Commons Health Committee (2010) that reported at the end of Labour's term in office, and pointed especially to failures on the purchasing ('commissioning') of care.

A second view comes from research that suggests that markets have improved care – and perhaps even saved lives. This research points to changes in particular clinical measures which, its advocates claim, have relationships with areas where market-like structures are most likely to have resulted as a consequence of Labour's market-based reorganisation (Cooper et al, 2011). This research was picked up by the Conservatives as justifying further market-based reorganisation (Secretary of State for Health, 2010), but also led to a series of academic responses suggesting problems with the research authors' approach and data (Bevan and Skellern, 2011; Mays, 2011; Pollock et al, 2011; Gaynor et al, 2012; Greener, 2012). Looking back at that debate (as one of the participants), it is fair to say that choice and competition did lead to changes of referral behaviour, especially in rural communities where patients appeared more likely to make choices about which hospitals to attend. It is harder, however, to justify the claim that market-based reorganisations 'saved lives', as some of the proponents of that debate appeared to be suggesting (Mays, 2011), or that the resources spent on choice and competition reorganisations could not have been better spent instead on the direct funding of healthcare.

Finally, because, as noted above, Scotland was largely free from 'choice and competition', and yet its measured performance during Labour's period in office was not significantly different than that of the NHS in England, this would also suggest that any gains from 'choice and competition' did not significantly contribute to an overall improvement in the performance of the NHS.

It is the case, however, that if we are to criticise market-based reorganisations, we need to offer an alternative. Scotland has avoided the costs of choice and competition while achieving the same measured improvements in healthcare as England by making greater use of collaboration and joint working between health and social care, with the most recent evidence suggesting that this approach is showing signs of success (Audit Scotland, 2017). The NHS in England also appears to be moving toward a more collaborative approach (Pym, 2017), suggesting that the tide may be turning against the use of market-based approaches. We return to this point in the Conclusion.

Private Finance Initiative

The outcomes of PFI are complex and messy. It is certainly the case that a number of new (and much-needed) hospitals and GP surgeries have been built – and a rate that would almost certainly not have occurred by making use of existing public financing schemes. However, the structure of the PFI process initially appeared to lead to a situation with experienced private contractors negotiating with public managers and officials who had not been through such a process before, and may have resulted in some very poor value contracts being signed (Appleby, 2017). Labour's need to conspicuously show they were being fiscally responsible meant that they continued with the policy, and that there was often little alternative to negotiating a PFI deal if a new hospital or school was needed (Clark et al, 2001). The legacy of PFI is unevenly distributed, but is clearly leading to financial problems for the worst affected trusts (Campbell, 2012), and to calls to bring PFI deals back into the public sector to avoid excessive financial commitments extending into the future – something which, for example, Tees, Esk and Wear Valleys NHS Trust did in 2011.

PFI is complex in that, on the one hand, a number of poor value deals have been signed that offer private organisations disproportionate returns, and that surely require that the state renegotiate them. That such deals continue as they were originally negotiated is hard to justify. Where private organisations have decided to exit from NHS contracts, such as Circle at Hinchingbrooke Hospital, no significant financial penalties have been imposed by the government (BBC News, 2015). It should not be the case that private organisations can exit public provision without significant penalty, while also requiring the public purse to pay out disproportionate returns for badly negotiated contracts that favour them.

However, it is also the case that PFI deals are not just about building new facilities, but also about maintaining them, and when calculating whether such deals are fair this also needs this to be taken into consideration. It does appear to be the case that the maintenance deals in some cases combine poor value for money and opaque accountability structures should things go wrong (Asenova and Beck, 2010). In other cases, however, taking maintenance costs into account may make PFI deals better value than they first appear, especially where that maintenance is being done in a flexible and responsive manner. To assess PFI fully, we need to take all of its aspects into account, even if there appears to be a prima facie case that many such deals have not offered good value to the public purse.

What we can say is that there is real evidence that some of the PFI deals negotiated in its first rounds represent poor value for money (Appleby, 2017). The programme theory of combining public sector need with private dynamism did prove in the early years of the scheme to be open to abuse through long-term, excessive return contracts, and it is important that the public sector learns from the poorly negotiated contracts to ensure that public–private partnerships of all kind, if they are to remain in use, again, are negotiated on an equal footing going forward, with an equal balance of risk and reward for all parties (Asenova and Beck, 2003).

Funding

Finally there is the 'funding' programme theory. Although it is difficult to directly attribute the gains of the 2000s to NHS funding, we can now see the effect of those funding increases coming to halt after 2010. Figure 12.1 shows UK real public health expenditure per capita from 1955 onwards, including Labour's above-trend NHS spending, and the subsequent slowdown.

While NHS budgets since 2010 have been protected in that they have not seen the significant reductions shown in other public services, there has been a marked slowdown in their growth, and in addition, local government budgets have seen real-terms reductions of well over a third (NAO, 2014). This has meant that community-based health services (including social care) have experienced significant reductions in funding. This has put additional pressures on the NHS, with patients who might have been treated in the community ending up in Accident and Emergency (A&E) departments, and hospitals struggling to discharge patients for lack of local support services. Since 2010, problems with

Figure 12.1: Real UK health expenditure per capita, 1955–2015

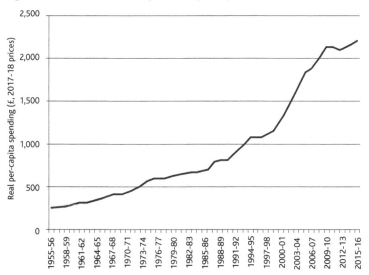

Source: Stoye (2017)

emergency services admissions and public concerns over the quality of care in both England and Scotland have reappeared (Bevan et al, 2014). This is not conclusive as suggesting the improvements between 1997 and 2010 were due to funding alone, but it does seem to suggest that the funding improvements were an important part of the health service improvements during the 2000s. Since the funding increases have come to an end, exactly the same problems that Labour were struggling with in the late 1990s, and that led to the funding increases in the first place, appear to have returned.

There is a deep irony here. In the 2010 General Election, Labour did not make the NHS a central focus of their election campaign (having done so in 1997, 2001 and 2005), being outflanked by the Conservatives who were promising to increase health funding year-on-year, and with a leader claiming his top priorities for government could be spelt out in just three letters, 'N', 'H' and 'S' (Prince, 2009).[2] Labour, with their model of welfare funding in pieces after the financial crisis of 2008, made a strategic error in not matching the Conservative's NHS funding promises (Timmins, 2012), despite NHS popularity being at record levels, and their previous funding increases having achieved so much. Post-2010 the promised increases in health expenditure that Labour felt unable to match have not really appeared, with the NHS having to find substantial efficiency savings while also undertaking an expensive reorganisation in England that appears to have achieved almost none of its intended goals.

Conclusion: what have we learned?

There is a range of important lessons from the above analysis, and that we can explore to consider what the case of the NHS offers us in terms of understanding debates about public reorganisation more generally.

A first general point is that Labour managed to put in place a remarkable amount of healthcare organisational change without the protests that were seen after the introduction of the internal market in the early 1990s, or the prominent criticisms and concerns that the medical profession has raised post-2010. One of the key reasons why the governments in 1989 and 2010 encountered such significant resistance was their insistence on trying to achieve a single, large-scale change tied to a particular piece of legislation, and that created, especially when combined with a lack of consultation with clinical leaders, a clear focal point for those who were opposed to change to mount their campaign against.

Labour, in contrast, first engaged with senior clinicians in consultation (especially in the NHS Plan) and did not engage in 'big-bang' healthcare reorganisation. Instead, Labour made a number of smaller changes but which added up together to form a significant programme of reorganisation, especially between 2000 and 2005. Whether this was intentional or not, it adds up to health reorganisation by stealth, a new approach to healthcare reorganisation in the UK compared to the big changes of the 1990s and 2010s. A slightly cynical lesson this appears to suggest is that, if policy-makers want to achieve large-scale health reorganisation, it might be more successful (at least in terms of getting policy change, as we have seen, implementation is a different thing) to do it by degrees rather than all at once.

A second point comes through the comparison of the 'delivery' in hospitals and GP practices. In hospitals there was extensive 'gaming' and a sense that the performance measures were political in origin. In GP surgeries many of those problems were avoided. The difference appears to be that the QOF proposals were consulted upon first, that they were linked in doctors' minds as being based on evidence and improving quality, and that they were rewarded for good performance through increased funding. Although the QOF made use of a degree of pay-for-performance, clinicians report that this is not the main motivating factor in complying with it (Grant et al, 2009), which was more to do with simply trying to do a good job. The comparison of the two cases of 'delivery' above certainly emphasises the importance of considering the exact means by which such systems are meant to work, and their potential effects on staff motivation using more sophisticated ideas than simple 'carrot and stick' models (Bowles, 2016). The QOF was not perfect, but it can give us clues as to how to better design performance management systems to support service improvement by working with public professionals rather than against them.

The main lesson of both 'choice and competition' and 'PFI' reorganisations is that we need more nuanced analyses of the exact institutional arrangements being put in place in public services. Discussions about the benefits of choice and competition appear to assume both that people want to choose their health providers (when they may not; see Fotaki et al, 2005), and that competition will drive improvements in public services (when the evidence supporting competition as a means of improving health is very limited; see Mays, 2011). That in 2017 the NHS in England appears to have had to find ways of 'bypassing' the competitive care markets introduced by the Coalition government of 2010 suggests that this lesson is slowly being learned on the ground (Pym, 2017), even if policy-makers might still be reluctant to acknowledge the increasing abandonment of 'choice and competition' as a means of trying to improve public services.

The lesson of PFI is that safeguards need to be put in place to ensure that public contracts that contain significant financial commitments are negotiated in a balanced and transparent manner. There is a real need for a full review of existing PFI deals to assess whether they represent good value for the taxpayer, and for an alternative capital funding process if PFI is not the best way of achieving this going forward.

Finally, for all the reorganisational change of the 2000s in England, it may be that the improvements in health and public satisfaction with the NHS that appeared under Labour came mostly from increased funding. It is certainly the case that public satisfaction has fallen since 2010 (Campbell, 2016), and that waiting time targets are now routinely being missed (Campbell, 2017). Budgets for the NHS have come under increased pressure while demands on services have continued to rise, and there is an increasing sense that the pressures on the NHS are threatening to overwhelm the service. England has also had to deal with another expensive and confusing reorganisation that has been all but abandoned. For all the attention reorganisations get, they do not seem to make the difference policy-makers imagine them to have, and based on the improvements in measurable outcomes achieved in the NHS between 2002 and 2010, the increase in funding in the 2000s seems to have been the most significant factor in improving measurable health outcomes.

While accepting fully that NHS expenditure cannot increase indefinitely, for almost all of its existence it has received less funding than similar nation's health systems, and this means not only that the funding in any given year is likely to be too little, but also that there is a cumulative backlog of under-funding. It is hard to assess exactly how much more investment it requires to address that shortfall. Post-2010 governments have refused to provide the funding the Chief Executive of the NHS says is necessary (Neville and Parker, 2017), while at the same not confronting the related challenge of under-funding in social care, leading the government to find itself under criticism from senior members of its own party as a result (Savage, 2017). It is certainly the case that the 'austerity'-based politics since 2010 has often created a hostile climate for arguments about increasing public funding, while at the same time public services have fallen back from the standards they were able to achieve in the 2000s, when better funded. The combination of reduced funding and lower service standards risks undermining public support while also making it more difficult for politicians to begin a debate about raising taxes to try and remedy the situation (Taylor-Gooby, 2015).

However, there is a real need to find ways of opening debates about how much funding NHS should receive, and of recognising public services as a crucial infrastructure for economic development and wellbeing, not as burdens on the economy (Galbraith, 1996). This is likely to lead to the better-off paying more in taxation to pay for much-needed improvements in public service funding, and as the findings above shows, has a much better chance of leading to service improvement than engaging in more needless and expensive reorganisation.

Notes
[1] In the UK a 'P45' is the tax form given when someone is dismissed from their job.
[2] This was a reference to Blair's 1996 Labour Party Convention Conference speech where he claimed his three priorities for government would be 'education', 'education' and 'education'.

References
Appleby, J. (2017) 'Making sense of PFI', Nuffield Trust (www.nuffieldtrust.org.uk/resource/making-sense-of-pfi).

Asenova, D. and Beck, M. (2003) 'The UK financial sector and risk management in PFI projects: A survey', *Public Money and Management*, vol 23, pp 195-202.

Asenova, D. and Beck, M. (2010) 'Crucial silences: when accountability met PFI and finance capital', *Critical Perspectives on Accounting*, vol 21, pp 1-13.

Audit Scotland (2017) *NHS in Scotland 2017*, Edinburgh: Audit Scotland.

Barber, M. (2007) *Instruction to deliver: Tony Blair, the public services and the challenge of achieving targets*, London: Portoco's Publishing.

BBC News (2015) 'Privately-run Hinchingbrooke Hospital returns to NHS', 1 April (www.bbc.co.uk/news/uk-england-cambridgeshire-32147907).

Bevan, G. and Hood, C. (2006) 'What's measured is what matters: targets and gaming in the English public health care system', *Public Administration*, vol 84, pp 517-38.

Bevan, G. and Skellern, M. (2011) 'Does competition between hospitals improve clinical quality? A review of evidence from two eras of competition in the English NHS', *British Medical Journal*, vol 343, pp 1-7.

Bevan, G., Karanikolos, M., Exley, J., Nolte, E., Connolly, S. and Mays, N. (2014) *The four health systems of the United Kingdom: How do they compare?*, London: The Health Foundation and Nuffield Trust.

Blair, T. (2010) *A journey*, London: Hutchinson.

Bowles, S. (2016) *The moral economy: Why good incentives are no substitute for good citizens*, London: Yale University Press.

Campbell, D. (2012) 'Hospital trusts offered £1.5bn emergency fund to pay PFI bill', *The Guardian*, 13 February.

Campbell, D. (2016) 'Public satisfaction with NHS drops 5% in last year', *The Guardian*, 8 February.

Campbell, D. (2017) 'NHS "waving white flag" as it axes 18-week waiting time operation target', *The Guardian*, 31 March.

Checkland, K., McDonald, R. and Harrison, S. (2007) 'Ticking boxes and changing the social world: Data collection and the new UK general practice contract', *Social Policy & Administration*, vol 41, pp 693-710.

Clark, T., Elsby, M. and Love, S. (2001) *Twenty-five years of falling investment*, London: Institute for Fiscal Studies.

Cooper, Z., Gibbons, S., Jones, S. and McGuire, A. (2011) 'Does hospital competition save lives? Evidence from the English NHS patient choice reforms', *Economic Journal*, vol 121, pp F229-F6.

Crisp, N. (2011) *24 hours to save the NHS: The Chief Executive's account of reform 2000 to 2006*, Oxford: Oxford University Press.

DH (Department of Health) (2001) *Extending choice for patients*, London: DH.

DH (2002) *Reforming NHS financial flows. Introducing payment by results*, London: DH.

DHSS (Department of Health and Social Security) (1983) *NHS management inquiry*, London: HMSO.

Dixon-Woods, M., Baker, R., Charles, K., Dawson, J., Jerzembek, G., et al (2014) 'Culture and behaviour in the English National Health Service: Overview of lessons from a large multimethod study', *British Medical Journal Quality and Safety*, vol 23, pp 106-15.

Doran, T., Kontopantelis, E., Reeves, D., Sutton, M. and Ryan, A. (2014) 'Setting performance targets in pay for performance programmes: What can we learn from QOF?', *British Medical Journal*, vol 348, pp 1595-602.

Fotaki, M., Boyd, A., Smith, L., McDonald, R., Roland, M., et al (2005) *Patient choice and the organization and delivery of health services: Scoping review*, London: National Coordinating Centre for the Service Delivery and Organisation (NCCSDO).

Francis, R. (2013) *Final report of the Independent Inquiry into care provided by the Mid-Staffordshire NHS Foundation Trust (Vol 1–3)*, London: The Stationery Office.

Galbraith, J.K. (1996) *The good society: The humane agenda*, London: Sinclair-Stevenson.

Gaynor, M., Moreno-Serra, R. and Propper, C. (2012) 'Can competition improve outcomes in UK health care? Lessons from the past two decades', *Journal of Health Services Research and Policy*, vol 17, pp 49-54.

Giddens, A. (2002) *Where now for New Labour?*, Cambridge: Polity Press.

Grant, S., Huby, G., Watkins, F., Checkland, K., McDonald, R., et al. (2009) 'The impact of pay-for-performance on professional boundaries in UK general practice: an ethnographic study', *Sociology of Health & Illness*, vol 31, pp 229-45.

Greener, I. (2004) 'The three moments of New Labour's health policy discourse', *Policy & Politics*, vol 32, pp 303-16.

Greener, I. (2012) 'Unpacking the evidence on competition and outcomes in the NHS in England', *Journal of Health Services Research*, vol 7, pp 193-5.

Greener, I. and Powell, M. (2009) 'The evolution of choice policies in UK housing, education and health policy', *Journal of Social Policy*, vol 38, pp 63-81.

HM Government (1989) *Working for patients, White Paper*, Cm 555, London: HMSO.

Hood, C. (2006) 'Gaming in Targetworld: The targets approach to managing British public services', *Public Administration Review*, vol 66, pp 515-21.

House of Commons Health Committee (2010) *Commissioning: Fourth Report of Session 2009–10, Volume I*, London: The Stationery Office.

Keegan, W. (2003) *The prudence of Mr Gordon Brown*, London: John Wiley & Sons.

Klein, R. (2006) *The new politics of the NHS: From creation to reinvention*, Abingdon: Radcliffe Publishing.

Le Grand, J. (2007) *The other invisible hand*, Woodstock: Princetown University Press.

Mandelson, P. (2011) *The third man*, London: HarperCollins.

Mays, N. (2011) 'Is there evidence that competition is healthcare is a good thing? No', *British Medical Journal*, vol 343, d4205.

Mays, N., Dixon, A. and Jones, L. (eds) (2011) *Understanding New Labour's market reforms of the English NHS*, London: The King's Fund.

McCartney, M. (2016) *The state of medicine: Keeping the promise of the NHS*, London: Pinter and Martin.

McDonald, R., Harrison, S., Checkland, K., Campbell, S.M. and Roland, M. (2007) 'Impact of financial incentives on clinical autonomy and internal motivation in primary care: ethnographic study', *British Medical Journal*, vol 334, p 1357.

Mohan, J. (2002) *Planning, markets and hospitals*, London: Routledge.

NAO (National Audit Office) (2014) *Local government: The Impact of funding reductions on local authorities*, London: NAO.

Neville, S. and Parker, G. (2017) 'Treasury resists calls for more money for NHS', *Financial Times*, 13 January.

Pawson, R. (2006). *Evidence-based policy: A realist perspective*, London: Sage.

Pawson, R. (2013) *The science of evaluation: A realist manifesto*, London: Sage.

Pawson, R., Greenhaigh, T., Harvey, G. and Walshe, K. (2005) 'Realist review: a new method of systematic review for complex policy interventions', *Journal of Health Services Research and Policy*, 10 July, pp 21-34.

Pollock, A., Macfarlane, A., Kirkwood, G., Majeed, A., Greener, I., et al (2011) 'No evidence that patient choice in the NHS saves lives', *Lancet*, vol 378, pp 2057-60.

Prince, R. (2009) 'David Cameron: the NHS is safe under the Conservatives', *Telegraph*, 20 August.

Pym, H. (2017) 'Stand by for a quiet revolution in the NHS', BBC News, 28 February.

Reid, J. (2004) 'Managing new realities – Integrating the care landscape', Speech given on 11 March.

Richards, S. (2010) *Whatever it takes: The real story of Gordon Brown and New Labour*, London: Fourth Estate.

Roland, M. and Guthrie, B. (2016) 'Quality and outcomes framework: What have we learn?', *British Medical Journal*, vol 354.

Savage, M. (2017) 'Senior Tories in budget backlash over NHS and social care cash', *The Guardian*, 25 November.

Secretary of State for Health (1996) *The NHS: A service with ambitions*, London: HMSO.

Secretary of State for Health (1997) *The new NHS: Modern, dependable*, London: HMSO.

Secretary of State for Health (2000) *The NHS Plan: A plan for investment, A plan for reform*, London: HMSO.

Secretary of State for Health (2010) *Equity and excellence: Liberating the NHS*, London: The Stationery Office.

Steel, D. and Cyclus, J. (2012) 'United Kingdom (Scotland), health system review', *Health Systems in Transition*, vol 14, pp 1-150.

Stoye, G. (2017) *UK health spending*, IFS Briefing Note BN201, London: Institute for Fiscal Studies.

Taylor-Gooby, P. (2015) 'Making the case for the welfare state', *Policy & Politics*, vol 43, pp 597-614.

Timmins, N. (2012) *Never again?*, London: The King's Fund and Institute for Government.

Wainwright, D. (1998) 'Disenchantment, ambivalence and the precautionary principle: the becalming of British health policy', *International Journal of Health Services*, vol 28, pp 407-26.

Wanless, D. (2002) 'Health care:the 20-year plan', *Public Money & Management*, vol 22, pp 4-5.

Watt, N. (2000) 'Blair's £12bn pledge', *The Guardian*, 17 January.

THIRTEEN

New Labour and adolescent disadvantage: a retrospective

Rikki Dean and Moira Wallace

When the Labour government came to office in 1997 the proportion of UK children in poverty was one of the highest in Europe, having doubled in the 1980s (UNICEF, 2000). The proportion of 18-year-olds in education was joint lowest in the European Union (EU) (OECD, 1997), and permanent exclusions had been rising (SEU, 1998). The UK had more 15- to 16-year-old drug users than any other EU country (EMCDDA, 1998), and the number of under-21s convicted of drug offences had doubled between 1990 and 1995 (Parker et al, 1998). Regular drinking by school pupils had risen in the 1990s, as had the mean number of units consumed by those pupils who drank (Becker et al, 2006). UK teenage pregnancy rates had been stuck at or above the early 1980s level, while rates in most of Western Europe had fallen, leaving the UK with the highest teenage birth rate in Western Europe (SEU, 1999b).

The new government was highly critical of the levels of youth disadvantage it inherited, both because of the negative impact on the lives and prospects of the young people affected, and the costs to society of the resulting high levels of unemployment, crime and ill health. Numerous policies designed to improve matters were introduced between 1997 and 2010. Now the children born in 1997 are young adults, it is possible to assess what happened to them during their teens, and whether their adolescence went better than that of their predecessors.

This chapter looks back at the policy changes Labour introduced in England[1] on nine key domains of youth disadvantage prioritised in Public Service Agreement (PSA) targets: child poverty, attainment at 16, secondary school exclusion and attendance, young people not in education or training, teenage conceptions, adolescent drug use, alcohol use, and youth crime.[2] It summarises the key policy changes, and analyses the data on outcomes, paying particular attention to the generation born in 1997 who turned 18 in 2015. The data show striking reductions across all of these domains. However, for subsequent cohorts, a number of these downward trends have stalled or begun reversing. If progress is not to be lost, it is important to understand what was achieved, how much of it can be attributed to policy, and how this can be built on. This calls for research that connects data across different domains of youth experience, investigating long-term outcomes, and costs and benefits, so as to help policy-makers understand how they can continue to reduce youth disadvantage in future.

Labour's approach to youth disadvantage

This section takes a dual approach to summarising Labour's diverse array of youth policies. First, Table 13.1 details specific policy interventions in nine domains of youth disadvantage and the PSA targets which were set.[3] Then there is an outline of the underpinning themes of Labour's approach: an emphasis on the cost and drivers of social problems; targeted prevention and redesign of services; increased investment and national targets; and cross-agency working and a focus on local areas.

Table 13.1: Labour key policy changes and targets on youth disadvantage

Child poverty	Education
Increases in child amounts in means-tested benefits	Free part-time early education for three- and four-year-olds
Introduction of Working Families Tax Credit and Childcare Tax Credit	Introduction of Sure Start, targeted on most deprived areas
Replacement with Child Tax Credit and Working Tax Credit	Reduced class sizes for five- to seven-year-olds
After-school childcare through extended schools	National literacy and numeracy strategy
Encouragement for lone parents to seek work	75% increase in secondary school spending, 56% in primary by 2008-09
From 2008 lone parents required to seek work as condition of benefit once youngest child over 12	Teacher numbers increased by 12%, and classroom assistants trebled
Aggregate cash transfers to families with children increased by £24 billion by 2009-10	Area-based initiatives such as Excellence in Cities
	'Teach First' and bursaries to attract new entrants to teaching
	Pressure on low performing schools through 'floor targets' and threat of closure
PSA targets to reduce the number of children in poverty by at least a quarter by 2004 and halve it by 2010-11	Collaboration initiatives such as London Challenge
	PSAs included targets for proportion of 16-year-olds with five or more A*-Cs at GCSE (later including English and Maths)
	Floor targets for proportion achieving 5 A*-Cs in every local education authority and school

(continued)

Table 13.1: Labour key policy changes and targets on youth disadvantage (continued)

School exclusion	Truancy
Statutory guidance on use of exclusion Targets for local authorities to reduce exclusions (until 2001) Behaviour Improvement Programme to drive good practice on truancy and exclusion In-school learning support units Duty on local authorities to make suitable provision for permanently excluded pupils from sixth day PSA target to reduce permanent exclusions by a third by 2002	Addressing causes including school disaffection, bullying and children falling behind Vocational GCSEs and increasing work-related learning opportunities for 14- to 16-year-olds Investment in electronic registration Parenting classes targeted at parents of low attenders Fines for parents who condoned truancy PSA targets first for a reduction in unauthorised absence, then total absence, then persistent absence
NEETs	**Teenage conceptions**
Educational Maintenance Allowance for low-income 16- to 18-year-olds in education or training (nationwide from 2006-07) Connexions, new support service for 13- to 19-year-olds, nationwide from 2003 Guaranteed place in learning for all 16-year-olds from 2007 and 18-year-olds from 2008 Education and Skills Act 2008 required participation to 17 from 2013 and 18 from 2015 PSA target to reduce proportion of 16- to 18-year-olds not in education, employment or training (NEET)	Addressing risk factors including school disaffection and truancy Improved access to contraception Improvements to sex and relationship education Coordinators working in local areas with at-risk groups National unit to coordinate strategy New incentives to GPs (2009) to raise awareness of long-acting reversible contraception methods PSA target to reduce the under-18 conception rate by 50 per cent by 2010 from 1998 baseline

(continued)

Table 13.1: Labour key policy changes and targets on youth disadvantage (continued)

Youth crime and justice	Drugs and alcohol
Creation of Youth Justice Board and local Youth Offending Teams New referral options for young people arrested or sentenced (eg to substance abuse treatment) Preventive programmes with at-risk young people, eg On Track, Youth Inclusion and Support Panels Establishment of local Crime and Disorder Reduction Partnerships Introduction of Anti-Social Behaviour Orders (ASBOs) Expansion of police numbers, creation of Police Community Support Officers (PCSOs) to deliver neighbourhood policing National targets for crime reduction and performance management of local police forces and areas Dissemination of good practice, eg hot spot policing, focus on hotspots and prolific offenders PSA crime targets to reduce vehicle crime, domestic burglary, robbery and overall crime PSA criminal justice targets to increase total 'offences brought to justice' (introduced 2001, dropped 2007) then from 2007 to reduce the number of first-time entrants into the Youth Justice System	Creation of National Treatment Agency to increase and improve drugs treatment and cut waiting times 'FRANK' website and advice line launched in 2003 as non-judgemental source of information Drugs workforce grew by 50% from 2002 and 2004 Drug Treatment budget increased from £50 million in 2001 to £360 million in four years Alcohol Harm Reduction Programme began in 2004 Home Office coordinated action campaigns from 2005 to drive enforcement of law on underage sales Industry introduced Challenge 21/25 to increase compliance 'Know your limits' advertising campaign on binge drinking Chief Medical Officer issued new guidance on adolescent drinking Alcohol Duty Escalator from 2008 (duty to rise by 2% above inflation each year) PSAs in all rounds had targets to reduce the proportion of people under 25 misusing illegal drugs. In 2007 alcohol and volatile substances were added In 2007 new PSA to reduce growth in alcohol-related hospital admissions (all ages)

Understanding costs and drivers

Labour's approach was heavily influenced by analysis identifying the social and economic cost of youth disadvantage. Government figures of £60 billion for the overall cost of crime (Home Office, 2000), £4 billion a year for serious drug misuse (Home Office, 1998), and £20 billion a year for alcohol misuse (PMSU, 2003) were powerful, both in making the case for increased resourcing and in shaping policy to focus on drivers of adolescent problems.

Government policy papers also highlight the evidence of associations between experiences such as poverty, truancy, school exclusion, educational underachievement, early parenthood, unemployment, substance misuse and offending. Teenage pregnancy was associated with a range of indicators of disadvantage including poverty, being in care, declining educational attainment between age 7 and 16, and being NEET (not in education, employment or training) at 16 and 17 (SEU, 1999b). Non-participation at 16–18 was closely associated with educational under-achievement/disaffection and family disadvantage/ poverty (SEU, 1999a). Policy on truancy was given added urgency by the link with crime, such as the estimate that 78 per cent of males and 53 per cent of females who truanted once a week or more committed offences (Graham and Bowling, 1995). Alcohol policy attracted attention for the same reason: around half of all violent crimes and a third of domestic violence incidents were estimated to be linked to alcohol misuse (PMSU, 2004).

Targeted intervention and redesign of services

Numerous preventive intervention programmes were introduced to try to reduce the prevalence of these linked youth problems (Walker and Donaldson, 2011). Prominent examples were: Youth Inclusion and Support Panels, which identified 8- to 13-year-olds at risk of becoming involved in anti-social behaviour and crime, providing them with tailored support overseen by a keyworker; Connexions personal advisers to help 13- to 19-year-olds overcome barriers to remaining in education or training; and Teenage Pregnancy Local Coordinators who identified and supported those most at risk.

Many public services aimed at young people were redesigned. Drug treatment for young people was reshaped, with more emphasis on youth justice referrals to treatment and a major investment in expanding the treatment workforce. To reduce exclusions and truancy, schools focused on effective behaviour management, developing Learning Support Units and new curriculum approaches to engage young people at risk of disaffection with school. Contraceptive services gave much more attention to accessibility and confidentiality, shown to be key to take-up by young people. Many of these redesigns drew on the insights of young people, frontline professionals and community leaders by involving them in policy formulation. However, community consultations often also drew attention to the problems caused in local neighbourhoods by children and young people engaging in persistent disorder, and the government's response, through its measures on Anti-Social Behaviour, set a punitive tone that was often resented by young people and those who worked with them.

Increased investment accompanied by outcome targets

The Treasury's attitude to funding investment became more positive with increasing exposure to the evidence on the costs of youth disadvantage, and because of Chancellor Gordon Brown's personal focus on tackling poverty. Education and policing budgets grew, enabling recruitment of more teachers, police officers, teaching assistants and community support officers. Cash transfers to families with children increased by more than 1 per cent of GDP to reduce the number of children living in poverty (Stewart and Obolenskaya, 2015). The Educational Maintenance Allowance was created with a budget of £500 million per year to support low-income adolescents in post-16 education. The Connexions service budget doubled from that of the Careers Service it replaced, to match its wider remit (NAO, 2004). Increased spending, such as that in education, was often tilted towards poorer areas, through deprivation-related grants or extra funding streams. Over the three years from 2005–06 these amounted to a real growth in the 'implicit free school meals premium' of 69 per cent for primary schools and 53 per cent for secondary schools, compared with a real growth in overall spending per pupil of 17 per cent (Chowdry et al, 2010).

Under Labour's approach to public service reform, investment was accompanied by outcome targets (PSAs). These exerted powerful pressure on ministers and officials to improve the design of policy (Barber, 2007; Panchamia and Thomas, 2014). This public accountability sustained the momentum on youth policies, but some targets created perverse incentives – for example, the 'offences brought to justice' target. Intended to increase crime clear-up rates, it had the effect of incentivising a criminal response to youth misdemeanours, which were easy for the police to 'detect'. For a period between 2001 and the target's abandonment in 2007, this drew more young people into the criminal justice system (Bateman, 2015). Overall, however, targets had the effect of sustaining government attention on youth disadvantage, and provided the quid pro quo for spending increases the sector had long advocated.

Cross-agency working and a local focus

Both in policy-making and implementation Labour founded cross-departmental and cross-agency institutions, recognising that youth disadvantage cuts across agency boundaries, and the costs of preventive intervention often fall in one agency while the benefits accrue to another. In Whitehall, new units such as the Teenage Pregnancy Unit, the Children's and Young People's Unit, the Drugs Unit and the Social Exclusion Unit were created to lead multi-departmental programmes of work, often bringing in external expertise from health, local government, the voluntary sector and policing. Cross-agency working was encouraged at local level through statutory partnerships such as Youth Offending Teams and Crime and Disorder Reduction Partnerships. In 2004 the government legislated to require every top-tier or unitary local authority in England to appoint a Director of Children's Services, to provide integrated leadership of education and social services functions. These new arrangements created pressures of partnership working but increased the prospects of joint action on the most difficult issues facing each agency in their respective caseloads.

Labour's approach to youth disadvantage was often area-based. Following the 'ameliorative logic' that underpinned the neighbourhood renewal strategy (see Chapter Ten, this volume), early initiatives were launched in multiply deprived areas with the deepest problems, which had often been adrift from national averages for decades. Excellence in Cities was one prominent example. Demanding national targets strengthened the need for Whitehall departments to understand where in the country problems were greatest and to develop plans to address them. This could mean extra resources, and guidance on good practice, but often also more scrutiny and the prospect of intervention if things did not improve. This was particularly obvious in education. From 2000 'floor targets' specifying minimum standards for GCSE performance were introduced, first at local authority level, and then applying to all English schools individually, with the threat of closure if improvement was not achieved. This represented a significant change in the role of central government in local delivery.

What does the outcome data show?

This section considers outcome data on the nine target domains of youth disadvantage. It presents the national data, and then, where possible, international comparisons and the local picture in England. In order to explore adolescent outcomes for the generation born when Labour came to office, it tracks outcomes for 18-year-olds until 2015, thus covering outcomes five years into the Coalition.

Child poverty

Labour did not meet its target to halve relative child poverty by 2010, but there was substantial progress. By 2010 there were over a million fewer children living in relative child poverty, a reduction of a third. Absolute child poverty fell by nearly two-thirds by 2010.[4] These gains were mostly for children aged under-11. The cohort of children born as Labour came to office thus benefited from declining relative poverty during their primary education. However, they were no less likely to be poor as adolescents. The risk of relative poverty for young people aged 11–15 remained relatively constant over this period, and there was a five-percentage-point increase for those aged 16–19 (Stewart and Obolenskaya, 2015).

From an international perspective, reductions in child poverty during the 2000s were unusual; child poverty in most countries was rising (OECD, 2008). Of the 23 countries covered by the Luxembourg Income Study only eight reduced child poverty between the mid-1990s and 2010, and the UK had the largest reduction (Bradshaw, 2016).

Local authority data shows that the reductions were larger in the poorest local authorities: over the (shorter) period from 2006 to 2011 for which we have local data, the poorest quintile of authorities in the base year saw a reduction of 15 per cent in the number of under-16s living in low-income families against a national average of 5 per cent.[5]

School exclusion and truancy

Permanent exclusions from state-funded secondary schools rose strongly in the 1990s, and stood at 10,190 in the year Labour took office, 0.33 per cent of the school population. By 2012–13, when permanent exclusions reached their lowest point, this had fallen to 3,900, or 0.12 per cent of the school population.[6] Both the absolute number and rate of permanent exclusions thus more than halved during this period.

Truancy showed less improvement initially and the targets were reframed several times, first to widen the focus from unauthorised to total absence as this was less prone to definitional arguments, and then in 2006 to focus on persistent absence – pupils missing more than 15 per cent of their timetable in a year. Persistent absence in state secondary schools fell every year from 2006–07 until 2014–15 when there was a slight rise. First measured at 12.5 per cent of pupils in 2006–07, the rate more than halved to 5.3 per cent by 2013–14.[7]

Every local authority in England saw their rate of persistent absence improve between 2006 and 2011, with an average reduction of 44 per cent. Moreover, on average, the quintile of local authorities with the highest rates in 2006 saw the largest falls, thus closing the gap between different areas.[8]

Educational attainment at 16

There was substantial progress on Labour's key target for achievement of five A*-C grades at GCSE. In 1997–98 more than 50 per cent of pupils failed to achieve this standard, whereas when the young people born in 1996–97 took their GCSEs in 2012–13, this had been reduced to less than 20 per cent (Lupton and Obolenskaya, 2013).

Educational attainment targets were, however, controversial. There were widespread criticisms that they led to disproportionate focus on pupils around the D/C boundary at the cost of other pupils (MacDonald and Marsh, 2005; McCombie and Pike, 2011). Using National Pupil Database data we analysed the bottom half of the attainment distribution, and found that gains in educational attainment at Key Stage 4 were widely distributed and not limited to those at the target threshold of five GCSEs at grade C, or 200 points (see Figure 13.1). The 5th, 10th and 25th percentiles all improved their GCSE and equivalent point scores more than the median, narrowing inequalities in attainment for a large proportion pupils. However, educational attainment for the bottom percentile of students showed no sustained improvement.

There were also criticisms that these measures inflate performance gains by including new, easier vocational qualifications that have questionable value in the labour market (Wolf, 2011; Lupton and Obolenskaya, 2013). However, what is not in dispute is that, in this generation, more young people remained engaged in schooling, gaining some qualifications rather than none.

International comparisons of educational attainment are notoriously difficult. There have been attempts to use international data to reflect on whether the increase in GCSE results reflected a 'real' increase in performance. However, these studies point to a number of methodological difficulties in drawing any firm conclusions. International comparisons are thus inconclusive about whether educational attainment was improving and whether this compared favourably to other countries (Jerrim, 2011; Heath et al, 2013; Lupton and Obolenskaya, 2013).

Figure 13.1: GCSE and equivalents points scores at selected population percentiles

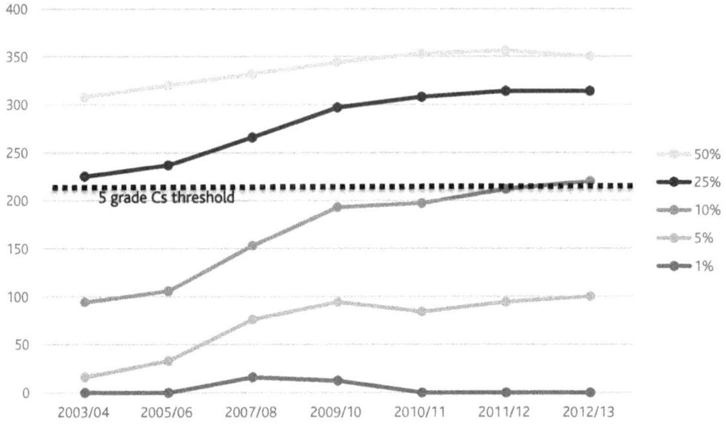

Source: National Pupil Database

To examine the geographical distribution of educational under-attainment, we created a measure of relative educational disadvantage – the percentage of students falling below half of their cohort's median GCSE points scores. Every local authority in England saw better performance on this measure between 2003–04 and 2011–12, with a mean reduction of 43 per cent. In addition, the quintile of local authorities with the largest share of 'below half median' students improved more than average, reducing gaps between areas.

Sixteen- and seventeen-year-olds not in education, employment and training

Participation in post-16 education in England began steadily increasing from around 2001. Between 2001 and 2014 there was an increase of almost 20 percentage points for 16- and 17-year-olds, and 12 percentage points for 18 year-olds.[9] However, employment of 16- to 18-year-olds not in education or training declined substantially, particularly for 16 year-olds.[10] Since many more young people stay in education than enter the labour market, the net effect was to halve the percentage of

16- and 17-year-olds not in education, employment or training (NEET) between 2005 and 2014.

The UK trend in the NEET rate for 15- to 19-year-olds, which is used for international comparisons, is not as positive as the steady reductions just described for 16- and 17-year-olds in England, and for most of this period was higher than the EU average.

Teenage conceptions

The teenage conception rate fell in all but two years after 1998, with an accelerated decline from 2008 onwards. Progress was not sufficient to hit Labour's target of halving the 1998 under-18 conception by 2010: by that stage the rate had only fallen by 27 per cent. However, by 2014 the reduction reached 50 per cent, and conception rates have continued to fall. By 2015 the rate had reached a record low of 21 conceptions per 1000 women aged under-18.[11]

These reductions in teenage fertility in England significantly outpaced the EU average (Wellings et al, 2016), although England started from a higher baseline. In the US, where significant efforts have also been made over a long period to tackle high rates, the teenage birth rate halved between 1998 and 2014.[12] It also halved in New Zealand between 2008 and 2016.[13] In all three cases the causes of the fall are thought to be multifaceted: a common feature in both the US and England is an increase in the use of contraception, especially highly effective forms of contraception (Hadley et al, 2016; Lindberg et al, 2016).

Every local authority area in England but one saw its under-18 conception rate improve between 2005 and 2012, with a mean reduction of 32 per cent. (The exception was Rutland, a small authority with very low rates.) Once more the local authority areas with the highest rates saw the largest reductions; for instance, the quintile of local authorities with the highest rates in 2005 saw conceptions down 40 per cent compared with 24 per cent for the quintile with the lowest rates.

Drug and alcohol use

Drug and alcohol use by adolescents both fell. The percentage of under-16s reporting using alcohol in the last week fell from 26 per cent to 8 per cent between 2001 and 2014.[14] Over the same period there were reductions of between 30 per cent and 50 per cent in the percentage of 11- to 19-year-olds using drugs in the last year. For secondary school pupils, regular drug use (at least once a month) fell even more dramatically – for instance, for 15-year-olds, from 15 per cent to 5 per cent between 2003 and 2012.[15]

These are self-report measures, but other data support them. Deaths related to illicit drug use have more than halved for under-20s since 1998, while rising for most other age groups.[16] Alcohol-related hospital admissions for under-18s have also almost halved since 2006–07.[17]

Adolescent alcohol use declined in some other countries too, but to different degrees. The trend in Scotland mirrored that in England (Bhattacharya, 2016). The international survey, Health Behaviour in School-aged Children, found that adolescent weekly alcohol use declined in 20 out of 28 participating countries between 2002 and 2010 (Looze et al, 2015). Nevertheless, the UK had the largest reduction, at 13 percentage points.

England and Scotland also saw very similar trajectories in reducing school-age drug taking (Crawford et al, 2016) at a time when this was not happening in most other countries. For example, while England saw the number of 11- to 15-year-olds who have ever taken drugs between 2003 and 2014 halve,[18] a survey of 15- and 16-year-olds in 25 European countries showed that overall the number of pupils who had ever taken drugs remained broadly constant between 2003 and 2015 (EMCDDA, 2015).

Youth crime

Crime fell significantly over Labour's period in office. The falls included the specific crimes – domestic burglary, robbery and vehicle crime – targeted by Labour with a strategy focused on young offenders. Proven offences by 10- to 17-year-olds fell by two-thirds between 2001–02 and 2012–13. This improvement encompassed all offence types, including violent crimes, with violence against the person down more than a third.[19] By 2012-13 there were 61,000 fewer 10- to 17-year-olds entering the criminal justice system[20] than in 2001–02 – a 69 per cent reduction. The overall downward trend in this indicator was interrupted by the impact of the 'offences brought to justice' target between 2003 and 2007, when both proven offences and young people entering the justice system rose.

Under-17s comprise around 10 per cent of the general population of offending age (that is, over 10) in England and Wales, but historically have accounted for a larger share of arrests. This has now changed. In 2000–01, 10- to 17-year-olds accounted for 25 per cent of arrests (Ayres,

2001), but by 2010–11 this had fallen to 15 per cent, and by 2015–16 it was down to 10 per cent, matching their population share.[21]

There is no long-run, cross-national time-series data on youth crime providing comparative figures on these trends. However, the number of total crimes recorded by the police has fallen substantially in England and Wales since the early 2000s, while remaining broadly constant in comparable European countries such as Germany and France.[22] Given that youth crime appears to account for a disproportionate share of this reduction, it is likely that England and Wales compare favourably on youth crime too. This is consistent with the European trends from 2008 (when Eurostat began collecting data) on juvenile prosecution, conviction and prison population, which have all seen significantly greater falls in England and Wales than the European average.

Between 2004–05 and 2012–13, every local authority area in England saw a fall in young people entering the criminal justice system, with an average reduction of 69 per cent. Again, gaps between areas narrowed: the quintile of local authority areas with the highest number of first-time entrants to the criminal justice system saw average falls of 74 per cent compared with 60 per cent for the quintile with the fewest.

The overall picture

These data present a striking picture of reductions across all the indicators of youth disadvantage targeted by Labour. The picture built up gradually, in many cases accelerated in the last years of the Labour government, and continued for some time under the post-2010 Coalition government. The gains were shared across all local authority areas, and places with the deepest problems improved most. This adds a youth dimension to other indicators of narrowing gaps between areas under Labour (Lupton et al, 2013).

The scale of these reductions is dramatic and has affected many hundreds of thousands of young people. But the degree of impact this has had on young people's lives is a complex question, and will have varied between indicators. So, for example, it makes an enormous difference to a young person not to have received a criminal sanction, to have avoided an early or unwanted pregnancy, and to have avoided being excluded from school. The impact of some other changes is more debatable. Commentators have queried the labour market benefits of some of the qualifications that contributed both to the improving GCSE figures (Wolf, 2011; Lupton and Obolenskaya, 2013) and to higher post-16 participation (Thompson, 2011; Maguire, 2013).

Can developments be attributed to policy?

It is difficult to establish to what extent the reductions in youth disadvantage documented above were the result of government policies. The policies were not controlled experiments, but overlapping innovations affecting the same people and areas. During this period other major economic, demographic, technological and cultural changes took place, including the post-2008 recession, and the rise of social media and increased internet access, which will have had their own impacts on outcomes for young people. To complicate attribution further, this cohort of young people were affected both by Labour policies and those of the Coalition, who changed some policies and kept others.[23] Still, examining the long-term picture remains valuable. The policies were intended to have a long-term effect, and childhood educational experience and family circumstances have a lifelong impact. There is no reason to assume that the benefits of a less poor childhood or a better funded education would disappear simply because the government that introduced the changes is no longer in office.

Despite the complications, the data in this chapter suggest a connection between policy and outcomes. The reductions are in most cases a notable departure from previous stagnation or worsening outcomes. Comparisons of international trends demonstrate that on child poverty, teenage pregnancy, drug and alcohol use, and youth crime, developments in England or the UK were more positive than other countries, often after years of being less positive. The timing of the changes relative to policy interventions, and the disproportionate reduction in the deprived areas where Labour invested more of its money, are also suggestive of a link. It seems highly improbable that, across all of these nine different policy areas, so many of the issues targeted began to change through other independent dynamics just at the moment that a concerted policy effort was directed towards them.

Other studies also offer some support for the connection between policy and outcomes. The connection between the Teenage Pregnancy Strategy and falling conceptions is widely accepted (Hadley et al, 2016; Skinner and Marino, 2016), and Wellings et al (2016) also note the role of higher educational attainment in the reductions. The link between Labour's benefits, tax credit and childcare policies and improving lone-parent employment and child poverty is also widely accepted (Brewer et al, 2006; Waldfogel, 2010; Hills, 2013). The Educational Maintenance Allowance, the Connexions Service and Vocational Diplomas have all been identified as drivers of improving participation rates in the 2000s

(Heath et al, 2013; Maguire, 2013). No studies exploring in detail the reasons for the fall in school exclusion and persistent absence were found. However, evaluations from the mid-2000s provide evidence of the benefits of Learning Support Units (Ofsted, 2006) and of other policies aimed at improving behaviour and attendance (Hallam et al, 2005; Halsey et al, 2005). Examinations of why adolescent drinking has fallen identify a variety of factors that featured in Labour's alcohol policies, including declining affordability of alcohol, increased awareness of health consequences and alcohol being harder to obtain for under-18s, as well as improved parenting (Birdwell and Wybron, 2015; Bhattacharya, 2016).

A recent study of the reduction in young people entering the criminal justice system (Sutherland et al, 2017) attributes the fall in part to the 2008 change to national targets and increased diversion of less serious young offenders out of criminal justice, and also suggests that reduced youth crime and reductions in the risk factors for youth offending contributed. There has been much discussion of crime drops in the UK and other countries over recent years, in some cases addressing the disproportionate role played by falling youth crime (Newburn and Reiner, 2007; Farrell et al, 2015; McAra and McVie, 2017). The many explanations posited include the continuing effect of increased security, but also point to policy changes described in this chapter such as increases in police numbers and improved police working practices, socioeconomic changes such as falling unemployment and reductions in child poverty, and cohort effects and youth policy changes. Improved drug treatment has been linked to a reduction in the number of drug users and/or reduction in crime in a variety of studies not limited to adolescents (Skodbo et al, 2007; Morgan, 2014; Ministry of Justice and Public Health England, 2017).

Implications for policy and research

The story of the last two decades is one of significant falls in adolescent disadvantage: these have paid a dividend in reduced public concern, and some reduction in pressures from adolescents in the justice and health systems. But what goes down can go up again, and a resurgence of past problems would bring both political problems and new pressures on public services. Sadly, this is just what is happening. A number of the trends in these indicators are now flat or rising again: relative child poverty,[24] permanent exclusions[25] and the percentage of students failing to get 5 A*–C GCSE grades (Lupton et al, 2016) all began increasing in

2013–14, and the latest survey data on drug use among under-16s shows a marked rise (although this is yet to be observed in other data sources).[26] The risks that the positive trends documented in this chapter are on the turn should not be ignored. It calls for a deeper analysis of what was effective in the past and whether it translates to the contemporary policy environment.

Labour made its investments during a period of growth in public spending. It is easy to assume that a preventive approach, encompassing many different public services, is simply an unaffordable luxury in more austere times. Before deciding something is unaffordable it is important to understand not only the costs of acting but also the implications of not acting. There is continuing debate about the costs of late intervention (NAO, 2013; Chowdry and Fitzsimons, 2016). There is, however, relatively little evidence on which to judge the cost-effectiveness of Labour's approach in this regard. Coles et al have shown through comparative case studies that the high public finance costs associated with teenage pregnancy, NEET status and youth crime can be avoided with 'modest investment in prevention' (2010, p 46), but do not evaluate particular policies. It has been argued that the estimated cost of preventing a conception through the Teenage Pregnancy Strategy was only a quarter of the estimated cost of social security payments to a teenage mother and child (Skinner and Marino, 2016). But there is an obvious risk of over-simplification in these inter-connected policy areas. It is unlikely to be the case that all reductions in, for example, teenage pregnancy, or youth offending, stem from interventions in that domain. Nor is it likely that all the benefits of investment in schools or on policing will be manifested only in better educational or crime outcomes. A richer understanding of these interlinkages would help policy-makers understand what the best value interventions were, and therefore what the priority actions should be to try to sustain some of the positive trends observed in the recent past.

The contemporary situation thus suggests a range of directions for further research, both to build on the progress documented in this chapter and to make the case for continued investment in youth policy. Three issues deserve particular attention. First, cross-cutting research: Labour policy treated issues of youth disadvantage as interlinked, with improvements in one domain likely to have benefits in other areas. The fact that all the indicators have moved together is some evidence that this was effective, but this needs much more rigorous examination, to connect data in different domains of youth experience. Second, and in the same vein, long-term research: the concept of early investment to reap long-term savings was key in designing the policies to reduce on youth disadvantage under Labour. But the evaluations of these policies concluded long ago and will not capture their long-term legacy, if there is one. There will be continued value in looking at the outcomes for this cohort in the years ahead, to see what the data shows for their fortunes as adults, particularly given that they are the youngest of the 'millennial generation' whose earnings and asset accumulation prospects are the subject of much current concern (see, for example, Corlett, 2017). Finally, and combining both these issues, policy-makers need stronger evidence to judge which investments are likely to have the biggest benefits and represent best value for money.

Conclusion

This chapter has outlined a remarkable improvement across a broad range of dimensions of youth disadvantage, an improvement that has been little noticed elsewhere. Perhaps its key contribution, then, is in drawing attention to an 'unknown known'. There is now a tendency to characterise successive governments as callous in their disregard for young people. However, this is a mischaracterisation, judged both by inputs and outcomes. Recent governments have benefited from a much improved picture of adolescent disadvantage compared with the late 1990s. Some of these positive trends have been sustained, but there are worrying signs that others are now beginning to reverse. Given the complexity of the interventions and the lack of research considering their cross-cutting impacts and cost-effectiveness, it remains difficult to draw clear-cut policy lessons for today beyond the important realisation that problems of youth disadvantage are tractable. Understanding more about how these outcomes came about, and how they can most cost-effectively be built on, is paramount if this progress is not to be lost. Social policy needs more focus on, and better methods for, disentangling the long-term and cross-cutting effects of policy interventions if we are to design effective policies to combat youth disadvantage in the future.

Notes
[1] These targets, and the data on outcomes, relate to England only in all cases except for youth crime and justice (England and Wales) and child poverty (UK). In some cases, similar policy changes were adopted in other countries of the UK during the period under discussion, but these are not considered in this chapter.

[2] One of the authors, Moira Wallace, was involved in some of these policies as Director of the Social Exclusion Unit from 1997-2001, and then as a Home Office senior official.

[3] Summarised from five separate PSA rounds in 1998, 2000, 2002, 2004 and 2007.

[4] Households Below Average Income, Department for Work and Pensions.

[5] Local Authority Interactive Tool.

[6] Permanent and fixed period exclusions statistics, Department for Education.

[7] Pupil absences in schools in England statistics, Department for Education.

[8] Local Authority Interactive Tool.

[9] Participation in education, training and employment statistics, Department for Education.

[10] Participation in education, training and employment statistics, Department for Education.

[11] Conception statistics for England and Wales, Office for National Statistics.

[12] US Department of Health and Human Services, Trends in teen pregnancy and childbearing.

[13] Statistics New Zealand, age-specific fertility rates data.

[14] 'Smoking, drinking and drug use among young people in England in 2014'.

[15] Crime Survey for England and Wales and 'Smoking, drinking and drug use among young people in England in 2014'.

[16] Deaths related to drug poisoning in England and Wales, Office for National Statistics, 2015.

[17] Local alcohol profiles for England, Public Health England.

[18] 'Smoking, drinking and drug use among young people in England in 2014'.

[19] Ministry of Justice, Youth justice annual statistics, 2016/17.

[20] Defined as someone receiving their first warning, caution, reprimand or conviction.

[21] Youth justice statistics, Ministry of Justice.

[22] Eurostat crime and criminal justice data.

[23] For more details on Coalition policies see, for example, Lupton et al (2015).

[24] Households Below Average Incomes statistics.

[25] Permanent and fixed period exclusions statistics.

[26] Smoking, drinking and drug use among young people in England statistics.

References

Ayres, M.A. (2001) *Arrests for notifiable offences and the operation of certain police powers under PACE* (http://webarchive.nationalarchives.gov.uk/).

Barber, M. (2007) *Instruction to deliver*, London: Politico's.

Bateman, T. (2015) 'Trends in detected crime and contemporary state responses', in B. Goldson and J. Muncie (eds) *Youth crime and justice*, London: Sage, pp 67-82.

Becker, E., Blenkinsop, S., Constantine, R., et al (2006) *Drug use, smoking and drinking among young people in England in 2005*, London: The Information Centre.

Bhattacharya, A. (2016) *Youthful abandon*, Institute of Alcohol Studies (www.ias.org.uk/uploads/pdf/IAS%20reports/rp22072016.pdf).

Birdwell, J. and Wybron, I. (2015) *Character and moderation*, London: Demos.

Bradshaw, J. (ed) (2016) *The wellbeing of children in the UK* (4th edn), Bristol: Policy Press.

Brewer, M., Duncan, A., Shephard, A., et al (2006) 'Did Working Families' Tax Credit work?', *Labour Economics*, vol 13, no 6, pp 699-720.

Chowdry, H. and Fitzsimons, P. (2016) *The cost of late intervention*, London: Early Intervention Foundation.

Chowdry, H., Greaves, E. and Sibieta, L. (2010) *The pupil premium: Assessing the options*, London: Institute for Fiscal Studies.

Coles, B., Godfrey, C., Keung, A., et al (2010) *Estimating the life-time cost of NEET: 16-18 year olds not in education, employment or training*, York: University of York (https://pure.york.ac.uk/portal/en/publications/estimating-the-lifetime-cost-of-neet-1618-year-olds-not-in-education-employment-or-training(09bb2803-f055-4637-8c90-7d7019e8ae3c)/export.html).

Corlett, A. (2017) *As time goes by*, Intergenerational Commission Report, London: Resolution Foundation (www.intergencommission.org/wp-content/uploads/2017/02/IC-intra-gen.pdf).

Crawford, C., Gohel, R., Heneghan, M., et al (2016) *United Kingdom drug situation*, London: Public Health England.

EMCDDA (European Monitoring Centre for Drugs and Drug Addiction) (1998) *Annual report on the state of the drugs problem in the European Union*, Lisbon: EMCDDA (www.emcdda.europa.eu/html.cfm/index37348EN.html).

EMCDDA (2015) *Results from the European School Survey Project on alcohol and other drugs*, ESPAD Report 2015, Lisbon: EMCDDA.

Farrell, G., Laycock, G. and Tilley, N. (2015) 'Debuts and legacies', *Crime Science*, vol 4, no 1, p 16.

Graham, J. and Bowling, B. (1995) *Young people and crime*, London: Home Office.

Hadley, A., Chandra-Mouli, V. and Ingham, R. (2016) 'Implementing the United Kingdom government's 10-year teenage pregnancy strategy for England (1999–2010): applicable lessons for other countries', *Journal of Adolescent Health*, vol 59, no 1, pp 68-74.

Hallam, S., Castle, F., Rogers, L., et al (2005) *Research and evaluation of the Behaviour Improvement Programme*, London: Institute of Education.

Halsey, K., Gulliver, C., Johnson, A., et al (2005) *Evaluation of Behaviour and Education Support Teams*, London: Department for Education.

Heath, A., Sullivan, A., Boliver, V., et al (2013) 'Education under New Labour, 1997–2010', *Oxford Review of Economic Policy*, vol 29, no 1, pp 227-47.

Hills, J. (2013) *Labour's record on cash transfers, poverty, inequality and the lifecycle 1997–2010*, Social Policy in a Cold Climate, Working Paper, London: Centre for Analysis of Social Exclusion.

Home Office (1998) *Tackling drugs to build a better Britain*, London: The Stationery Office.

Home Office (2000) *The economic and social costs of crime*, London: Home Office.

Jerrim, J. (2011) *England's 'plummeting' PISA test scores between 2000 and 2009: Is the performance of our secondary school pupils really in relative decline?*, DoQSS Working Papers, London: UCL Institute of Education (https://ideas.repec.org/p/qss/dqsswp/1109.html).

Lindberg, L., Santelli, J. and Desai, S. (2016) 'Understanding the decline in adolescent fertility in the United States, 2007–2012', *Journal of Adolescent Health*, vol 59, no 5, pp 577-83.

Looze, M.D., Raaijmakers, Q., Bogt, T.T., et al (2015) 'Decreases in adolescent weekly alcohol use in Europe and North America', *The European Journal of Public Health*, vol 25, suppl 2, pp 69-72.

Lupton, R. and Obolenskaya, P. (2013) *Labour's record on education: Policy, spending and outcomes 1997–2010*, Social Policy in a Cold Climate, Working Paper, London: Centre for Analysis of Social Exclusion.

Lupton, R., Fenton, A. and Fitzgerald, A. (2013) *Labour's record on neighbourhood renewal in England*, Social Policy in a Cold Climate, London: Centre for Analysis of Social Exclusion.

Lupton, R., Burchardt, T., Fitzgerald, A., et al (2015) *The Coalition's social policy record 2010–2015*, London: Centre for Analysis of Social Exclusion.

Lupton, R., Thompson, S. and Obolenskaya, P. (2016) 'Schools', in R. Lupton, J. Hills, T. Burchardt, et al (eds) *Social policy in a cold climate*, Bristol: Policy Press.

MacDonald, R. and Marsh, J. (2005) *Disconnected youth?*, Basingstoke: Palgrave Macmillan.

Maguire, S. (2013) 'Will raising the participation age in England solve the NEET problem?', *Research in Post-Compulsory Education*, vol 18, no 1-2, pp 61-76.

McAra, L. and McVie, S. (2017) 'Developmental and life course criminology', in A. Liebling, S. Maruna and L. McAra (eds) *The Oxford handbook of criminology*, Oxford: Oxford University Press, pp 607-38.

McCombie, J. and Pike, M. (2011) 'The problem of young people not in employment, education or training: Is there a "Neet" solution?', in P. Arestis (ed) *Microeconomics, macroeconomics and economic policy*, Basingstoke: Palgrave Macmillan, pp 54–71.

Ministry of Justice and Public Health England (2017) *The impact of community-based drug and alcohol treatment on re-offending*, London: Ministry of Justice and Public Health England.

Morgan, N. (2014) *The heroin epidemic of the 1980s and 1990s and its effect on crime trends*, Research Report 79, London: Home Office (www.gov.uk/government/uploads/system/uploads/attachment_data/file/332952/horr79.pdf).

NAO (National Audit Office) (2004) *Connexions Service: Advice and guidance for all young people*, London: The Stationery Office.

NAO (2013) *Early action: Landscape review*, London: NAO.

Newburn, T. and Reiner, R. (2007) 'Crime and penal policy', in A. Seldon (ed) *Blair's Britain, 1997–2007*, Cambridge: Cambridge University Press, pp 318-40.

OECD (Organisation for Economic Co-operation and Development) (1997) *Education at a glance 1997*, OECD Indicators, Paris: OECD Publishing.

OECD (2008) *Growing unequal?*, Paris: OECD Publishing.

Ofsted (2006) *An evaluation of Learning Support Units*, London: Department for Education.

Panchamia, N. and Thomas, P. (2014) *Public Service Agreements and the Prime Minister's Delivery Unit*, London: Institute for Government.

Parker, H., Bury, C. and Egginton, R. (1998) *New heroin outbreaks amongst young people in England and Wales*, Crime Detection and Prevention Series, London: Home Office.

PMSU (Prime Minister's Strategy Unit) (2003) *Alcohol misuse: How much does it cost?*, London: Cabinet Office.

PMSU (2004) *Alcohol harm reduction strategy for England*, London: Cabinet Office.

SEU (Social Exclusion Unit) (1998) *Truancy and school exclusion*, London: The Stationery Office.

SEU (1999a) *Bridging the gap: New opportunities for 16-18 year olds not in education, employment or training*, London: The Stationery Office.

SEU (1999b) *Teenage pregnancy*, London: The Stationery Office.

Skinner, S.R. and Marino, J.L. (2016) 'England's Teenage Pregnancy Strategy: A hard-won success', *The Lancet*, vol 388, no 10044, pp 538-40.

Skodbo, S., Brown, G., Deacon, S., et al (2007) *The Drug Interventions Programme (DIP): Addressing drug use and offending through 'Tough Choices'*, London: Home Office.

Stewart, K. and Obolenskaya, P. (2015) *The Coalition's record on the under-fives*, Social Policy in a Cold Climate, Working Paper, London: Centre for Analysis of Social Exclusion.

Sutherland, A., Disley, E., Cattell, J., et al (2017) *An analysis of trends in first time entrants to the youth justice system*, Ministry of Justice Analytical Series, London: Ministry of Justice (www.gov.uk/government/uploads/system/uploads/attachment_data/file/653182/trends-in-fte-to-the-youth-justice-system.pdf).

Thompson, R. (2011) 'Individualisation and social exclusion: the case of young people not in education, employment or training', *Oxford Review of Education*, vol 37, no 6, pp 785-802.

UNICEF (2000) *A league table of child poverty in rich nations*, Florence: UNICEF Innocenti Research Centre.

Waldfogel, J. (2010) *Britain's war on poverty*, New York: Russell Sage Foundation.

Walker, J. and Donaldson, C. (2011) *Intervening to improve outcomes for vulnerable young people: A review of the evidence*, London: Department for Education.

Wellings, K., Palmer, M.J., Geary, R.S., et al (2016) 'Changes in conceptions in women younger than 18 years and the circumstances of young mothers in England in 2000–12', *The Lancet*, vol 388, no 10044, pp 586-95.

Wolf, A. (2011) *Review of vocational education*, London: Department for Education.

Index

Note: page numbers in *italic* type refer to Figures; those in **bold** type refer to Tables.